Preface

The final version of this book project has been thirteen years in the making. It has spanned births, deaths, theater productions, an extended department chairmanship, and sundry other obstacles. Indeed, so long has the completion of this book been delayed that some of the people whom I will subsequently thank here might not remember ever having discussed its ideas with me!

I am first and foremost indebted to the two institutions where this project began and ended: the Center for Hellenic Studies in Washington, DC and the Faculty of Classics at Cambridge University. My work on the meaning of the Athenian Asklepieion commenced during a term in 1993–94 as a Junior Fellow at the Center when I thought I was writing a book on Euripides. I am extremely grateful to the Center's directors at that time, Deborah Boedeker and Kurt Raaflaub, not just for extending a fellowship to me at a critical moment, but also for fostering such a truly collegial and friendly environment, and to the other Junior Fellows for their incredible range of knowledge and their lively conversation, especially Eric Csapo, Ahuvia Kahane and Dirk Obbink. At another critical moment in 2005, Pat Easterling and Robin Osborne helped me secure a Visiting Fellowship at Wolfson College, Cambridge, and made me feel welcome as a Visiting Scholar in the Faculty of Classics at the University. It was during a visit to Cambridge early in 2004 when I realized that I had, actually, been writing a book about the great plague of Athens. I hope that the completion of this book is some form of adequate thanks for the help of my colleagues at the CHS and Cambridge. At Cambridge I enjoyed in particular also the intellectual companionship of Tim Duff, Elaine Fantham, William Fitzgerald, Simon Goldhill, Emily Gowers, Richard Hunter, Liz Irwin and Julia Shear. Aside from the intellectual community of classicists at both institutions, my work particularly benefited from their magnificent libraries which each keeps their stacks open and with all aspects of the study of Classics together in one large room. To a scholar whose work has always been interdisciplinary, the time saved in not running to different floors, if not to different buildings, in order to fetch books from the range of disciplines that compose Classics is almost incalculable.

Early versions of my work on Euripidean drama and the Asklepieion were given in 1994 as talks at the Center for Hellenic Studies, at Harvard University, and at Jesus College, Oxford, at the invitation of Don Fowler. More on Don later. I also presented my ideas on Euripides' *Heracles* to the fall 1994 meeting of the Classical Association of the Atlantic States in Philadelphia, and on the *Phoenissae* to the spring 1995 CAAS at Rutgers University. In more recent years I tested versions of my chapter on the *Philoctetes* at the 2003 Annual Meeting of the Classical Association of the United Kingdom, held at the University of Warwick, the 2004 Annual Meeting of the APA in New Orleans, the University of Pennsylvania, and Cambridge. The chapter on the *Trachiniae* was presented at the 2005 Annual Meeting of the Classical Association of the United Kingdom, which was held at the University of Reading, at Stanford University and the University of Edinburgh. The friendly classicists at Swarthmore College hosted a version of the *Oedipus* chapter in 2006. From these performances and other conversations, I am grateful to have had the responses of Douglas Cairns, David Konstan, Albert Henrichs, Ian Rutherford, Oliver Taplin, Richard Seaford, Mark Padilla, Andromache Karanika, Sheila B. Murnaghan, Ralph Rosen, C. W. Marshall, Mike Lipman, Tom Harrison, Nick Lowe, Richard Martin, Lowell Edmunds, Peter Burian and Kirk Ormand. I would be extremely remiss not to single out for special thanks Michael Sharp of Cambridge University Press and the two anonymous readers, who all made valuable contributions to the final form of this book.

A shorter version of my chapter on Sophocles' *Philoctetes* appears in *TAPA* 137 (2007).

In the final stages of this work I acknowledge the support of Temple University, for a Research Leave in spring 2005 and a grant for summer 2006, and the Loeb Foundation for further support in the summer of 2006.

Through all stages of this project I have been blessed with the support of my wife, Amanda, and my children have kindly allowed its completion to interfere with their normal time with me!

Back to Don Fowler. In 1992 I received a letter from Don, shortly after the publication of my first article on the *Aeneid*, indicating a desire for conversation since we had similar interests. He included his e-mail address. Those were the early, heady days of the internet, so he had no idea whether I might be one of the first adopters as well. I was. His became one of the friendships I have treasured most in this profession. Don's generosity, both personal and intellectual, has never ceased to inspire me, and many others, and I hope to carry it with me for the rest of my life. Don's own life ended prematurely in 1999. Others have written about that loss far more eloquently than I could. I thus simply dedicate this book to his memory. I wish he could have read it.

Last in this beginning, I acknowledge that parts of this work are speculative and conjectural and I ask my readers to approach them with an open mind. Readers who prefer concrete, unassailable proof for all arguments will not be happy here, but I believe that, if they are patient, they might still find benefits to my approach.

Prologue

Our knowledge of late fifth-century Athens in general and of the plague of 430–426 BCE in particular has largely, and at times exclusively, rested on the broad, cantankerous shoulders of the historian Thucydides. Indeed, Thucydides' own strong opinions on his native city, the possibility that he wrote some sections of his *History* well after their events, his very skill as a writer, and his proven capacity to shape his narrative creatively have sometimes led to the scholarly suspicion that he had at least embellished some of the more gripping parts of his discourse, including the section on the plague. However, during the 1990s, construction projects for the 2004 Olympics in Athens yielded numerous exciting discoveries involving Classical Athens; among them, in 1994 a burial pit at the ancient Kerameikos cemetery that can be dated, based on vases found in the site, to the early years of the Peloponnesian War.[1] This, however, was no ordinary sepulcher, but is characterized by a neglect of traditional burial customs. The roughly 150 skeletons found there were interred in a plain pit composed in an irregular shape, with the bodies of the dead apparently having been laid out in a disorganized, random fashion. Further, no soil had been deposited between the layers of corpses. The bodies were found in outstretched positions, though a number had their heads pointed to the outside and their feet toward the center of the grave. Moreover, the lower levels seemed more orderly composed and the upper in apparent chaos, with evidence that, at the later stages of internment, bodies had simply been dumped on top of one another. The number of votive offerings found in the pit were inappropriate in both number and scale, further suggesting a rushed and unplanned burial. Clearly, some catastrophe was afflicting Athens at this time. We know from the imaginative works of Greek literature from Homer through Sophocles, from the archaeological record and from historical documents that the proper burial of the dead human body was one of the most

[1] See Baziotopoulou-Valavani 2000.

overriding values in ancient Greek culture. In Thucydides' own narrative, the account of the plague immediately follows the account of the extremely structured burial of the first soldiers who had fallen in the Peloponnesian War, and Thucydides' telling of the effect of the plague depicts those burial customs quickly being thrown into confusion. All told, the recently discovered archaeological evidence suggests a city in a state of panic, disregarding its most fundamental and sacred customs of burial, desperate to dispose of the infected bodies as quickly as possible. Thucydides' picture of Athens at that time suddenly seems more powerful, indeed more unquestionably accurate, than ever.

In this book, I explore the consequences of this plague for the imagination of Athens during its course and for the two decades following its conclusion in 426. The plague enters Athenian discourse immediately and is visible, once one accepts how deeply it had affected Athens, throughout a number of texts and through their relationship with a major construction project on the south slope of the Acropolis, the Athenian Asklepieion, next to the Theater of Dionysus, where Athenians watched performances of dramas that engaged the plague and its aftermath much more meaningfully than has previously been thought. This, then, is not a book about the plague or "what it really was," but it examines the effect of the plague on selected elements of Athenian culture from the epidemic's onset in 430 to the production of Sophocles' *Philoctetes* in 409.[2]

---

[2] Papagrigorakis *et al.* 2006 now show through an analysis of DNA in the skeletons that typhoid fever was almost certainly the cause of the plague.

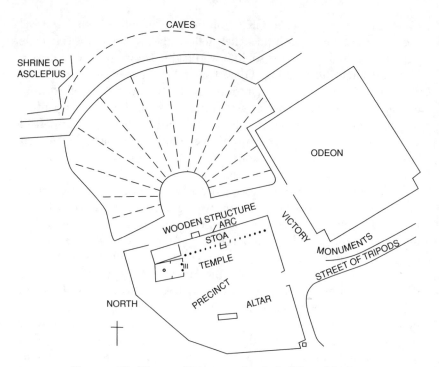

Figure 1. The Theater of Dionysus, after the building of the Stoa
at the end of the classical period
(Source Wiles 2000: 101)

CHAPTER I

Introduction

τίς δῆτ' ἰατρός ἐστι νῦν ἐν τῇ πόλει;
Who is the doctor now in the city?

Aristophanes, *Wealth* 407

τῆς δὲ πόλεως <κακῶς > βουλευσαμένης ἰατρὸς ἂν γενέσθαι
You would become a doctor for this badly counseled city.

Thucydides 6.14 (Nicias on the debate over the Sicilian expedition)

If this road, before it opens into the grove of the Muses, leads us over by the temple of Asclepius, so is this for acquaintances of Aristotle only further proof that we are moving in the right footsteps.

Jacob Bernays[1]

This study, an examination of the effect of the great plague of Athens on the Athenian imagination, will try to show that Jacob Bernays, the first great proponent of the medical interpretation of Aristotelian *katharsis* (and the uncle of Dr. Sigmund Freud's wife), himself stepped closer to a truth about Athenian tragedy than he had realized, because the Muses indeed sit quite close to the temple of Asclepius on the south slope of the Acropolis in Athens. For, assuming Aristotle did visit the Theater of Dionysus in Athens to witness dramatic performances, an activity he subordinated to reading them as texts, a few steps, even a brief glance over his shoulder, would have taken him into the Athenian City Asklepieion, the shrine of the Greek god of healing (see Figure 1). The Athenians had placed this temple at the upper western edge of their great theater dedicated to Dionysus in the last quarter-century of their finest era of tragic drama, a few years after a devastating plague had killed from a quarter to a third of their city's population. One wonders what, if anything, Aristotle made of this congruence, since his

---

[1] "Führt uns dieser Weg, ehe er in den Hain der Musen mündet, am Tempel des Aesculap vorüber, so ist dies für Kenner des Stagiriten nur ein Beweis mehr, daß wir in den richtigen Spuren gehen." Bernays 1880: 14. I have provided my own translation instead of the one by Barnes, as my more literal translation preserves more of Bernays' sense that he was following Aristotle's medical footsteps.

own concerns with drama were primarily formal and secondarily ethical; Dionysus has "nothing to do" (to play on the ancient proverb on the dramas themselves) with the philosopher's theory, and Aristotle's work on drama seems to go out of its way to minimize Athenian tragedy's very relationship with the *polis* of Athens.[2] However, since I am not focusing on Aristotle's *Poetics* here, I shall postpone the consideration of its concerns for a while to concentrate on a triangular relationship between *polis*, healing and theater. Dionysus aside, what does Asclepius have to do with Athenian drama? After all, Asclepius is only mentioned in a handful of the extent dramas that were produced in Athens. However, the adjacency of the Asklepieion to the Theater of Dionysus was an important part of their performative environment after 420 and the construction of the Asklepieion itself was part of the Athenian reaction to the plague.

Over the last two decades scholars have increasingly paid attention to a more historically rigorous situating of Greek drama in its context of performance; such studies have examined, for example, how drama concerns itself with certain social tensions and their resolution in the democracy of Athens, and here I pursue a line of inquiry that builds on this preceding discussion, with a focus on the relationship between the plague that struck Athens during the first part of the 420s BCE and the dramas that were produced then and during the next fifteen years.[3] Simon Goldhill (Goldhill 2000: 35) sums up much of the work on Athenian drama at the turn of the millennium: "That the event of the fifth-century drama festival in Athens is political (on the broadest understanding of that term) and that its specific rituals and language are integrally democratic is a starting point of much recent writing on tragedy."[4] This will be my starting point as well. The following study investigates the effect of the great plague of Athens on the imagination of its literary artists and the social imagination of the city as a whole. This work thus involves the complex interplay among the theme of mortality and the imagery of disease in drama, along with the development of the cult of the healing hero/god Asclepius in fifth-century Athens, during a period of war and increasing civic strife. The *History of the Peloponnesian*

---

[2] The modern import of the proverb is considered in the Introduction by Winkler and Zeitlin to *Nothing to Do with Dionysos?* On the absence of the *polis* in the *Poetics* see Hall 1996.

[3] See in particular the work, following the lead of Vernant and Vidal-Naquet, of Foley, Goldhill and Seaford. Against this movement, Jasper Griffin 1998 has argued for a return to more esthetic appreciation of Greek drama, albeit from a more rigorously historical viewpoint than Heath 1987. Against Griffin see Seaford 2000 and Goldhill 2000.

[4] The relationship between democracy and City Dionysia is further elaborated in Seaford 1994 and Connor 1989, 1996. See also Raaflaub 1989: 49–54. The cautions by Rhodes 2003 against the overemphasis on democracy, as opposed to the ideology of the *polis*, in studies of Athenian drama, are salutary.

War of Thucydides will also be a recurring concern, both as a source for this period and as an example of the effect of the plague on the Athenian imagination. Imagery and themes of illness, once situated in the contexts of the new cult and the social turmoils in Athens, take on resonances far beyond the health of the diseased character in a particular play. Athenian drama produced after the plague of the 420s and next to the Asklepieion will come to be seen as part of the discussion of the political health of Athens. I use the term "political" in a more literal sense than normal; that is, as Goldhill observes, "political" connotes matters pertaining to the order of the *polis*, including its religious life.

My argument will have three threads that will work their way throughout the succeeding chapters, but they will be stressed in the order I now list them. First, I shall show how the imagery and language of disease becomes a living, not dead, metaphor after 430 (if, in fact, it had ever died); second, that the construction of the Athenian Asklepieion next to the Theater of Dionysus starting around 420 was a result of the Greek belief in the healing powers of song and then the shrine itself had an effect on a number of dramas composed after its construction; and, third, that the specific metaphor of the sick city, which appears several times before 430, becomes particularly potent during the plague and then newly powerful as the political unity of Athens begins to fail during the subsequent decade. It is necessary to make Asclepius a central, though not necessarily *the* central, component in all three areas because of the timing of the construction and the placement of the Asklepieion.

In brief, I argue that, because of traditional associations between song and healing in Greek culture, tragedy becomes a form of therapy for the diseased *polis* that is projected on to the space of the Theater, a space overlooked, after 420, by Asclepius, a hero/god of healing. I use the ambivalent designation hero/god for Asclepius because of the different statuses this figure held in cultic practice and myth; in the former he functions as a divinity to whom a worshipper sacrifices and prays, while in the latter he heroically defies the gods by trying to reverse death, a rebellion for which he pays with his own life. This ambivalence suggests Heracles' analogous duality, and we shall return to this comparison later when discussing Euripides' *Heracles* and Sophocles' *Trachiniae* and *Philoctetes*, for there are telling correspondences between Heracles and Asclepius. However, it is clear that Asclepius was worshipped from a fairly early time as a hero. Thus, Bruno Currie observes (Currie 2005: 355), "it seems likely that Pindar and his audience would have known Asklepios as a figure of cult, whether as hero or god." In the texts of tragic drama, Asclepius generally functions as a mortal hero, though in the context of the Athenian Theater of Dionysus his cult is more important. The language of disease in tragedy, I shall show over the next two chapters, sharpens in intensity and multiplies in frequency after the great plague of Athens that began in 430 and then again after the construction of the shrine to Asclepius next to the Theatre of Dionysus around 420, and it broadens in import because of political instability in Athens during the same era, which is imagined first in drama and then in the philosophical works of Plato as a type of disease.

However, I do not wish my interest in context to overwhelm the vital, complex texts of the dramas themselves, since I find impoverished both the excessive concentration on history that denies much of Greek drama's richness and the rigid formalism of the New Criticism.[5] All critical movements generate their own excesses, and it certainly was instructive, during the last stretch of the twentieth century, to watch proponents of the New Historicism and Cultural Studies increasingly resemble traditional philologists in their dismissal or lack of interest in the realm of the imagination. It is even more instructive to observe Stephen Greenblatt, the founding father of New Historicism in Renaissance studies, more recently lament how "phobic" such scholars of Renaissance literature have become about the power of imaginative literature.[6] The Greeks themselves knew the power of poetry and song,[7] and a scholarly, even mildly historicist, account of Greek drama neglecting this power leads to the strange irony of its own form of ahistoricism. I thus, once I enter the specific chapters on the dramas of Euripides and Sophocles, shall be working from inside the texts outwards, using context as a complement to, not a substitute for, formalism, in a method I shall dub "contextual formalism." In other words, context will be used to answer the questions raised by the close attention to form that form itself cannot answer.

In general, this examination shall serve as a study of how Greek tragedy, just as Shakespearean theater does 2,000 years later, absorbs and deploys certain structures taken from its culture, but extrinsic to itself as poetry, and transforms them into an essential, intrinsic part of its activity as art. I assume here an operative homology between different segments of Athenian

---

[5] I have found that the blankly dismissive, even openly hostile, attitude to "formalism" in Seaford 1994 detracts from a work I otherwise admire. Fully forty years before Seaford's book, Ehrenberg 1954 (who does not appear in Seaford's bibliography) lamented the tyranny of the cult of literary genius in the study of Greek tragedy.

[6] Greenblatt 2001: 4. One wonders how much the pendulum will swing, since, despite the frequently polemically historicist stance of Goldhill's work on Greek drama, words such as "emotions" and "pleasure" are seen creeping into Goldhill 2000 (albeit on his own terms).

[7] Walsh 1984.

culture in the mid- to late fifth century along the lines of Michel Foucault's conception of *épistèmes*, "regimes of truth," which encompass all of a given age's cultural activities.[8] I am thus pursuing an "archaeology of knowledge" (Foucault 1972), which examines the vertical linkages among drama, medicine, politics and ritual. I am not so much concerned with whether the tragic poets read the Hippocratic corpus, which particular disease from the Hippocratic texts a stage character might have, or how much, in one particular passage, a given medical writer influenced Euripides, since the distinction between "literary foreground" and "social background," to borrow and transform Stephen Greenblatt's terms (Greenblatt 1988: 6), seems particularly permeable here; I see the relationship between texts and contexts as dialectical. Further helpful for us is W. R. Connor's appropriation of Benedict Anderson's concept of the "social imagination," which, Connor argues, "is a highly metaphorical activity, in which specific practices from one realm are envisioned as operating in another realm" (Connor 1996: 223).[9] Last, in addition to not engaging in source study as an end in itself, neither is my argument genetic, positing a special origin for tragedy or a foundational relationship between Greek drama and healing.

Rather, my goal here is to discuss how a specific set of historical circumstances and cultural practices produced a theater deeply preoccupied with social illnesses and their cures; the actual great plague of Athens that accompanied the upheavals of the onset of the Peloponnesian War reenergized tragedy's concern with social conflict and stability through a particular system of metaphors. The dynamics of post-plague tragedy thus are transformed and we see this most clearly in Euripidean drama, though Sophoclean drama, once one sorts through the more relatively oblique signs it gives, also engages these dynamics, particularly in the *Trachiniae* and *Philoctetes*. Now, part of this higher visibility rests on the vagaries of manuscript survival which left us with roughly one dozen more dramas by Euripides than by Sophocles, but Euripides' greater open involvement with the specific intellectual, political and moral questions of his time has been recognized at least since the first performance of Aristophanes' *Frogs*, though, I shall suggest in my chapters on Sophoclean drama, the increasingly contested notion of Sophocles' Olympian detachment needs to be further reconsidered, if not retired.[10]

---

[8] For a quick, insightful overview of Foucault's work by a classicist, along with relevant bibliography, see Morris 1994: 10–12. The approach of Lloyd 1979 is comparable here.

[9] Connor contends, persuasively to me, that elements of the Dionysian cult were transferred "from the sacral sphere into the realm where day-to-day decisions about the polis were located." Connor here builds on his 1989 article.

[10] On Euripides and Athenian life see Gregory 1991.

So, despite the traditional association of Sophocles with the cult of Asclepius, I find that Euripides seems particularly concerned with developing a
tragic pharmacology in which often the *pharmakon* (cure) for the *polis* is
to purge the *pharmakos* (scapegoat).[11] Sophoclean drama, I shall argue, is
more concerned with cures that rebalance social systems which have become
unstable, whether through the transformation of the problematic element
(Heracles in the *Trachiniae*) or the new incorporation of a diseased, expelled,
individual (Philoctetes). I shall thus link early theories of medicine, tragic
plots involving the destruction of "ill" heroes, and ritualized expulsion. Yet
pharmakos myths and rituals were not the only structures in Greece that
predicated the safety of the community on the removal of a particular individual. Conceptually similar to scapegoating in its equation of one for the
many, ostracism furnished the Athenian *polis* with a means of preserving
political stability through the expulsion of an individual, and tragic drama,
I shall argue later in this study, forms part of the discourse of symbolic
ostracism in "reminding aristocrats of the power of the *demos*" (Forsdyke
2000: 233).[12] Sophocles maintains an active interest in the dramatic implications of disease, yet seems reluctant to extend these implications as openly
as Euripides to the realm of the metaphorical; in some ways Sophocles simply makes us work harder for that knowledge. However, recognizing the
importance of these interrelationships in Euripidean drama may allow us
to see Sophocles' interest in disease, and thus in the problems of Athens, in
a new way. In this light, I shall also provide a more complex, and more historically secure, synthesis of the "Girardean scenario" that I have discussed
elsewhere,[13] in an attempt to explore "the poetics of culture" (Greenblatt
1988: 6) in post-plague Athens. This interpretive process also requires that
we pay more attention to the critical blindnesses generated by the lack of
awareness of scholars to their own position in history. After establishing the
discursive structures operative at this moment in Athenian history, I shall
return to a more rigorously textual approach to show how these structures
permeate and are transformed in Athenian tragic drama, moving through

[11] Craik 2001 suggests that, among the tragedians, Euripides was especially interested in medical
ideas. Bremmer 1983 remains the starting point for any discussion of scapegoat rituals in ancient
Greece, along with Parker 1983: 258–80. See also Seaford 1994: 311–18 and Mitchell 1991, with further
bibliography.

[12] Forsdyke 2000 does not mention tragic drama at all, yet her theory of symbolic ostracism seems,
to me, powerfully suggestive in the light of the work in Seaford 1994 on the political importance of
the depiction of the destruction of royal households in Athenian tragedy. Seaford 1994: 312–13 also
examines the two ends of the spectrum when Greek mythical thinking sees the expulsion of the one
as the cure for the ills of the many.

[13] Mitchell 1991 and Mitchell-Boyask 1993, 1996.

close readings of a group of tragedies in the order in which I believe they were produced.

I shall further suggest that it was the earlier associations among poetry, healing and immortality that contributed to the installation of Asclepius' shrine above the Theater of Dionysus. Therefore, I shall need to move through a number of diverse and complex issues: the cult of Asclepius, the direct evocations of Asclepius in dramatic texts, the relationship of Apollo and Dionysus in cult, shrine locations, the Mysteries, the City Dionysia, the genre of the paean song, *katharsis*, the great plague, and the imagery of illness in the works of the tragedians. The *Hippolytus*, *Oedipus Tyrannus*, *Trachiniae*, *Heracles*, *Phoenissae* and *Philoctetes* will be of particular concern. And a study of plague and the Athenian imagination requires, of course, considerable attention to the writing of Thucydides. The primary focus will be on networks of conceptual associations, some easily recognizable, ✓ some latent, and thus for the latter especially I ask my reader to withhold judgment until all the ballots are counted, including those from the outlying districts.

I shall try to demonstrate that, while the plague changed the nature and effect of disease language in the theater, there were two main waves of transformation: the attacks of the plague itself and then the construction of the Asklepieion roughly a decade later. I thus introduce two series of studies of individual dramas with two chapters, "Materials," the first on the language of disease in tragic drama and the second on the cult of Asclepius. Chapter 3, the discussion of nosological discourse, covers the sweep of the fifth century, and after that the chapters are arranged in a historical sequence. That said, the sequence that moves from the *Hippolytus* to the *Oedipus Tyrannus* to the *Trachiniae* does not imply my conclusion that that was their order of production. I do, in fact, believe that the *Hippolytus* was produced first, but the relative order of the three is inconsequential to my broader concerns. All that really matters, taking the three together, is that they were composed and produced during the plague years.

CHAPTER 2

Death, myth and drama before the plague

I begin with broad and general (and, probably to some, overly simplistic) thoughts about the poetics of mortality in Greek thought and their pertinence to discussing subsequently the response of the Athenian imagination to the plague. This foundation is a necessary prelude to the consideration of both disease language in Chapters 3–6 and the relationship between healing, poetry and theater in Chapters 7–9. From its beginnings in Homer's *Iliad*, Greek poetry broadly concerns itself with man's attempts to grapple emotionally and intellectually with the basic reality of his own mortality. As Sheila B. Murnaghan observes (Murnaghan 1992: 242), early Greek epic is "preoccupied with defining human life by exploring the line that separates men and gods." In archaic epic, the heroic code posits that the hero receives "immortal glory" (*kleos aphthiton*) in return for risking an even earlier death than the normal men whose name dies with them, although they do live longer (Redfield 1975; Nagy 1979). The heroes live on through the songs of the poets. Near the beginning of the most important era of Greek drama, Pindar, in poems such as *Pythian* 3, promises to preserve the *kleos* of mortals through song and urges his listeners not to hope for more than their mortal lot. Athenian tragic drama itself, which draws its plots from the epics of the heroic age, thus by necessity continues the concern with the inevitability of death. Because its plot revolves around the problem of murderous revenge, mortality forms an important theme in Aeschylus' *Oresteia*, the trilogy that also features the first reference in extant Greek drama to the myth of Asclepius.[1] In its closing drama, the *Eumenides*, Apollo, in his role of defender of Orestes against the Furies, explains the magnitude of Agamemnon's murder by emphasizing the irreversibility of death (647–51):

---

[1] The myth of Asclepius appears earlier in narrative and lyric poetry: Hes. Fr. 125, Pi. *P.* 3. On allusions to Asclepius in Homer's *Iliad*, and links between Achilles and Asclepius that suggest in turn a larger role for Asclepius in Greek myth and literature than is apparent and thus normally recognized, see Mackie 1997 and 1998.

ἀνδρὸς δ' ἐπειδὰν αἷμ' ἀνασπάσῃ κόνις
ἅπαξ θανόντος, οὔτις ἔστ' ἀνάστασις.
τούτων ἐπῳδὰς οὐκ ἐποίησεν πατὴρ
οὑμός, τὰ δ' ἄλλα πάντ' ἄνω τε καὶ κάτω
στρέφων τίθησιν οὐδὲν ἀσθμαίνων μένει.

But whenever the dust drinks the blood of a man once he's dead,
there's no getting up again.
My father did not make charm songs for these things,
although he can turn everything else up and down,
not even breathing hard with effort.

About to launch his now infamous defense of matricide, that the father alone is the true parent, Apollo especially stresses the tragedy of the dead male (*andros*), and he indicates that the preferred method of raising the dead hero would be (if it ever could be preferred) songs with magical powers (*epôidas*). But, despite Zeus' omnipotence, men, no matter how beloved by the gods, will not be resurrected, for the barrier between mortal and immortal is final and must not be crossed. Apollo here recalls similar sentiments in the *Agamemnon*, the first play of Aeschylus' trilogy, as the Chorus sings shortly before the Cassandra scene (1019–24):

τὸ δ' ἐπὶ γᾶν πεσὸν ἅπαξ θανάσιμον
πρόπαρ ἀνδρὸς μέλαν αἷμα τίς ἂν
    πάλιν ἀγκαλέσαιτ' ἐπαείδων;
οὐδὲ τὸν ὀρθοδαῆ
τῶν φθιμένων ἀνάγειν
Ζεὺς ἀπέπαυσεν ἐπ' ἀβλαβείᾳ;

How might one call back by singing incantations
the dark mortal blood of a man
once it has fallen to the earth?
Not even the one who knew how
to bring back men from the dead did
Zeus restrain in a harmless way.

The Chorus thus sets the stage for Apollo's later plea, as it recalls the story of Apollo's son Asclepius, whom Zeus destroyed for raising the dead; the Chorus might even weaken slightly Apollo's later rhetoric by allowing that resurrection, while strongly discouraged, seems possible under the Olympian order. In the *parodos* of the *Agamemnon*, the Chorus already evokes, as the potential savior of Iphigenia, Apollo Paean, "Apollo the Healer," the cult title given elsewhere to Asclepius, and it further laments the paeans (songs of victory or healing) Iphigenia sang at her father's feasts (245–47). Cassandra herself, who so strikingly and multiplicitly recalls Iphigenia,

denies the possibility of paeans for her own situation (1248 ἀλλ'οὔτι παιὼν
τῷδ' ἐπιστατεῖ λόγῳ); a paean can neither heal her nor return her from
the death that Cassandra knows is inevitable and imminent. The text here
thus links the death of the paean-singing Iphigenia with Cassandra's fate,
and Aeschylus plays with one overlap between Apollo and his son and
another between paean song of victory and paean song of healing, two
relationships I shall explore later. It is further noteworthy that in both
passages songs or magical incantations (the Greek terms overlap) are the
possible means cited to return the dead to life. In any case, these hints cast
Asclepius' entrance into Greek drama as a means of focusing on the tension
between heroic action and death, and on the relationship of both to poetry.

The line between mortal and immortal is one of the most important
conceptual demarcations for the ancient Greek, beginning with Homer's
heroes, whose inevitable deaths give their life meaning, and reaching
through the protagonists of Athenian drama and beyond, as I shall now
sketch very briefly, though with the awareness that oversimplification here
can misrepresent reality. The Archaic sense of death, as represented most
completely in Homer' *Iliad*, represented death as a finality that even the
greatest of heroes cannot surmount, though Hesiod's *Works and Days* (170–
73) preserves an early strand of belief that heroes move on to the Isles of the
Blessed after death, a concept also glimpsed briefly in Book 4 of the *Odyssey*
when Proteus prophesies that Menelaus and Helen will live there and not in
Hades.[2] Confronting the living Odysseus in Hades, the Homeric Achilles
laments that death's endless emptiness utterly negates the value of heroic
existence (*Od.* 11.487–91). With its depiction of the ambiguous status of the
Dioscouroi (11.301–04) and of Heracles (11.601–05), the *Odyssey* certainly
opens the door to a less strict division between mortality and immortality,
but the lament of Achilles in Hades and the decision of Odysseus to reject
Calypso's offer of immortality indicate that the Iliadic vision remains active
and interested in not letting that door open too much.[3]

During the fifth century, however, the continued growth of Pythagoreanism and its belief in the immortality of the soul, as well as the increasing
importance of the Eleusinian Mysteries, weakened the Greeks' sense of
futility before their seemingly inevitable demise. Increasingly, poets such as

---

[2] On these issues see Griffin 1977, 1980 and Rutherford 1982. But Nagy 1979 argues that the presence
of Homeric heroes in Hades is transitional, not eschatological.

[3] Johnston 1999: 12–13 argues against using epic passages that admit to alternative lots after death to
establish that at the time of Homeric epic people already believed in a range of possible afterlives:
"these passages concern extraordinary individuals." Johnston locates the first tangible signs of a shift
in Pindar.

Pindar (e.g. *Ol.* 2.79–83) chose, essentially, Hesiod's over Homer's account of the afterlife and represented Achilles not as imprisoned in Hades but immortal on Leuke in the Isles of the Blessed as a reward for his heroic excellence.[4] In the fourth century, Plato, in Book 10 of his *Republic*, will take the next step in this progression and imagine the souls of the Homeric heroes (though, intriguingly, not Achilles) lining up to choose their next incarnation. Euripides represents the tradition of Achilles on Leuke in a very untragic, almost bizarre, moment at the end of the *Andromache*, when Thetis consoles Achilles' father Peleus with this information while he laments the demise of Achilles' son Neoptolemus (who is curiously ignored at that point). Tragic drama thus can contain both the older pessimistic vision of death and the newer more optimistic stance. This growing optimism was accompanied by the development in the fifth century of a practice of medical healing that gave new hope that men could overcome the physical ailments so frequently shortening their lives. Typical of the paradoxical concomitance of reason and irrationality in fifth-century Athens that Dodds so brilliantly elucidated in *The Greeks and the Irrational*, this new scientific medicine, seen in the Hippocratic texts, was accompanied by an increasing belief in religious therapy; alongside the practice of surgery, many continued to believe that sleeping in certain temples and singing the right charm songs could produce good health.[5] It remains open to question whether the belief in magical healing grew as a response to the inevitable failures of early scientific medicine or merely as a supplement to the raised hopes of an ailing, increasingly urbanized, population.

Just as tragedy encompasses both the optimistic and pessimistic visions of death, so too does it give expression to the belief in both kinds of medical therapy, the religious and the scientific. The Chorus, during the

---

[4] On Pythagoras, the growth of Pythagoreanism and its effect on the fifth century (including authors such as Pindar) see Burkert 1972. More recently Currie 2005: 31–46 contrasts the Homeric with the Pindaric views of death along the same lines I sketch here.

[5] Dodds 1951: 193: "But nothing illustrates better the polarisation of the Greek mind than the fact that the generation which paid such honor to this medical reptile saw also the publication of some of the most austerely scientific of the Hippocratic treatises." On the other hand, Parker 1983: 249 is careful not to polarize Greek thought in this period so excessively into the binary opposition of science and cult: "Cooperation between doctors and priests of Asclepius is not demonstrable, nor is hostility; and, though there are important differences between scientific and temple medicine, there are also important similarities . . . It is therefore only partially correct to see the triumphant rise of the Asclepius cult as a symptom of growing irrationalism. The genuine achievement and programmatic aspirations of Hippocratic medicine had aroused large expectations as to the possibility of curing all forms of disease, which, naturally, it was in no position to fulfill." See also Krug 1993: 120–21 and Lloyd 2003 on the coincidence of the growth of medicine and healing cult. One might compare the growth of alternative medicine in our own time, which, arguably, might have arisen from the excessive expectations raised by modern medicine.

first stasimon of the *Antigone* of Sophocles, exclaiming its confidence in human ability to master all of the earth's obstacles, closes, in a brief moment of supreme optimism, with the recognition that, while man still cannot flee death, he has now found "escapes from intractable diseases," νόσων δ' ἀμαχάνων φυγάς (363), through the strength of his own intelligence; this optimism proves unfounded in the rest of the drama as various forms of *nosos*, both literal and metaphorical, inhabit the play's discourse (421, 732, 819, 1015, 1052, 1140). The residents of Thebes, in the *parodos* of the *Oedipus Tyrannus*, pray first to Apollo Paean, "Apollo the Healer," to free them from the plague afflicting their city (151–57). Their prayers are heard not only by Apollo and Oedipus as the internal audience on stage, but also in the theater by an external Athenian audience that a plague has recently devastated (Knox 1956). In fact, this Athenian plague is one of several reasons, we shall see, that disease becomes a more important metaphor in drama and the tragic theater a site of healing for the *polis*, especially in the last quarter of the fifth century. In general, illness and its cure remain a recurring concern for tragic drama throughout the fifth century in Athens, though at varying levels of intensity.

Let us return to the Aeschylean Apollo's remarks about the irreversibility of death, as they may indicate a certain self-consciousness on the dramatist's part about the implications of his art form.[6] In an important sense, the only one who has the power to resurrect Agamemnon and allow him to walk the earth (or at least a part of it) is the tragic poet; those charm songs cited by both Apollo and the Aeschylean Chorus can be seen as embodied in the drama itself. While the narrative and lyric poets preserve the hero's *kleos* through words alone, the dramatist revivifies the hero and allows him again to inspire, and terrify, future generations of humans. C. J. Herington has written eloquently of how the greatest achievement of Thespis was to have disguised his performers with masks: "I, for one, find it hard to imagine fully the shattering impact of that single technical innovation, even in the first moments of the first performance, whatever its nature" (Herington 1985: 97).[7] The dead were suddenly alive again. One might compare here the recent suggestion by Stephen Greenblatt that Shakespeare's theater, which was itself regularly threatened with closure by plague epidemics, was a "cult of the dead" (Greenblatt 2001: 258).

This interest in the relation between the dead and the living suggests hero-cult, an institution of great significance for both ancient Greece in general

---

[6] On possible metatheatrical elements in the *Oresteia* see Wilson and Taplin 1993.
[7] Herington discusses the impact of the audience "meeting" the embodied heroes in the theater rather than hearing about them in song or seeing their images in painting and sculpture.

and Athens, and its tragic theater, in particular.[8] The Greeks believed that the tombs of heroes possessed the capacity to bless and curse; heroes thus maintained some vitality after death. Families and cities could often take pride in their connections to the heroes of epic. In Athens Cleisthenes reorganized the city after the advent of democracy into ten tribes, each named after a hero, with ten *hêrôa*, their imagined tombs, in the agora. Thus hero-cult took on a new integrative social role as the cult of the tribal hero could promote group unity among citizens bound by neither blood nor locality. Yet, as Sarah Iles Johnston has shown, the growth of hero-cult in the classical *polis* also was marked by a sense that, unlike in the Homeric world, the dead were not cut off from the living, and that, in the world of hero-cult, they could affect those who still inhabit the earth. Commenting on "tragedy's obsession with the dead," Johnston observes, "if even in those plays where they do not occupy a central role, death and the dead persistently manifest themselves, then these were indeed topics that longed for expression and resolution in the fifth century" (Johnston 1999: 25). Shakespearean theater again provides an apt and instructive comparison, as recent scholarship has shown how the explosion of the concern with the dead, starting in *Hamlet*, was driven by the upheavals, both political and religious, in late fifteenth-century England, especially by the ruptures in traditional forms of mourning and the denial of purgatory.[9] Hence arose the concern I just noted in Aeschylus with the irreversibility of death and its relation to the theater, which also seems, through hero-cult and the portrayal of heroes in the theater, to be deeply associated with problems of social cohesion.

This power of resurrection the tragic poet shares with Asclepius, the figure who is sometimes hero, sometimes deity, and who is said to have introduced medicine to humankind. Pindar draws a direct comparison between Asclepius the doctor and the poet. Pindar, whose ode on Asclepius advocates the immortality the poet bestows as a safer alternative to what Asclepius attempted, describes Asclepius' iatric artistry as *epaoidai* (ἐπαοιδαῖς, *P.* 3.91), precisely what the Aeschylean Apollo claims Zeus had not made for men. This healing function Asclepius derives from his father Apollo; father and son thus share the title Paean. But the dramatist shares more with the son of Apollo than mere necromancy, for Asclepius, I shall

---

[8] The bibliography on hero-cult is enormous. A good starting point is Burkert 1985: 204–08. Among the central modern studies are Boedeker 1992, Antonaccio 1995, Kearns 1989, de Polignac 1995, Morris 1987, Seaford 1994: 106–143 and Johnston 1999. Johnston and Seaford in particular are concerned with hero-cult and tragedy.

[9] See Greenblatt 2001 and 2004 on the absorption of religious concerns and discourses in the theater of the Renaissance. On the changing nature of the conceptualization of the dead and its impact on the theater see Gittings 1984 and Frye 1984.

argue, hovers around the edge of the Theater of Dionysus both spatially and spiritually. At the risk of falling into the quagmire of Nietzsche's *The Birth of Tragedy*, I observe that, although the father of Asclepius is Apollo, his rites in Athens partake of two separate festivals closely tied to Dionysus, the City Dionysia and the Eleusinian Mysteries; I discuss the relationship of Asclepius to those festivals in subsequent sections of my argument. This involvement with two deities normally thought to be polar opposites is one of several paradoxes Asclepius embodies.

Recognizing in this study the link between medicine and drama that the Athenians drew, I shall attempt to show that the placement of the god of physical healing near the Theater of Dionysus turns it into a locus of therapy for the *polis*. Greek poetry, from its beginnings, presents itself as being able generally to make men forget their troubles and take rest from cares (e.g. *Th.* 52ff. and *Od.* 1.337ff.), and specifically to heal men of their spiritual and bodily illnesses (e.g. Pi. *P.*3 and *N.* 4). In Homer (*Od.* 19.455–88) the sons of Autolycus heal the bleeding wound of Odysseus on Parnassus with song (ἐπαοιδῇ, 457).[10] The Sophist Gorgias argued (*Hel.* 14) that just as a *pharmakon* affects the body, so does the *logos* affect the soul, which is an idea echoed, as Pucci observes, in the Nurse's observation in Euripides' *Medea* (199–200) that there is a gain in healing griefs for mortals by song (Pucci 1977: 167–68). In Sophocles' *Trachiniae* the agonized Heracles, his body wracked with pain due to the poisons from the Centaur Nessus, wonders what healer he might find, and his first option is "What singer?" τίς γὰρ ἀοιδός (1100). Heracles, ultimately, realizes that the only healers possible are Zeus and Death, which turn out to be one and the same for him (1035, 1208–09). Aristophanes, in his *Wasps*, has Bdelycleon talk of how the task of the comic poet is "to heal the ancient disease in the city," ἰάσασθαι νόσον ἀρχαίαν ἐν τῇ πόλει (651). Tragic drama, then, I shall try to show in subsequent chapters, draws its civic setting into that circle of healing.

The dramatist, as I have already begun to observe, resurrects the hero and places him before the assembled *polis*. An aspect of the performance of drama often overlooked by scholars is the basic reality of the physical presence of the characters on stage (Griffith 1998; Murnaghan 1987–88). Unlike all other forms of literature, drama insists on the body's reality, especially in its suffering. Following Vernant's lead, it has been often said that Greek tragedy brings into conflict the cooperative values of the *polis* with the aristocratic ideals of the hero, but drama in performance sharpens

---

[10] On the connection in Greek thought between poetry and healing see Laín Entralgo 1970, Flashar 1956, Cordes 1994, Machemer 1993, Pucci 1977 and, more generally on poetry's effect, Walsh 1984. Renehan 1992 discusses *Od.* 19.455–58.

the split even further by embodying these values and making them walk the stage. Solon, Plutarch reports (*Sol.* 29.5), allegedly left the theater once in disgust, accosting the semi-legendary playwright Thespis, after having seen these realized figures from the past, pursuing their own needs at the expense of those of their communities, undermining the political harmony he had endeavored to achieve. While a likely apocryphal story, this nonetheless shows the real power that the embodiment of heroes has in the theater. The poet, like Asclepius, returns to life the heroes of the legendary past, though the tragedian's resurrection of the hero is often a far more ambivalent enterprise, since his concern is not just with the hero's glory but also with the effect of his pursuit of glory on his community. Aristophanes, whose comic dramas show a thorough acquaintance with the cult of Asclepius, plays on this practice in the *Frogs*, as his Dionysus, god of theater, specifically aims to resurrect, albeit ironically, not a hero, but a poet who will save Athens, thus turning the poet himself into a hero. Aristophanes confers immortality not on a hero or athlete, but on another poet, and thus his parody shows a metatheatrical awareness of the dramatist's Asclepian powers. And it is especially interesting here that it is Dionysus who will return a poet from the dead, since the myths of Dionysus and Asclepius have much in common, a subject to which I shall return in my later chapter on the cult of Asclepius.

Before Aristophanes and Euripides, Pindar's *Pythian* 3 epitomizes a recurrent Greek belief, dating back to the Homeric tradition, in the immortality that song confers as a recompense for inevitable death. The poet uses the myth of Asclepius to convince Hieron of Syracuse to hope not for the type of eternity Apollo's son tried to provide, but for what only song can bestow.[11] As Pindar tells the story, Asclepius was himself all too human, and tried to resurrect men for the love of profit (that classic Pindaric human foible), for which Zeus destroyed him; not, as the tragedians say (e.g. the opening lines of the *Alcestis*), for the mere attempt at resurrection. To hope for such immortality is thus to flout the will of the gods. Neither Asclepius still lives, nor does Chiron, the Centaur who taught him. Moreover, Pindar reminds Hieron, none of even the greatest heroes achieved a life free from pain or escaped death; not even Achilles, who was born from a goddess. Pindar closes this ode by comparing his activity of song to the doctor's art (Θεραπεύων, 193), through which excellence (ἀρετά, 201) becomes ageless,

---

[11] The traditional view of *P.* 3 is that it presents an antithesis between literal immortality and immortality in song. Currie 2005: 344–405, however, now argues that, instead, "the poem presents an antithesis between different types of literal immortality" (2005: 403). The poem's first half thus explores the raising of the dead through song and incantation, while its second half "explores the eschatological possibilities offered by the Mysteries."

as opposed to the human body, which withers with time; the poet's song is safer than Asclepian resurrection and more effective than the doctor's medical arts, so the poet is the true healer. The poet thus places himself in competition with the doctor. David Young has further argued that Pindar composed the ode in opposition to the rapidly developing science of medicine, which was encouraging men to think arrogantly about immortality (Young 1968: 63).[12]

As so often happens, moving from Pindar to tragedy greatly complicates matters, for the immortality of heroic fame becomes often a problematic goal, given the ambivalence about the heroic in tragic drama, and due to the sheer complexity of tragedy's engagement with disease, which involves trauma to the body and to the psyche, both imagined with the same word, *nosos.* Ruth Padel (1992) observes that the texts of Greek drama continually exhibit interest in the relationship between physical and mental states, but, although these same texts also are concerned with disease, both literal and metaphorical, illness in drama has received comparatively little attention from scholars, apart from the occasional attempt to link the language of the Hippocratic texts to the plays. Such sporadic forays usually have aimed to show that the dramatists were acquainted with Hippocratic doctrine or that a character has a particular illness.[13] The most recent of these studies, Jennifer Clarke Kosak's use of the Hippocratic texts (Kosak 2004) to examine figures of healing in Euripidean drama, has also been the most successful, not least because its inquiry is much more holistic than older studies and thus integrates Hippocratic medicine into a sustained interpretive strategy. The past identification of specific medical language in the tragic corpus has been a fruitful activity, but recognition of a set of words or images does not in itself sufficiently account for the function of that imagery or for the systems of meaning in the work as a whole. While this pursuit helps set the tragic language in its proper intellectual context, it is also fraught with the danger of the assumption of an empirical one-for-one correspondence between medical and dramatic discourse that neglects the larger structure of sense or the deeper cultural networks of associations. In such a restricted

---

[12] Machemer 1993 discusses how in the *Fourth Nemean* Pindar asserts poetry's superior healing powers compared to medicine.

[13] I must stress that I mean no disrespect to these previous scholarly efforts, since they are a necessary step to all subsequent work. A fine early example of recognizing the importance of medical language for tragedy is Dumortier 1935, whose concern is Aeschylus. Bernard Knox's *Oedipus at Thebes* (1957: 139–47) is still probably the most successful attempt to integrate medical language into a larger, more sustained, interpretation of an entire tragic drama. Most recently, see Biggs 1966, Jouanna 1988, Worman 2000 and Lloyd 2003. Craik 2001 and Kosak 2000, 2004 show a more far-reaching and subtle engagement with medical language in Euripides, largely based on the role of Hippocratic language in tragedy.

framework, the repetition in a drama of medical terminology that designates a particular condition indicates the presence of a particular symptom
in a character, and typically scholarship has been content with this literal
philological diagnosis.

But often in tragedy the language of disease and cure moves beyond the
human body to other semantic fields, such as the body politic. Despite
this range, few have asked whether the symptoms point to a larger, or
more metaphorical, structure of meaning. Adam Parry's important work
(Parry 1969) on the representation of the Athenian plague in Thucydides,
a study which acutely questioned the case for precise medical terminology
in Thucydidean narrative, should serve as a warning against looking too
much into the Hippocratic corpus by itself for answers to medical problems
in Greek drama. Parry, indeed, seems to have been more willing to see the
metaphorical aspects of medical language in Thucydides than have his
counterparts in studies of Greek drama, which is especially striking since
Parry himself draws so much on Greek tragedy, as I shall show later in my
study of the *Trachiniae*.[14] It seems strange to deny a mode of thought to the
tragedians that Thucydides obviously found so productive, especially since,
as Finley (1967), Macleod (1983) and Parry (1969) have shown, Thucydides'
thought and language shared so much with the tragedians, Euripides in
particular. An examination of instances of *nosos* (disease) in Thucydides
will show that this particular fifth-century writer never uses it loosely or
casually; every single time it means real illness or plague. Clearly *nosos* was
an important term for Thucydides, one chosen with care. Let us thus see
what happens when we take seriously the language of disease in tragic drama
and allow it a freer range over our own imagination.

[14] Similarly see Holladay and Poole 1979 and 1988. Morgan 1994 resurrects the case for precise medical
terminology, but also concedes the importance of metaphoricity and of the literary resonances in
the narrative of Thucydides.

CHAPTER 3

Materials 1: The language of disease in tragedy

A few decades ago, after philological examinations of very specific terms for types of bodily woes, scholars tended to dismiss the metaphorical aspects of disease in general out of hand, as "mere metaphor." These scholars erred, I believe, in making sweeping assumptions about poetic language in its historical situation, in underestimating how rapid shifts in that situation could affect metaphoricity, and in not considering how their own historical conditions might have affected the way they read the Greek texts. Recently, G. E. R. Lloyd has more fundamentally cast doubt upon the traditional conception of metaphor as an analytical tool for Greek discourse, especially for studying the Greek terminology for disease (Lloyd 2003: 8–9):

> It is unhelpful because it sets up a rigid dichotomy between a supposed primary, literal use and other deviant ones. Over and over again the key terms used in relation to health and disease pose severe problems for anyone who seeks an original "literal" sphere of application. I accordingly prefer to think of all the terms we shall be considering as possessing what I call "semantic stretch." Indeed in my view all language exhibits greater or less semantic stretch.[1]

In other words, can we really be so sure which use of *nosos* designates real illness and which is a trope? And could there not sometimes be slippages between the real and metaphorical applications of a word even inside the same text? Such slippages will quickly become apparent when I turn to examining specific dramas. My broader argument shares Lloyd's concerns about the assumptions of metaphoricity that have dominated the history of scholarship on disease language in tragedy. "Semantic stretch" is a bit cumbersome as a descriptive term, and I shall thus keep using the more traditional term "metaphor," but with the understanding that to call a Greek city "sick" is not to deploy a "mere" or "dead" metaphor. Lloyd's qualms concerning traditional thinking about metaphor, however, are consonant with developments over the past few decades in the study of the

[1] Lloyd first questions the notion of *metaphora* in Lloyd 1990.

theory of metaphor that have incorporated advances in cognitive science and cognitive linguistics. Such work has increasingly put into doubt the distinction between the literal and the metaphorical in language, and it has stressed that the projection of the human body into our environment and into our representation of that environment entails that the concept of the dead metaphor is dead (Fludernik, Freeman and Freeman 1999: 385): "Since all language is embodied, dead metaphors can no longer be regarded as 'dead.'"[2] And the functioning of the body and its disfunctioning when subject to illness is certainly one of these metaphors. We first need, though, to see how assumptions among classical philologists about disease metaphors developed and why.

In 1944, a seminal article by H. W. Miller recognized that medical language in tragedy was "derived ultimately . . . from the vocabulary of Ionic medicine" (Miller 1944: 156–57) and was used consciously so by the poets, but then, when explaining his decision to concentrate on the terminology for very specific symptoms, he rejected any larger discussion of words such as *nosos* and *iatros* (doctor) because they were too common in everyday language. Miller thus makes fairly substantial assumptions about everyday, let alone poetic, language in fifth-century Athens, and further does not account for whether the ritualized setting of the dramatic performance in the Theater of Dionysus motivated many aspects of Greek language which might have been unimportant in the agora. More recent scholarship has concluded that disease language has more potency, and freshness, than was previously believed to be the case. Roger Brock, for example, has reexamined the evidence in extant tragedy and discovered that, in the *Oresteia*, Agamemnon's threatful promise, upon his return to Argos, to restore civic health by surgery (*Agamemnon* 848–50) is unique in literature of the classical period, and so certainly not an overused and thus dead metaphor (Brock 2000: 31–32). Moreover, if, as Miller admits, the tragedians were actively interested in the new science imported from Ionia, then it is entirely possible, even probable, that this interest could have breathed new life into dead metaphors, if they were indeed even dead at the time.

One finds a similarly broad dismissal of disease symbolism in Robert Goheen's 1951 study of imagery in Sophocles' *Antigone*. We cannot take

---

[2] Fludernik, Freeman and Freeman 1999 is a valuable and clear overview of developments in metaphor theory that have been influenced by cognitive science. See further Lakoff and Johnson 1980, Lakoff 1987 and Kövecses 2005. Many of these issues are discussed from the perspective of classical philology in Kirby 1997, who also shows how Aristotle's approach to metaphor actually has important adumbrations of Lakoff's cognitive methodology and that the two views can be reconciled through a semiotic model.

such language seriously, says Goheen, because "[t]he expression of almost any adverse condition as a *nosos* (disease, diseased state) can be found in Greek poetry" (Goheen 1951: 41), and, moreover, "in Greek tragedy the idea of a *nosos* seems to be transferred often to distress and sorrow or to mental disorder and to the causes of great commotion, without necessary supernatural connection." Again, this is in part true, but it is a large assumption from a relatively small number of texts, and there does seem to be a supernatural connection at least in the *loimos* affecting Thebes in the *Oedipus Tyrannus*. I also do not understand why Goheen lumps mental disorder in with general distress and does not see it as a legitimate illness in itself, since the madnesses of Ajax and Heracles seem real enough illnesses to those two and their *philoi*. The operating scheme of thought here as with Miller is that the actual use of a metaphor by a poet kills it. In 1962, N. E. Collinge, following Goheen's lead, is slightly more willing to admit the metaphorical implications of disease language in tragedy, but here also the scope of examination is quite limited and the author ultimately merely lists medical terminology and briefly discusses psychological pathology.

Subsequently, and more productively, during the latter part of that period, the importance of disease as a theme in Sophoclean drama was examined in a 1966 article by Biggs, who followed Knox's lead in his earlier study of the *Oedipus Tyrannus*, and in Welsey Smith's 1967 article on Euripides' *Orestes*. These studies grazed the tip of the proverbial iceberg that remained floating in the frozen north of Greek drama studies.[3]

Part of the problem here, I think, is that such discussions had, for the most part, become excessively detached and distanced from the real trauma in Athens and the imagined suffering in the Theater of Dionysus, as they neglect the corporeal ailments of the characters, overlooking their physical agony before an audience composed of people suffering from a variety of ailments that we no longer experience in significant numbers in the modern world. I further do not believe that we can so simply assume that a culture lacking immunization shots, antibiotics and anesthetic would have let connections of bad things to the language of disease slip by too easily. We can talk all we want about historicizing the study of tragedy by focusing on the role of the *polis* or rejecting a universal psychology that makes Oedipus the cousin of Hamlet, but the sheer fragility of life itself in antiquity, and how the ancient imagination responded to it, seem to me at least as an important historical factor in how we read the texts that survive

---

[3] For an excellent overview of recent scholarship on the relationship between fifth-century medical writings and tragic drama see Kosak 2004: 6–11.

to us. I submit that there does not seem to be any convincing reason to believe that the Greeks of the fifth century BCE found so little meaning in calling certain woes *nosoi*, particularly in dramas where characters (and their societies) literally ail.

Perhaps these doubts about metaphoricity are reasonable and true, since it is not unreasonable to posit that some metaphors ossify, die and lose their force in everyday speech, but on the other hand it might be more unreasonable to assume that metaphors which seem bland and worn to us and in our everyday language would have also sounded similarly to Athenians 2,500 years ago. One would also have to engage in some rather fine hairsplitting about which specific instances retain their metaphorical import, and to posit that poetic language operates at the same motivational level as conversational speech. The context of such language, and the relationship between text and context, should be taken more seriously. It would seem more helpful, I suggest, to ask new questions and see whether a drama's use of *nosos* and related words participates in a larger structure of signification for the drama and the culture that produces it. The modern reader, I propose, needs to examine his or her own assumptions in addition to those of the fifth-century audience.

Thus, understanding the force of the imagery of disease in the Theater of Dionysus requires resituating the dramatic texts historically, both in the era of Euripides and Sophocles and in ours. At the risk of banality, I suggest that we need to imagine more vividly what it was like to live without the hygienic comforts of modernity and the possible impact more precarious health might have on our reception of Greek terms. We must more concretely imagine "a world," in John Gould's words (Gould 1985: 6),[4]

constantly vulnerable to crop failure and sickness and far closer to present-day India than to anything in our own experience, a world in which the expectation of life was appallingly low and in which medicine (the most articulate and sophisticated of ancient sciences) was all too often an unavailing witness of human suffering, disease and death.

Gould's observation should be weighed heavily against the doubts about both the reality and the metaphoricity of disease in texts from ancient Athens and should help us guard against modern complacency. Further, the work of the three earlier scholars of medical language in drama that we have just discussed was all published between 1941 and 1962, a time of

---

[4] More recently Stephens 1995: 157–59 forcefully questions the complacency of the modern scholar in the light of the very different physical conditions the Athenians experienced.

tremendous scientific optimism, when medicine had ameliorated, if not eliminated, most major curable diseases, and there was even hope for a cure for cancer; and the social unrest spawned by the Vietnam War had not destabilized America and Europe. 1962 was also, oddly enough, the publication year of Rachel Carson's landmark book *Silent Spring*, which exposed the damage modern man had done to the environment through DDT in his attempts to control nature. We forget that, before the relatively recent introduction of antibiotics in the twentieth century, even a cut in one's skin could kill through infection, though the alarm, early in the twenty first century, over infections suddenly resistant to treatment and virulent illnesses spread quickly through globalization shows a potential mnemonic recovery.[5] This earlier time of rapid medical progress was also, perhaps not coincidentally, the era of the birth of the New Criticism, which, while it offered important new insights into the rhetoric and structure of literary works, also sealed off texts from the messy circumstances of their production as self-sustaining artifacts to be admired solely for their beauty or as timeless works of art. Art, like disease, could be contained, even at the cost of quarantine. For these reasons, I thus suspect that metaphors of illness might not have had the appropriate resonance for those scholars and their colleagues. My impression of the modern history of the language of health is that words like "disease" and "plague" have much greater power now, in the era of AIDS (not to mention the various newly lethal viruses that could be spread quickly thanks to globalization), than they did three or four decades previously.

It is in the word *nosos* that I am particularly interested, and not in terms for specific illnesses and maladies, as these have been variously catalogued and further do not seem as persistently central thematically as the more general word *nosos*. The focus on individual maladies can be an interpretive dead-end, as it often remains decoupled from the larger patterns of thought in a text. While examining *nosos* and derived words, I shall also try to explain the strange neglect of the more precise word for plague, *loimos*. I pursue this study mindful of the sage warnings from my predecessors concerning the excessive concentration on a single word or vocabulary group,[6] but I hope that my attempts to work comparatively among a range of authors

---

[5] For a brief and informative account of how much medicine has changed our lives in the last century see M. F. Perutz's review essay, "The White Plague," in the May 26, 1994 issue of *The New York Review of Books*. Perutz reviews Frank Ryan, *The Forgotten Plague: How the Battle against Tuberculosis Was Won — and Lost*; Sheila Rothman, *Living in the Shadow of Death: Tuberculosis and the Social Experience of Illness in American History*; and Alan Kraut, *Silent Travelers: Germs, Genes, and the Immigrant Menace.*

[6] See, for example, M. Griffith 1977: 147, with bibliography.

and to take into account certain important features of historical context will mitigate the potential dangers of such a study, not least of which is the loss of perspective. I seek to discover the general metaphorical and literal semantic ranges that *nosos* had in the Theater of Dionysus, and Greek usage itself appears to support concentrating on this word. The plague that began in 430 BCE in Athens, and its recurrence for several years thereafter, surely deepened an Athenian audience's sensitivity to a dramatic poet's deployment of such language, which itself had been inspired by the plague. And this is probably an understatement. If Thucydides' description of the plague is at all accurate, then we·cannot underestimate the power words like *nosos* had in the theater, especially when they were articulated at key moments of pressure in dramatic action. We thus must ask how acknowledging this affects the way we read the relevant representational practices in Athens. I begin with words, the vehicle of those representations. I start, however, not with *nosos*, but with the more specific term for plague, *loimos*.

THE RARITY OF *LOIMOS* IN TRAGEDY

Since tragic language builds so much on Homer, one wisely starts there, and *loimos* only occurs once in all of Homer: this is, not surprisingly, in the description of the plague Apollo sends against the Achaean army (*Il.* 1.61, λοιμός). Elsewhere in archaic poetry, Hesiod solely uses *loimos* when he describes the two woes Zeus sends against men as *loimos* and *limos*, famine (*Op.* 243), a combination possibly driven in part by poetic needs, since the word *laoi* (people) completes the line, thus tripling the alliteration.[7] This relative avoidance of *loimos* in archaic poetry sets the stage for the lyric poets; Pindar, for example, never uses it.

Before turning to the tragedians, I should widen our scope briefly, to see whether other writers of this general era eschew *loimos*. It never appears in Pindar, whose career antedated the Athenian plague, and only three times in the vast output of Herodotus, who likely lived at least to the beginning of the plague but away from Athens.[8] In one passage (7.171.2), Herodotus, like Hesiod before him, pairs off *limos* and *loimos* as the twin afflictions of Crete. That Herodotus, as recent scholarship has shown, had a thorough acquaintance with early Greek medical writings, makes the persistence of

---

[7] Bremmer 1983: 301, while citing this passage from Hesiod, notes that plague, famine and drought are "events which of course can hardly be separated."

[8] Hdt. 6.27, 7.171, 8.115. On scholarly controversies over the publication date of Herodotus see Thomas 2000: 20.

such Archaic thought patterns even more noteworthy.[9] Plato, who was born born during the plague years in Athens (428 BCE) and who thus grew up hearing the stories elders and friends told about it, can only bring himself to write the word four times, two times each in the *Laws* (4.709a, 10.906c) and *Symposium* (188b, 201d), and in that last passage, a description of Diotima's wisdom, Plato refers specifically to the great plague of 430, but also in the same sentence, like Thucydides, then uses *nosos* to designate the identical event. However, authors who had no contact with the fifth century do not share this aversion to the word *loimos*. In the fourth century, in an oration originally attributed to Demosthenes, *Against Aristogeiton*, the speaker asks the jury to convict "the scapegoat, the plague," ὁ φαρμακός, ὁ λοιμός (25.80).[10] Given the tendency we have observed in fifth-century writers to avoid the word *loimos*, the power of this language in the fourth century might have been remarkable.

Still later, Plutarch summons up the courage to write it six times, though predominantly in texts concerning figures central to the plague years, with one of these in *The Life of Nicias* and four in *Pericles*, the latter scattered over three chapters.[11] Pausanias differs even more starkly from his predecessors with nineteen instances of forms of *loimos*, some of which in passages about the great plague of 430.[12] Thus, during the fifth century, the authors of still extant texts avoid *loimos*, probably out of superstition, and, especially in its last three decades, *loimos* virtually disappears as part of fifth-century literary vocabulary.

Similarly, the fifth-century writer Thucydides is most concerned with the broader term *nosos*, occasionally combining it with more specific adjectives like *loimôdês* (pestilent), but his descriptive language remains surprisingly non-specific. *Loimos* itself is strangely rare in Thucydides, but in his report scorning religion, at the end of the plague narrative, he repeats the Hesiodic coupling I mentioned in the previous paragraph. An oracle

[9] On Herodotus on early Greek medical treatises see Lateiner 1986 and Thomas (2000).

[10] *Pharmakos*, scapegoat, should not be confused with *pharmakeus*, poisoner or sorcerer, which is what the Loeb translator does in rendering ὁ φαρμακός, ὁ λοιμός as "this poisoner, this public pest." There are no instances in Classical Greek that justify such a translation, especially when, as here, *pharmakos* is combined with a word such a *loimos*, which would be the precise condition, plague, that warrants a scapegoat; compare Lys. 6.53 (another speech wrongly attributed) which asks its audience to "cleanse the city . . . and send away the scapegoat" (τὴν πόλιν καθαίρειν . . . καὶ φαρμακὸν ἀποπέμπειν). The Loeb translator, who might have been unduly influenced by an actual word for sorceress a few lines before (φαρμακίδα, 79), thus seems to repeat the reluctance of the Athenian writers 2,500 years previously.

[11] *Cim.* 19.4; *Nic.* 6.3; *Per.* 34.3, 36.1, 36.3, 38.1.

[12] Pausanias writes of the great plague at 1.3.4. Other instances of *loimos* occur at 1.43.7, 2.32.6, 3.9.2, 4.9.1, 5.4.6, 5.13.6, 7.7.1, 7.10.3, 7.17.2, 8.41.2, 8.41.8, 9.5.1, 9.5.9, 9.8.2, 9.22.1, 9.36.3, 9.38.3, 10.11.5.

allegedly foretold (2.54.3) that "a Dorian war (*polemos*) will come and with it plague (*loimos*)," with the assonance of *polemos* and *loimos* surely further linking them conceptually. There followed, Thucydides reports, a dispute whether the oracle foretold a famine, *limos*, or plague, *loimos*, but the Athenians chose the latter because "they made their memory fit with what they had suffered." Thucydides thus shows his awareness of the role of language in the public perception of disease and suffering. Perhaps significantly, because the oracle in Thucydides repeats in its two readings the combination of two disasters in the aforementioned Hesiodic passage, and again in Herodotus (7.171.2) plague and famine, *loimos* and *limos*, seem to be related conceptually, which then the strong assonance reenforces; I shall try to show later how the associations between plague and famine are also present in Euripides' *Hippolytus*. *Nosos* itself frequently pairs off with another calamity, war; often Thucydides tends to cluster *nosos* with *polemos* (war) in alliance, as seen already just in the dispute over the oracle, and this combination continues a line of thought from the Archaic Age, as I shall examine later, that closely linked the two catastrophes.[13] Herodotus (7.171.2) also links plague with his account that Cretans who fought in the Trojan War returned home only to find themselves and their flocks afflicted by famine and pestilence to the extent that Crete was made desolate. Moreover, given the aforementioned scholarly commonplace that *nosos* is too generalized a word that designates bad things in general to be meaningful itself, one wonders why Thucydides never uses it directly for anything other than actual, specific bodily disease.[14] *Loimos* and *nosos* are completely interchangeable in Thucydides' narrative; for example, at the beginning of his account of the plague, the first mention of it is as *nosos* – ἡ νόσος πρῶτον ἤρξατο γενέσθαι τοῖς Ἀθηναίοις, "the plague first began to occur to the Athenians" (2.47.3) – and then, in the same sentence, only a few words later, it is *loimos*. All four occurrences of *loimos* are confined to these two brief passages, joined only by the adjective *loimôdês* in Book 1 (1.23.3), which is, moreover, combined with *nosos*. All subsequent passages, especially those in the body of the plague narrative, refer to the plague as *nosos*. I shall defer for a short space a fuller account of disease language in Thucydides.

Tragic language confirms this pattern of avoidance. Both before and after the plague strikes Athens, *nosos* is also the predominant, if not exclusive, choice of the tragedians Aeschylus, Sophocles and Euripides to represent

---

[13] *Nosos kai polemos* in Thucydides: 2.59.3, 3.3.1, 5.41.2, 6.12.1, 6.26.2.
[14] Thucydides does cluster other medical vocabulary metaphorically; see Kallett 1999.

disease. *Loimos* appears twice in the extant dramas of Aeschylus (the only tragedian among these three who died well before the Athenian plague) and thus twice as often as in the substantially larger combined output of Euripides and Sophocles, and, as with the other passages already discussed, plague is paired off with war or strife as one of the two disasters which can afflict an individual or state. In the first passage, from Aeschylus' *Persians*, the ghost of Darius questions his wife Atossa, who has heard before her husband's reappearance about the swift and unexpected disastrous loss of the Persian forces to the Athenians, concerning her sudden plunge into despair: τίνι τρόπῳ; λοιμοῦ τις ἦλθε σκηπτὸς ἢ στάσις πόλει; "How did it happen? Did some stroke of plague or factional strife come upon the *polis*?" (715–16). Given the strong associations, later in the fifth century, between disease and *stasis*, this passage might significantly indicate the predilection in older Greek to associate the two forces; if nothing else, it builds on the wider link between war and disease that stretches back to Homer.[15] In the second instance in Aeschylus, from the *Suppliant Women*, the Chorus of fugitive women, overjoyed at their reception by the Argives, pronounces a series of blessings over Argos that again combine *loimos* and strife, and, although here strife in Greek is the more generic *eris*, the context of its effects on the land's inhabitants suggests a meaning more like *stasis* (659–62):

> μήποτε λοιμὸς ἀνδρῶν
> τάνδε πόλιν κενώσαι·
> μηδ᾽ ἐπιχωρίοις <ἔρις>
> πτώμασιν αἱματίσαι πέδον γᾶς.

> May plague never empty this city of its men
> nor may strife ever bloody the plain of the land
> with the blood of its fallen inhabitants.

Note that in the Aeschylean excerpts plague attacks not the land but the city, the human creation of the body politic, again preparing the later more open conceptualization of the sick city. One would perhaps expect plague to strike the land instead and cause famine, but tragic language seems more interested in the malfunctioning of civic structures than in agricultural stability.

The successors of Aeschylus follow his lead. In Sophocles' *Antigone*, probably produced sometime in the later 440s or early 430s, we hear of Antigone's mental *nosos* (according to Creon, 733), Creon's similarly described delusion (by Tiresias, 1052), the dust storm at Polynices burial described by the

---

[15] On *stasis* and disease in general, and in Thucydides in particular, see Price 2001.

Sentry as "divine plague," θείαν νόσον (421), and two references to the sick city of Thebes (1015, 1141).[16] The movement of *nosos* among characters and between characters and *polis*, merely hinted in the *Antigone*, is then picked up and developed by post-plague tragedy, as I shall show in my later studies of Euripides and Sophocles.[17] The specific term for plague, *loimos*, does not occur in the extant dramas of Euripides, and is found only once in Sophocles, line 28 of the *Oedipus Tyrannus*, the tragedy where one would most expect to find an abundance of instances, and, given Sophocles' persistent interest throughout his career in illness, this singularity seems remarkable. This usage persists through the dramatic mode, for Aristophanes restricts his medical vocabulary in his comedies exclusively to *nosos*, and *loimos* thus never appears in comedy. Since *loimos* does not present any metrical difficulties for a poet, as evinced by its appearance twice in Aeschylus, this rarity most likely does not entirely lack cause. Aside from superstition, perhaps *nosos* becomes, paradoxically, the word of choice for Thucydides and the tragedians because it came to be used to designate bad things in general outside of the theater; that is to say, its very vagueness there thus would lend *nosos* a greater metaphorical potential or semantic resonance which the poet can redirect as needed.

Moreover, because Greek tragedy tends to universalize or, we might say for lack of a better term, allegorize, contemporary events, the shift from the specific *loimos* to the more general *nosos* would seem typical of the relationship between history and tragic drama; perhaps *loimos* would too directly remind the Athenians of their recent troubles, which is suggested when the Theban priest in the *Oedipus Tyrannus*, with decidedly unminced words, calls the *loimos* "most detestable" (*echthistos*). It could be that any tragedian producing dramas which include the word *loimos* too soon after 430 could run the risk of suffering the same fate as Phrynicus did several decades earlier, when he was fined 1,000 drachmas for reminding the Athenians of their losses at Miletus in his tragedy *The Sack of Miletus* (Hdt. 6.21). The presence of *loimos* might turn the relationship between stage world and audience world, in the words of Sourvinou-Inwood, "transgressive," in making the two spheres too similar (Sourvinou-Inwood 2003: 16). Or, put in analogous Aristotelian terms, *loimos* would represent "something too close to the experience of those in the audience," and thus arouse "in them extreme sorrow for themselves, which, like the kind of extreme fear

---

[16] *Nosos* and its cognates appear a total of seven times in S. *Ant.*: 360, 421, 733, 1015, 1052, 1141.

[17] On the date of the *Antigone* see Lewis 1988, who argues, convincingly to me, for 438. On *nosos* in the *Antigone* see Winnington-Ingram 1969: 5–6 and Scullion 1998.

mentioned in *Rhetoric* 1386a17–24, is incompatible with pity" (Belfiore 1992: 232).[18] Indeed, in my chapter on the *Oedipus*, I shall thus suggest here a possible solution for the mystery of how the *Oedipus Tyrannus*, a drama admired both by Aristotle and countless modern audiences, could have finished second. Since *loimos* seems taboo, our attention must focus on the broader term *nosos*.

THE USE OF *NOSOS* IN TRAGEDY

At this point, I believe it is helpful to include two tables that represent the surviving fifth-century tragic dramas (and I thus exclude Euripides' satyr play, the *Cyclops*), their years of production (which are admittedly often conjectural) and the frequency of forms of *nosos* in them. These tables contain the same data, only arranged differently, with the first focused on *nosos* and the second on chronology. The totals for the *nosos* frequency in both of them include cognate forms such as verbs and adjectives. I shall then draw some preliminary observations and conclusions from the data in the tables before turning to a more detailed discussion of *nosos* in the dramas of Aeschylus, Euripides and Sophocles.

From these tables I can deduce some broad, though not absolutely consistent, patterns that can be linked first to the plague, then to the construction of the Asklepieion starting in 420 and finally to reactions, I suspect, to the oligarchic coup of 411. One must, however, be ever aware that we only possess a small sample of dramas produced in ancient Athens, and we further lack absolutely secure dates for many of the ones we do have, and thus any conclusions must be tentative. Please note that I discuss controversies concerning the dating of tragic dramas in subsequent chapters, and thus do no provide arguments and citations on that subject here.

Three of the highest six in *nosos* frequency are either definitely or likely dated to the first half of the 420s, and the top pair to the years subsequent to the oligarchic revolution of 411, but here I shall proceed chronologically through the set as a whole. We have secure external evidence for the date of the *Hippolytus*, and the *Oedipus Tyrannus* seems about as surely placed during the plague years as is possible without direct testimony. In my chapter on the *Trachiniae* I shall argue that internal evidence suggests a strong case for its production during the first half of the same decade; the eighteen instances of *nosos* are part of that equation. *Prometheus Bound*

---

[18] Both Sourvinou-Inwood and Belfiore in their respective passages discuss the failure of *The Sack of Miletus*.

Table 1: *Tragedies ranked according to frequency of forms of nosos.*

Play	Poet	Year	*Nosos* frequency
Orestes	Euripides	408	45
Philoctetes	Sophocles	409	26
Hippolytus	Euripides	428	24
Prometheus Bound	Aeschylus??	??	17
Trachiniae	Sophocles	429–425?	18
Oedipus Tyrannus	Sophocles	429–425?	14
Ajax	Sophocles	440s?	13
Ion	Sophocles	418–412	12
Andromache	Euripides	425?	8
Antigone	Sophocles	442–438	7
Phoenissae	Euripides	411?	7
Iphigenia at Tauris	Euripides	413?	6
Iphigenia at Aulis	Euripides	407–406	6
Alcestis	Euripides	438	5
Agamemnon	Aeschylus	458	5
Medea	Euripides	431	3
Heracles	Euripides	422–416	4
Oedipus at Colonus	Sophocles	406	4
Trojan Women	Euripides	415	3
Suppliant Women	Aeschylus	460s	3
Electra	Euripides	417–413	3
Choephoroe	Aeschylus	458	3
Helen	Euripides	412	3
Bacchae	Euripides	407–406	3
Eumenides	Aeschylus	458	2
Electra	Sophocles	413?	1
Suppliant Women	Euripides	423?	1
Heraclidae	Euripides	430–427?	1
Persians	Aeschylus	472	1
Rhesus	Euripides??	??	1
Seven against Thebes	Aeschylus	467	0
Hecuba	Euripides	424?	0

clearly does not conform to this trend, and I shall attempt to account for its uniqueness shortly later in my argument. Sophocles' *Ajax* also is ranked unusually high, with thirteen instances of *nosos* placing it seventh, but those are motivated by the madness of its hero. Starting around 425, *nosos* then decreases in frequency with the *Andromache*, drops to one with Euripides' *Suppliants*, and disappears completely in his *Hecuba*; again taking into account the limited evidence available, I would surmise that, with the conclusion of the plague's waves of attack, Euripides at least decided to put

Table 2: *Tragedies ranked according to likely year of composition or production.*

Play	Poet	*Nosos* frequency	Year
Persians	Aeschylus	1	472
Seven against Thebes	Aeschylus	0	467
Suppliant Women	Aeschylus	3	460s
Agamemnon	Aeschylus	5	458
Choephoroe	Aeschylus	3	458
Eumenides	Aeschylus	2	458
Prometheus Bound	Aeschylus??	17	??
Ajax	Sophocles	13	440s?
Antigone	Sophocles	7	442–438
Alcestis	Euripides	5	438
Medea	Euripides	3	431
Heraclidae	Euripides	1	430–427?
Trachiniae	Sophocles	18	430–425?
Oedipus Tyrannus	Sophocles	14	429–425?
Hippolytus	Sophocles	24	428
Andromache	Euripides	8	425?
Hecuba	Euripides	0	424?
Suppliant Women	Euripides	1	423?
Heracles	Euripides	4	422–416
Ion	Euripides	12	418–412
Electra	Euripides	3	417–413
Electra	Sophocles	1	413?
Trojan Women	Euripides	3	415
Iphigenia at Tauris	Euripides	6	413?
Helen	Euripides	3	412
Phoenissae	Euripides	7	411?
Philoctetes	Sophocles	26	409
Orestes	Euripides	45	408
Bacchae	Euripides	3	407–406
Iphigenia at Aulis	Euripides	6	407–406
Oedipus at Colonus	Sophocles	4	406–405
Rhesus	Euripides??	1	??

its language and metaphors aside for a while, possibly because of audience fatigue or the poet's need for innovation. Construction on the Asklepieion commenced in 420, and, perhaps coincidentally, Euripides' *Ion*, a drama about another son of Apollo, was likely produced around 418 and is ranked eighth in *nosos* frequency. The Asklepieion, I shall argue in later chapters, helps to keep disease as a theme and metaphor current. Once one moves into the middle of Table 1 and the bottom third of Table 2, the numbers become insignificant in themselves for some dramas or, for others, the relatively low total of instantces, such as four for the *Heracles*, is balanced with the recognition that they all come at key moments, as I shall demonstrate in my extended discussion of the *Heracles*. With the *Philoctetes* of 409 and the *Orestes* of 408, *nosos* explodes in frequency, an outcome, I believe, of the oligarchic revolution of 411 and the consequent political upheavals, as both Euripides and Sophocles came to exploit more fully the metaphors of the sick body politic, something which Euripides had begun in the *Phoenissae* of (probably) 411.

A few more comments are needed here concerning dramas that do not conform to these tendencies. I first note that Euripides' *Heraclidae*, which is generally thought to have been produced between 430 and 427, and thus possibly during the heart of the plague years, falls near the bottom of Table 1; this could be because Euripides did not imagine a connection between its themes and the plague, or because, if it were produced at the City Dionysia of 430, it would have been composed before the plague struck that summer. One could thus in general draw a distinction between dramas in which characters literally ail, such as the *Ajax*, and which as a result feature *nosos*, those which deploy it metaphorically and thus need some kind of motivation, such as the *Trachiniae*, and those in which neither is the case, such as those about, for example, the murder of Clytemnestra. Following this overview of *nosos* in Greek tragedy, I now turn to an assessment of its general deployment among the works of the three poets.

AESCHYLUS AND *NOSOS*

Aeschylus, the only tragedian to use *loimos* twice in the extant plays, employs *nosos* and cognates either thirty-one or fourteen times, depending on how one regards the authenticity of the *Prometheus Bound*.[19] Since seventeen instances are in the *Prometheus*, let us begin there. Indeed, the sheer relative abundance of this word in the *Prometheus* might either add to the case against its Aeschylean authenticity, or further establish it as influencing other tragedies later in the century, or even suggest it marks a shift in the conceptualization of disease in tragic drama. Because of major stylistic differences from the other six plays attributed to Aeschylus, some scholars, in particular Mark Griffith (1977), have argued that the *Prometheus Bound* is likely the work of another, probably later, poet, and thus date

---

[19] *A.* 542, 835, 850, 1002, 1016; *Ch.* 70, 279, 282; *Eu.* 479, 942; *Pers.* 750; *Supp.* 561, 587, 684. *Pr.* 225, 249, 378, 384 (twice), 473, 478, 483, 596, 606, 685, 698, 924, 977, 978 (twice), 1069.

the play anywhere from 479 to 415, with a date between 450 and 425 (that is, after Aeschylus' death) most likely.[20] Indeed, a quiet, but persistent, series of studies have noticed similarities between the *Prometheus Bound* and Euripides' *Heracles*, which is itself most commonly thought to have been produced around 415, that are so striking as to suggest they are not coincidental; *nosos* would be part of the web of connections between the two dramas (Mullens 1939 and 1941; Jouan 1970; Aélion 1983: II, 127–32 and 358–63; Papadopoulou 2005: 120–22). With nineteen instances of *nosos* and its derivatives, the frequency in the *Prometheus* makes it look more like a play by Sophocles or Euripides later in the century (not even to hint of a possible authorship by either), as the two tables provided earlier suggest.[21] Generally, the later plays feature this word and theme more prominently, mainly because of the plague of 430 and then, I argue below, under the influence of the construction of the Asklepieion next to the Theater of Dionysus. And the range of possible dates for the *Prometheus* allows for the influence of either of those events; I should note, however, that the *Ajax* almost certainly dates before 430, although Sophocles' plays are notoriously impossible to pin down in years and, after the redating of Aeschylus' *Suppliant Women*, we should always be careful about relying solely on stylistic criteria.[22] Two further cautions. First, word counts in themselves are not absolute proof of anything, but they can show us tendencies and thus suggest possible lines of reasoning. Second, my own ultimate judgment of the authorship of the *Prometheus Bound* remains fairly conservative and even the idea of placing it after 430 (a full quarter-century after Aeschylus' death) remains for me on the side of uncomfortably radical. Still, we need to consider the range of issues involved and their relationship to our larger concerns. Another difference between the *Prometheus Bound* and the rest of Aeschylus is that here the author uses *nosos* in its more general or metaphorical sense, while Aeschylus tends to restrict its usage to mean specific physical illness, though a passage from the *Agamemnon*, we shall see shortly, shows differently.[23]

One point of contact between the *Prometheus Bound* and the rest of the Aeschylean corpus, though, that also points us toward the later stages of

[20] In support of Griffith see Taplin 1977: 460–69 and West 1979. In support of an Aeschylean authorship see Herington 1979 and Hammond 1988: 9–16.

[21] M. Griffith 1977: 174 finds it "curious that [*Prometheus*] has so many explicit uses of the word *nosos* and its derivatives . . ." On medical language in the *Prometheus* in general see now Kosak 2004: 44–49.

[22] The *Suppliant Women* was originally thought to be a relatively early play, based on the prominence of its chorus, but the discovery of *P.Oxy.* 2256.3 proved it to be late. See the discussion in Jones 1962: 65–72. I return to this problem in more detail in my chapter on the *Trachiniae*. On doubts about style to date the plays of Euripides see Michelini 1987: 334–37.

[23] Cf. *Pr.* 227, 251, 381, 386, 473, 596, 607, 632, 686, 924, 1069.

this study, is that in both the *Prometheus Bound* and the *Agamemnon* political instability is compared to illness. If, as Herington suggests (1979), the *Prometheus* comes very late in Aeschylus' career (i.e. just after the *Oresteia*), then this shared metaphor marks the development in Aeschylean thought of a linkage between the body and the body politic that becomes pervasive later in the fifth century. In the *Oresteia*, King Agamemnon, in his opening speech to the Argive elders after his return from a decade fighting the Trojan War, announces his intention to reconvene the assembly and casts himself as the doctor who will heal any civic malady of dissent (*A.* 848–50):[24]

> ὅτῳ δὲ καὶ δεῖ φαρμάκων παιωνίων,
> ἤτοι κέαντες ἢ τεμόντες εὐφρόνως
> πειρασόμεσθα πῆμ᾽ ἀποστρέψαι νόσου.

> But whenever there is a need for healing drugs,
> whether by burning or cutting carefully
> we will try to turn away the woe of disease.

Those disloyal to the king, and thus, presumably, to the *polis*, are to be purged – literally. The king would be the doctor of the polis. Of course, it turns out that Agamemnon himself is the substance that will be burnt and cut, an idea which typifies the Oresteian dynamic that the agent is always successively the acted upon. The king is the state and thus its physician cannot operate on himself, an idea that recurs more explicitly in the *Prometheus Bound*.[25]

Prometheus, then, recounting the ingratitude of King Zeus after Prometheus had helped him overthrow the Titans, pronounces Zeus' attitude as characteristic of the tyrant's illness: ἔνεστι γάρ πως τοῦτο τῇ τυραννίδι / νόσημα, τοῖς φίλοισι μὴ πεποιθέναι, "For this is the disease of tyranny: to fail to trust friends (*philoi*)" (*Pr.* 225–26). Prometheus elsewhere casts himself as the healer, yet he is repeatedly told that he himself is sick, not just in terms of his physical distress but in his unyielding hostility to Zeus' reign, transforming the physical suffering into a social one. Both Zeus and Prometheus suffer diseases that threaten not their bodily health, but their places in the social and political order, and, since Prometheus carries a secret that can destroy Zeus, the disease threatens that order itself. By placing itself above the welfare of the *kosmos*, the unyielding spirit of Prometheus endangers all. Attempting to dissuade him, Okeanos thus reminds the stricken Titan that "words are doctors of the diseased temperament," ὀργῆς νοσούσης εἰσὶν ἰατροὶ λόγοι (380). This metaphorical

---

[24] On these lines see Brock 2000: 31.
[25] See, for example, 473–75, and the notes for those lines in M. Griffith 1983.

See p 38
Ar. V

field even extends to the Io scene when Io, whose own bovine illness is one of the themes that link her to Prometheus, ultimately replies gnomically when she asks the reluctant Prometheus for true prophecy, not flattery: "I say the most shameful disease is fake ('synthetic') words," νόσημα γὰρ / αἴσχιστον εἶναί φημι συν[θέτους λόγους] (685–6). The bodily suffering of Prometheus thus is transfo[rmed, through] Zeus' mistrust and Prometheus' intransigence, into a politi[cal metaphor, an] illness that only proper speech can cure. If Zeus does no[t ...]el, the disease could spread; in other words, if the patien[t ...]nt, then the doctor must resort to more cathartic means o[f ...]

PHARMAKOS

NOSOS I[N ...] ND EURIPIDES

Thus concludes my ov[erview ... Aesch]ylean (and possibly pseudo-Aeschylean) drama, and s[...] two tragedians active before and after the plague struck. S[...]ore plays by Euripides than his two peers one inevitably [...]s to examine the possible role of nosological imagery for t[... Dion]ysus in general, a choice further motivated by the prod[... exta]nt Euripidean drama save two after the plague's first on[... e]arly as the ancient *Life*, was long associated with medici[...]s cult, and, of course, we see a clear evocation of the plague at the opening of Sophocles' *Oedipus Tyrannus*, produced sometime between 430 and 425 BCE, and disease figures prominently in his penultimate play, the *Philoctetes* of 409, whose hero suffers exile because of a festering wound. Already in the earlier *Antigone* Sophocles associates *nosos* with the events in the *polis* of Thebes (421, 1015, 1141) and with the conduct of specific characters (732, 1052), but here Sophocles does not develop the metaphor and it remains, at most, episodically deployed, especially in comparison with later Sophocles; I wonder, though, whether the *nosos* in Thebes in the *Antigone* became a seed which only sprouted in Sophocles' imagination a decade later. Thus, the *Oedipus Tyrannus* and the *Philoctetes*, along with the *Trachiniae*, show the most thorough interest in disease as a theme, and these texts, and a paean (a song of healing, woe or victory) to Asclepius attributed to Sophocles' authorship, led to an early tradition that Sophocles himself introduced the cult of Asclepius to Athens; I shall return to the origins and function of this story later. Sophocles throughout his career took a great interest in characters and communities under the threat of disease, but Sophoclean drama deployed these illnesses not out of any clinical interest; as Biggs observes (Biggs 1966: 223), "the Sophoclean description of diseases is fully subordinated to their

PHARMAKOS

development as dramatic symbols." Because Sophoclean drama has for so long been connected to medicine and the plague because of the plague in the *Oedipus Tyrannus*, and since Bernard Knox lucidly and thoroughly demonstrated the function of medical language in it (Knox 1957: 139–47), I shall, after a briefer discussion of the *Oedipus* that supplements Knox, concentrate my energies on the *Trachiniae* and *Philoctetes* later in this study, where the potential of *nosos* is more fully exploited and Asclepius is evoked as a healer for the suffering hero in the latter.

Despite the reasonably frequent occurrence of specific terms for maladies both physical and psychological in Aeschylus and Sophocles, the language of disease achieves almost startling prominence in Euripidean drama, especially after 430, when the plague begins. Sourvinou-Inwood, as part of her argument that Euripidean drama does not deny traditional religion, as is frequently thought by modern critics who write under the influence of Aristophanes, but that rather Euripides explores or, at most, "problematizes" it, contends that in Euripides "a tendency had begun at around 430, intensified very strongly by 428, to articulate tragedies through a dense deployment of rituals, and to intensify religious problematization" (Sourvinou-Inwood 2003: 405–07).[26] While Sourvinou-Inwood only peripherally touches upon the plague in her discussion as part of more general environment of anxiety in Athens, still her articulation of a shift in ritual intensity in tragedy is consistent with a focus on the plague's effect, and, I think, it supports my larger argument for a fundamental change in the use of disease imagery and language, joined with an increasing use of paeans and references to Asclepius, because disease is seen as sent by the gods. The dramas with the least amount of ritual density are the *Alcestis* and *Medea*. In the dramas written before the plague of 430 – that is, the *Alcestis*, produced in 438, and to a lesser extent the *Medea* of 431 – words such as *nosos* are present, though not central, as the *Alcestis* has five occurrences and the *Medea* only three, while, for example, the *Hippolytus*, composed in the aftermath of the plague's first and most virulent attack and produced in 428, while the plague was still recurring, has twenty-four. Lest I appear overconfident that there is any neat formula at work here, I note that some late plays reduce severely their nosological language. One of Euripides two final dramas, the *Bacchae*, has only three instances, and these are all clustered together.[27] This

---

[26] For the view that Euripides was more traditional in his attitude to the gods than normally thought see also Lefkowitz 1989.

[27] *Alc.* 203, 237, 885, 1047 (twice); *Med.* 16, 471, 1364; *Hipp.* 40, 131, 176, 179, 186, 205, 269, 279, 283, 293, 294, 394, 405, 463, 477 (twice), 479, 512, 597, 698, 730, 766, 933, 1306; *Ba.* 311, 327, 353. On the *Bacchae* passages see Lloyd 2003: 91–94. Could the reduction in such language be a result of

reduction might show the effect of the passage of time on the power of the metaphor, or the effect of Euripides' sojourn from Athens in Macedonia. Internal plot motivations can explain such imagery in the two early plays. The *Alcestis* deals with the untimely death of a woman, and (as I shall discuss later) the death of Asclepius lurks in the background of that story, while in the *Medea* love is depicted as a disease, and poetry as a cure for suffering, according to traditional Greek thought about the power of Aphrodite. The increase of intensity and much greater pervasiveness of the love-as-disease metaphor in the *Hippolytus*, produced a couple of years after the *Medea* and the plague's onset, possibly indicates the poet's expanded awareness of the range of the metaphor, or at least a greater interest in deploying it.[28] The metaphor of disease thus runs powerfully through the plays written during and after the great plague of Athens, perhaps climaxing in the late drama, the *Orestes*, one of the few texts where scholars have recognized this metaphor's potency. Wesley Smith's early important study of the *Orestes*, though, still continues the focus on psychological illness, on pathology, while neglecting the sociopolitical implications of the diseased aristocracy of the drama's community; and the *Orestes* is a very political play.[29] Thus, in the next chapter I shall attempt to sketch out the more metaphorical or symbolic possibilities for disease in Euripides' *Hippolytus*, a line of inquiry I shall pursue through Sophocles' *Oedipus Tyrannus* and *Trachiniae*, shifting focus more to politics in the dramas of Euripides after 420, until I close with similar concerns in Sophocles' *Philoctetes*.

ARISTOPHANIC COMEDY AND THE PLAGUE

The persistent interest in nosological language and imagery in tragic drama becomes especially thrown into relief when one compares it to the relative scarcity in Aristophanes. Since Athenian comedy deals more directly with contemporary social concerns than does tragic drama, one might expect to find the plague to have factored into Aristophanes' plays from the 420s, yet

the composition of the *Bacchae* outside of Athens and thus away from the physical environs of the Theater of Dionysus? However, recently Scullion 2003 has argued that the Macedonian exile was one of those Euripidean biographical fallacies that Lefkowitz has exposed. One also wonders about the nosological language of Euripides' lost *Philoctetes*, produced the same year as *Medea* and any connections Euripides might have drawn between these two dramas through shared language and imagery, especially given the strong thematic connections of betrayal and abandonment shared by the two myths.

[28] On poetry as a cure in the *Medea* see Pucci 1980, although this work is, to my mind, fairly obscure at times.

[29] Smith 1967. Of *Orestes*, J. Peter Euben (1986: 222) writes: "Euripides' *Orestes* is about political corruption." "Corruption in Euripides' *Orestes*," in Euben 1986.

Aristophanes seems to have skirted it. Here I shall examine Aristophanes' use of *nosos*, possible references to the plague, and why Aristophanes avoided the plague. Aristophanes debuted, during the plague years, with the *Banqueters* of 427, followed by the *Babylonians* in 426, neither of which, based on the available information and fragments, seems to have engaged the plague, and then the *Acharnians*, the first comedy to have survived antiquity, and that play is devoid of any direct sense that the plague had recently concluded its attacks on Athens, an elision which suggests its two predecessors steered clear of the subject as well.[30]

One would have to surmise that a disaster like the plague was terrible fodder for comedy, especially for a young, ambitious playwright who proclaimed his desire to win at every available opportunity. One might consider here that in our day comedians generally do not make jokes about AIDS or cancer. Aristophanes certainly relished ridiculing savagely politicians, sophists and charlatans of all stripes, yet, when it came to attacking the war, he was careful to restrict his comedies to lampooning blustering generals, joking about the mismanagement of the conflict by politicians, or war's effects on conjugal relations and the livelihood of small businessmen. There were no references to bodies impaled by spears or trampled by horses, and certainly no grieving widows, children or parents. Indeed, the mortality of war was given a very wide berth. If I am correct in my argument later in this study that the depiction of the Theban plague in the *Oedipus Tyrannus* during or just after the plague of Athens had something to do with its second-place finish, then Aristophanes would have seen a negative model for himself that would have been even more urgent for a comic poet whose first job was to entertain and please. On the other hand, according to Michael Vickers (1991), Aristophanes might have alluded to the suffering of plague victims in the *Clouds* of 423, in his depiction of the agonized Strepsiades, lamenting the assaults on his body by bed-bugs after Socrates had ordered him to lie down and think (707–16). If the comic use of the dire distress in Athens of just a few years before registered with the audience and judges, it might have contributed to the discomfiture that led to its defeat, a loss that clearly rankled Aristophanes, who complained about this decision at great length in the main section of the *parabasis* in the *Wasps* (1015–50) the following year and then rewrote the *Clouds* itself.

The *Wasps* is, curiously enough, then also the only Aristophanic comedy in which disease is a theme, and Aristophanes thus transfers it into the

---

[30] If, however, in the *Acharnians*, Aristophanes speaks through Dicaeopolis, as Reckford 1977: 298 argues, it might be significant that the specific Euripidean tragedy parodied there is the *Telephus*, whose hero, like Philoctetes, needs to be healed.

safer metaphorical realm.[31] In the *Wealth*, as I shall discuss in my concluding chapter, the god Wealth is healed in the Asclepius sanctuary, but its
vocabulary is free of *nosos*, which Aristophanes seldom uses. There are only
twelve lines in all of Aristophanes in which a form of *nosos* appears (*Av.* 31,
104, 473; *Nu.* 243; *Ra.* 1033; *Lys.* 1088; *V.* 71, 76, 80, 87, 114, 651); thus, one
half occur in the *Wasps*, Aristophanes' comic exploration of the excesses of
the Athenian legal system. The old man Philocleon suffers from a "strange
illness" (71), which takes the form of being a "lover of trials," φιληλιαστής
(87), so that he "lusts," ἐρᾷ (88, 753), for judging. On one level we see here
a parody of the linkage in tragedy, found in the *Hippolytus* and *Trachiniae*,
between *eros* and *nosos*. Sidwell (Sidwell 1990: 10) notes "the strong reliance
of Aristophanes on an intuitive grasp of tragic patterns," and thus that the
nosos pattern and its relation to *eros* must satire recently produced tragedies.
Philocleon's son Bdelycleon has tried various cures for the father, including
an incubation at the Asclepius sanctuary on Aegina (121–25), but manages,
ultimately, to cure his father by redirecting Philocleon's energies toward
more traditional debaucheries. In the process, however, Bdelycleon, who
at times seems to become the voice of Aristophanes,[32] indicates that the
task of the comic poet is "to heal the ancient disease in the city," ἰάσασθαι
νόσον ἀρχαίαν ἐν τῇ πόλει (651). This disease, which Bdelycleon fears,
perhaps in a statement of false modesty, is too much for the comic poet
to heal, and is not just a mania for the courts, but the entire set of civic
ills, embodied in the demagogue Cleon, that has afflicted Athens since the
death of Pericles. As Reckford observes on these lines (Reckford 1977: 298),
"[t]he longtime, deeply ingrained disease of Philocleon merges with that of
Athens." The city is sick, as tragic drama intones repeatedly during these
years, and needs a healer, and here Aristophanes suggests himself, building
on traditional Greek associations between poetry and healing that will be
subtly echoed later in the *Frogs* and, as I shall show later, in forms both
more direct and more indirect, in the *Wealth*.

   In sum, then, Aristophanes in general avoided the plague because it was
a poor source for comedy and its use risked the disapproval of the audience
on which he depended for success and acclaim. In 422, during the period
when disease imagery recedes in tragic drama (at least as it seems to in the
small sample that survives), it becomes safe enough for Aristophanes to
apply metaphorically to the condition of Athens.

---

[31] See Sidwell 1990. Beta 1999 sees resemblances between the madness of Philocleon and that of the
Euripidean Heracles and thus argues for an earlier version of the *Heracles* than the one we currently
have and to which the *Wasps* alludes.
[32] On Aristophanes and Bdelycleon see Olson 1996: 144 and Reckford 1977: 297–302.

MEDICINE, POLITICS AND TRAGIC DRAMA

Athenian comedy, unlike tragedy, is often openly and aggressively political, yet Aristophanes does not exploit the metaphorical possibilities of illness in and of the city. Tragic drama drew these metaphors from early medical writings. Thus I shall now examine briefly the language of early Greek medicine, not only, as is typical scholarly practice, as a source for dramatic speech, but more for its use of political language to describe physical malady, an image seen frequently in tragedy, and so we can begin to see the discursive homologies among medicine, politics, poetry and sacrifice that circulated throughout Greek culture. Jean-Pierre Vernant, building on the work of Charles Kahn and Gregory Vlastos, has already explored such homologies as they pertain to Greek cosmology and politics. Vernant shows how Anaximander's theory of a universe is viewed geometrically with the independent Earth, dominated by nothing, at its center, equidistant from all points of the celestial circumference in a space of symmetrical and reversible relationships, a structure which Vernant compares to the rise of the *polis* centered around the open and free agora which no individual dominates.[33] Just as Anaximander's cosmology deploys political concepts to describe a universe governed by *isonomia* (equal rights) and subject to law, so too does the Greek *polis* become based on the idea of a center which gives all members equal right to speak and act.[34] The political idea of *isonomia* thus circulates through cosmology and, we shall see shortly, medicine, before moving into the discourse of drama. I shall suggest then that Euripides later reverses the equation in employing medical language to depict political turmoil. Hence, identifying disease imagery in the texts of Athenian drama is only a first step to understanding the multivalent, suggestive power of its discourse in the Theater of Dionysus.

Two concepts central to early Greek medicine that are especially relevant here are that diseases enter the body from the outside through *poroi* (holes, paths) and that health depends on a proper balance of the body's different components. Early Greek thought held that the human body continually experiences attack from external sources; some of them enter the brain and are manifested in thought or sensation, and others introduce disease.

---

[33] On these issues see Chapter 6, "Geometry and Spherical Astronomy in the First Greek Cosmology," and Chapter 7, "Geometrical Structure and Political Ideas in the Cosmology of Anaximander," in Vernant 1983. These essays were first published in the French *Mythe et pensée* in 1965. Vlastos 1953 links Anaximander's cosmology to Alcmaeon's medical theory. Wiles 1997: 63–86 takes this idea of the center and links it to the basic structure of the Greek theater.

[34] Lloyd 1979: 246–64 discusses the conceptual relationships among Greek science and politics.

Padel observes (Padel 1992: 54): "Outside cause, therefore, is cardinal in Hippocratic nosology. Disease comes from *ta esionta*, 'the things coming in,' *exôthen*, 'from outside'." Early in the fifth century, the pre-Hippocratic writer Alcmaeon, whose concepts profoundly influenced the Hippocratic texts, believed that good health arose from the equilibrium of the powers in the body, and he cast this balance in strikingly political language (DK24 B4):[35]

Ἀλκμαίων τῆς μὲν ὑγιείας εἶναι συνεκτικὴν τὴν ἰσονομίαν τῶν δυνάμεων, ὑγροῦ, ξηροῦ, ψυχροῦ, θερμοῦ, πικροῦ, γλυκέος καὶ τῶν λοιπῶν, τὴν δ᾽ ἐν αὐτοῖς μοναρχίαν νόσου ποιητικήν· φθοροποιὸν γὰρ ἑκατέρου μοναρχίαν . . . τὴν δ᾽ ὑγίειαν τὴν σύμμετρον τῶν ποιῶν κρᾶσιν.

Alcmaeon maintains that the bond of health is the "equal rights" (*isonomia*) of the powers, moist and dry, cold and hot, bitter and sweet, and the rest, while the "monarchy" of either is destructive . . . Health on the other hand is the proportionate admixture of these qualities.

Health thus is cast as a political struggle between warring factions, almost a *stasis* (the Thucydidean overtones of my language are not accidental and their implications will become apparent shortly). Health is *isonomia*, equality of power or rights, one of the hallmark terms of Greek democracy in the fifth century.[36] The universe, the *polis* and the body all rely on the same basic principles. The comparison between the balance of the parts in a body and the state should sound familiar to students of Plato, and indeed Alcmaeon's theories influenced not just the Hippocratic writers, but also philosophers beginning with Empedocles, as "political ideas increasingly articulated an image of health in society and government as a balance of inner powers that may be upset, either by the emergence of a single stronger power or by the intrusion of an alien, outside force" (Padel 1992: 57). Herodotus, while describing the troubles of Miletus, notes that the Milesians for two generations "were very sick with civil strife," νοσήσασα ἐς τὰ μάλιστα στάσι (5.28), until the Parians made them orderly by selecting as rulers those who managed well their own farms; this is the only metaphorical instance of *nosos* in Herodotus. Thus from Thucydides to Aristotle the idea of a mixed polity, based on the Hippocratic ideals of a balance in physical properties,

---

[35] Kirk, Raven and Schofield 1983: 260, no. 310. Longrigg 1963: 167. See also Belfiore 1992: 35, Longrigg 1993: 47–81, Padel 1992: 58–59, Ostwald 1969: 97–99 and Kosak 2004: 157–58. Longrigg 1993: 51 argues for Alcmaeon to have been active in the second quarter of the fifth century. Price 2001: 121 suggests that Thucydides likely knew Alcmaeon's teachings.

[36] On *isonomia* and the language of democracy see Vlastos at 1947, 1953. Vlastos discusses the Alcmaeon fragment at 1947: 156–58 and 1953: 363–66.

becomes common.[37] Plato in the *Republic* (556e) compares the sick body (σῶμα νοσῶδες) and the divided city as two entities subject to *stasis*, and, in the *Sophist* (228a), the Eleatic Stranger says that *nosos* and *stasis* are the same. In the Platonic dialogues, such language, and the noetic structure it implies, while relying ultimately on the Hippocratic texts, might also stem directly from tragic discourse, a reliance that might be suggested by Plato's insistence on the word *nosos*.

Moreover, in the account of the sick body the image of the one standing apart from the others, gaining control and thus threatening the whole sounds not only like a common political scenario, but also like a fairly typical basic plot structure for much of Greek drama, and in turn it suggests a more powerful metaphorical potential for disease than we have suspected. Typically, as Vernant has shown, tragedy sets in opposition the conflicting values of the democratic polis and the aristocratic hero, who is usually a member of the royal household that rules the city of the play's locale.[38] Hence, by mirroring a constant political concern of fifth-century (not to mention sixth-century) Athens, drama enacts the tensions between the needs of the many and the desires of the one. Given this political current in Greek medical thought, the obvious acquaintance of the tragedians with the Hippocratic writings, and the political setting of the City Dionysia, it should not be surprising that disease becomes a live, not a dead, metaphor for the crises afflicting the political communities on stage. This metaphor becomes especially common after the outbreak of the plague in Athens, and perhaps can be seen even in Thucydides' text, to which I shall now briefly detour.

The great plague of Athens that began in 430 and recurred sporadically for several years figures prominently in Thucydides' analysis of the breakdown of Greek society during the Peloponnesian War. By placing the plague description directly after Pericles' Funeral Oration and restricting the detailed accounting of the plague's effects primarily to this section of Book 2, Thucydides' description condenses the extended time frame so that the reader experiences the plague as intensely, if not as dramatically, as possible. Indeed, unless the reader pays careful attention, she is led to think that the plague did not last more than the time devoted to it in that particular section of the *History*.[39] And while Thucydides does detail the disease's

---

[37] See Connor 1984: 228–29, who discusses Thucydides Book 8 and the proposal of a mixed constitution. Note 35 lists a fragment of Euripides, *TGF* (II) 21, as a source for metaphor, and cites its medical origin. See also de Romilly 1976.

[38] On this tension see the important work in Seaford 1994.

[39] On Thucydides' manipulation of his reader's perception of the duration and intensity of the plague see Mikalson 1984.

symptoms, the historian focuses mainly on the plague's psychological and ethical effects. The narrator creates a sense of overwhelming despair that leads directly to a severe weakening of the moral, and, ultimately, the political structure of Athens: "For the catastrophe was so overwhelming that men, not knowing what would happen next to them, became indifferent to every rule of religion or law" (2.52). The consequential human behavior seems almost to be a disease itself. If we believe that the placement of this narrative directly after Pericles' Funeral Oration, with its glorification of Athens at its orderly civilized apex, is intentional and thus significant, then this change from structure to anarchy suggests the political metaphor of disease in Alcmaeon. As with the later civil war in Corcyra, the change in the hierarchy of values and expectation breeds a diseased polis. Ruth Padel observes (Padel 1992: 53):[40]

Change in the body is an image for change in the body politic. Thucydides' parallel between the plague in book 2 of his *History* and *stasis*, "civil war," in book 3 rests on his culture's familiarity with this sort of comparison. His comment, "so *ômê* [raw] did *stasis* become," introduces the symptoms and effects of *stasis*, summed up by *toiautai orgai*, "such angers," using for *stasis* an image of "rawness" applied in tragedy to *orgê, daimôn, phronêma*, "anger," *daemon*, and "(arrogant) thought." In tragedy, *ômotês* is "cruelty, savagery." In biology it appears as "indigestion." *Stasis* in book 3 behaves as an exterior overriding destroyer, like a disease or daemonic tragic passion . . . The image of *stasis* resonating against it adds a political dimension to the moral, physiological, and social disintegration possible in a Greek "body."

Thucydides' analysis of the plague is important not just for its diagnosis of the illness, but also for the disease's broader implications. Until Adam Parry, Thucydidean scholars tended almost exclusively to worry about the exact identification of the disease, or how Thucydides employs precise medical language from the Hippocratic texts. Parry, however, showed that the historian's language tends not toward technical, but to normal, everyday, usage, and may even have been taken from drama, and this non-technical language can lend itself in turn to a larger system of associations and metaphors.[41] Parry even seems to take the metaphorical potential of Thucydides' language more seriously than do his counterparts in the study of Greek tragedy, for he recognizes that, as early as the first book of the *Iliad*, Greek thought

---

[40] Also see the related thoughts in Price 2001: 28–30.

[41] Parry 1969 argues most pointedly against Page 1953. More recently, see Allison 1983, Morgan 1994, Swain 1994, and Kallet 1999. Hornblower 1991: 316–18 has an excellent overview, with bibliography, of the controversies over Thucydides' language in the plague narrative and its debt, or lack thereof, to the medical writers. Hornblower's wise words of caution (1991: 317) that "we should always remember that there was more than one Thucydides" should be kept in mind throughout any reading of the plague narrative.

equates war and plague. Thucydides' first mention of the plague i
Book 1, with its rare deployment of the more specific adjective *loi*
in combination with *nosos*, could recall the sole occurrence of *loin*
Homer, the description of the plague Apollo sends against the Achaean
army in Book 1 of the *Iliad*. Thucydides thus seems aware of the resonance
of disease in the Greek imagination as symptomatic of moral and political
disintegration; for example, he begins his litany of the plague's consequences
by observing (2.53.2) that plague was the beginning of lawlessness, *anomia*,
language that is distinctly evocative of Alcmaeon's political metaphor for
disease. Plague breeds lawlessness, which in turn thus becomes a societal
illness; recall here that Nicias later in Thucydides urges the presiding officer
of the Athenian Assembly to reopen debate over the Sicilian Expedition,
and thus to become a doctor for the disordered state. When Thucydides
lists early the disasters Athens experienced during the war, the catalogue
climaxes with the plague, in one of the longest spans between an article
and its noun in Greek literature, redundantly piling adjective on adjective:
ἡ οὐχ ἥκιστα βλάψασα καὶ μέρος τι φθείρασα ἡ λοιμώδης νόσος, "the
not least harmful and in part devastating pestilential disease" (1.23.3). As
I noted earlier, Thucydides links *nosos* and *polemos* a number of times in
his sentences, and verbs normally describing the onset of diseases he uses
for the turmoils of battle and civic *stasis* (Swain 1994: 306–07). For Thucydides, writes Parry (Parry 1969: 116), "[t]he plague is a *paralogon* [something
outside of expectation] beyond all others, and is essential part of the war.
It represent the most violent incursion of the superhuman and incalculable into the plans and constructions of men." The idea of something
irrational, monstrous and unexpected exploding into human affairs suggests more than one Euripidean tragedy, but in particular the *Heracles*, one
drama where *nosos* figures as a powerful image of civic and psychological
disintegration.[42] With Euripides we move from the Thucydidean interest
in the social and psychological effects of disease to a discourse where society
and the mind are literally diseased.

    Thus concludes my overview of the language of disease in Athenian
tragic drama, which presents the introductory materials to the succeeding
three chapters on Euripides' *Hippolytus* and Sophocles' *Oedipus Tyrannus*
and *Trachiniae*. In these three subsequent chapters I shall proceed chronologically through a series of dramas in the order in which I believe they
were produced. After the three case studies on the plague which focus on

---

[42] On the similarities between Thucydides and Euripides see Finley's (1967) and Macleod's (1983)
chapters on this topic.

close readings of the dramas' language, I establish a second set of introductory materials. In these, I discuss the role of the development in Athens of the cult of the healing hero/god Asclepius, as it was, I believe, after the plague an important part of the performative context of tragedy, especially of the *Heracles*, which was first produced shortly after the construction of the Asklepieion, the temple of Asclepius, on the slope immediately above the Theater of Dionysus, and then of Sophocles' *Philoctetes*, which directly engages the Asklepieion. The construction of the Asclepius sanctuary adjacent to the Theater of Dionysus seems to have given new life to nosological discourse, especially as that discourse became joined to growing political conflicts in Athens in the course of the Peloponnesian War.

CHAPTER 4

Plague, cult and drama: Euripides' Hippolytus

Plague struck the Athenians in 430, and its impact, multiplied by the confinement of the area's population inside the city walls for protection against the Spartan attacks (a condition the rustic Dicaeopolis laments at the opening of Aristophanes' *Acharnians*), is felt in Sophocles' first tragic drama about Oedipus. Moving further inside the walls, to the heart of the *polis*, Asclepius enters the south slope of the Acropolis by 420, yet thematically he occupies the lower part of the slope several times before then. The social energy released by the increased concern with disease and Asclepius may be seen circulating through Euripides' *Hippolytus*, which was produced in 428 BCE.[1] The extant drama is the second Euripides composed on this subject and, given the timing of the drama's production and the prominence of nosological imagery in its language, it is conceivable that the plague was one of Euripides' motivations in returning to this myth; if nothing else, the plague informs and gives resonance to the tragedy's preoccupation with illness.[2] In this chapter I examine the intersection of disease language and imagery with myths and rituals that involve the threat of famine, with initiatory rituals, and allusions to Asclepius himself.

Troezen, the drama's setting, functions historically as an intermediary city for the Asclepius cult in Athens, and this history may even help explain why Euripides chose to set his tragedy there, and not in Athens, which was the traditional home of Hippolytus' father Theseus, and the setting both of Euripides' first play on this subject, which antedated the plague, and of Sophocles' *Phaedra*.[3] According to Pausanias (2.32.6), the plague of 430 afflicted the residents of Troezen, but less extensively than it had the

---

[1] I acknowledge the healthy skepticism of Gibert 1997, who argues that evidence is not conclusive that the *Hippolytus* of 428 is in fact the second *Hippolytus*.

[2] On medical language in the *Hippolytus* and its relationship to Hippocratic discourse see Kosak 2004: 49–65.

[3] Barrett 1964: 10–30 provides the basic information on these three dramas about Phaedra and Hippolytus. On the setting of the *Hippolytus* in Troezen see Jeny 1989, who does not make any historical or political arguments. Wiles 1997: 216–17 persuasively (to me, at least) rebuts Barrett's reluctance

Athenians, and this difference might imply that the plague was brought there from Athens by refugees; on the opposite side of the Saronic Gulf, Troezen is close enough for escape yet distant enough for safety. Burford, observing how the old relationship between the two cities featured a period when the Athenians evacuated women and children to Troezen in 480 to avoid the Persians, argues that the Athenians must have similarly fled there in 430 and 427, where they then learned in detail of the powers of Asclepius (Burford 1969: 21); even here we see the combination of *nosos kai polemos*, plague and war. The *Hippolytus*, if it evokes or is intended to resonate in contemporary events, may support this theory, for Aphrodite in the Prologue clearly states that Theseus arrived in Troezen (35) "fleeing the *miasma* from the blood of the Pallantids." Theseus thus is a refugee due to pollution, a word that has strong associations in tragic diction with plagues; for example, near the beginning of the *Oedipus Tyrannus*, Creon refers to the source of the plague as an "incurable" (ἀνήκεϲτον) *miasma* (97–98), thus mixing the language of pollution and disease, and then the unknowing and ironic curse of Oedipus against the unknown killer of Laius identifies the source of the Theban plague as *miasma* (241).[4] Moreover, *nosos*, used both by Euripides to describe first Phaedra's disease (e.g. 40, 176, 179, 186) and then the experience of Hippolytus (936), and by Thucydides to narrate the Athenian plague, figures very prominently in the play's vocabulary,[5] and the text further hints that *miasma* is not something Theseus can escape so easily, for he has brought it with him; indeed this language suggests the incipient concepts of contagion in Thucydides' plague narrative. Both Phaedra, believing she follows a familial curse of fatally illicit passions, and Theseus, stained with the blood of his family, are cast as people who are trying to flee from previous pathologies, but who find in the end that they cannot escape (Reckford 1974).

But the god of healing Asclepius himself appears in this drama, obliquely, though not insignificantly. Theseus curses his son first with death and then with banishment, and so, when Hippolytus goes off into exile, he travels along the coast toward Epidaurus, the home of Asclepius, who,

---

to make anything of the setting, arguing instead that the setting's significance rests on the repeated attempts by Athens to acquire and keep this city under its control. Wiles does not mention the plague.

[4] *Miasma* and its cognates also appear at *OT* 313, 353 and 1013. Scullion 1998 argues that, in the *Antigone*, *nosos* arises from *miasma* and that the two should not be equated.

[5] *Nosos* and its cognates appear in the *Hippolytus* at lines 40, 131, 176, 179, 186, 205, 269, 279, 283, 293, 294, 394, 405, 463, 477 (twice), 479, 512, 597, 698, 730, 766, 933, 1306. The observation by Kosak 2004: 51 that *nosos* is used in different ways by different speakers suggests a Euripidean interest here in the intersections of literal and metaphorical meanings.

according to the traditional myth in the Archaic epic *Naupactia,* at the request of Artemis will resurrect Hippolytus, dead from the wounds the huge bull has indirectly inflicted at the seashore, a tradition excised by Euripides except for one small item.[6] The final geographical detail given by the Messenger who brings the report of Hippolytus' disaster, after a series of references to Theseus' heroic exploits that mark the topography as significant for the drama's action, is that the wave carrying the monstrous bull which fatally panics Hippolytus' horses hides the "rock of Asclepius" (πέτραν Ἀσκληπιοῦ, 1209), a feature whose exact identity is unknown, but surely must lie at the shore below Epidaurus, given that this city was Asclepius' birthplace and the center of his cult.[7] A small detail, perhaps, but, given the themes and specific language of this drama, I do not think it is an insignificant one. Why the rock of Asclepius? This tragedy features characters who are struggling with a condition called a *nosos,* which in turn leads to the destruction of much of the family of the leader of Athens, and, toward the drama's end, one of the characters is pointed in the direction of Asclepius in Epidaurus. Phaedra closes her final speech before suicide by announcing that her revenge against Hippolytus will make him share in her illness, *nosos* (νόσου, 730), and, having caught Phaedra's disease, Hippolytus travels toward the home of the great healer himself, ignorant that he ails and needs healing. But, as with Thucydides' description of the Athenian plague, what matters most is not the corporeal effect of Phaedra's illness, but its impact on the behaviors of all who come in contact with it. Euripides, however, could be evoking the cult ironically, since the "rock of Asclepius" is hidden by the huge wave from the bull, suggesting the obliteration of any hope of salvation. Because the drama gives no hint of Asclepius' resurrection of Hippolytus (a myth to be discussed shortly) and even covers the healer's traces, Euripides could be suggesting that the cult of Asclepius can be of no real help to the people of Athens in the plague, just as it remains "hidden" from Hippolytus. Euripides thus locates his tragedy in Troezen, not with the purpose of making some simple point about the cult of Asclepius, but to exploit the resonances of the plague and the Athenians' attempts to deal with it. In turn, the drama can provide us with an indication of the state of the activity of the cult of Asclepius in Athens, or at the very least the Athenian acquaintance with it.

---

[6] See Barrett's account of the journey (1964) and the map in his comments on lines 1198–200. The map clearly shows that Hippolytus is traveling toward Epidaurus.

[7] Mitchell-Boyask 1999: 49–52 argues for the general mythological significance of the topography of the journey of Hippolytus as the Messenger narrates it.

While the traditional resurrection of Hippolytus in myth cannot be directly narrated because it would violate the finality of tragic mortality, the allusions to Asclepius and to Hippolytus' initiation into the Mysteries (24–26), like that of Asclepius before him, suggest an underlying pattern of myth whereby Hippolytus functions as a doublet for Asclepius. This process is, I propose, similar to how, as Seaford argues, in a later drama, the *Bacchae*, "Euripides consciously alludes to the Dionysiac mysteries for a dramatic effect dependent on the religiosity of his audience" (Seaford 1981: 252). Hippolytus and Asclepius are closely linked in myth and ritual. The resurrection of Hippolytus was featured in the opening lines of another Euripidean drama a decade earlier, when Apollo began the *Alcestis* by reporting his own fury at the destruction of Asclepius by Zeus, and this action, normally viewed as coming in exchange for the revival of Hippolytus,[8] became part of the knowledge and expectations of the tragedian's audience. Thus, there are a number of correspondences between the myth and cult of Asclepius and Euripides' tragedy. Hippolytus is an initiant into the Mysteries, as Aphrodite explains (25), and Phaedra first was smitten with him when he traveled to Athens for his initiation, a journey Pausanias reports Asclepius made as well (2.26.8). Hippolytus closes his speech to the votive statue on stage with a wish (87): "May I round the turning-post (*telos*) of my life as I began it." Hippolytus here uses the metaphor of the farthest point in the race course to describe the conduct of his life, but the distinct overlap between Aphrodite's language of the Mysteries (*telê*) and Hippolytus' athletic imagery (*telos*) suggests a meaning beyond what the character might intend.[9] The belief in the immortality of the soul, cycled into new bodies, that was vital to the Mysteries could be represented as an end that resembles the beginning, as a circular course. Moreover, Hippolytus' description of himself in his first speech as a virgin plucking flowers in a meadow suggests the figure of Kore, or Persephone, Demeter's daughter, whose abduction and return by Hades (Death) is the founding myth, as the Homeric *Hymn to Demeter* shows, of the Eleusinian Mysteries (Cairns 1997: 63–68). Even Hippolytus' refusal to reveal his sworn secret to his father Theseus could mark the secrecy of the initiant into the Mysteries (Zeitlin 1985: 85–86). Asclepius himself was so strongly associated with the Eleusinian Mysteries that his annual arrival into Athens was celebrated on the first day of the festival of the Great Mysteries (Parke 1977: 135; Garland

---

[8] The resurrection of Hippolytus by Asclepius is told in Apollodorus 3.10.3. See in general Gantz 1993: 288 on the ancient sources for this myth.

[9] Thomson 1941: 124 quotes Plutarch, Porphyry and Plato, who use athletic metaphors to describe the Mysteries, and says that this image goes back to drama.

1992: 123–24). There was even a close enough tie between Hippolytus and
Asclepius for an image of one to be confused for the other's, as Pausanias
reports of one statue in Troezen (2.34.4). Also, the initial part of the incuba-
tory healing procedure in the sanctuary of Asclepius was a three-day period
of sexual abstinence, which evokes the avoidance of sexuality so important
to Hippolytus. In his discussion of the interrelations of Asclepius and the
Mysteries, Burkert also notes that a drink in the Asclepius ritual, called the
Hygieia, resembles the *kykeion* of Eleusis, and a piglet was sacrificed in both
rituals (Burkert 1985: 267–68). Again, I would not push these ideas too far
and argue that Euripides' sole point in the drama is some kind of allegory
about Asclepius and his cult, but there do seem to be some evocations
of it which form a reasonably important part of the drama's structure of
meaning; Asclepius resonates in Hippolytus. It is worth noting, however,
that, eight years after this drama's production, when the Athenians constructed the City Asklepieion on the south slope of the Acropolis above
where the masked actor brought the son of Theseus briefly back to life,
they also installed a grave mound to Hippolytus and a sacred precinct next
door (Barrett 1964: 4–5). The implications of the intersection of myth, cult,
drama and Acropolis topography seem particularly rich here and suggestive
for my larger thesis about the placement of the Athenian Asklepieion. This
network of correspondences, taken together, does not seem accidental. The
Hippolytus thus reflects the plague's immediate impact and anticipates the
arrival of the Asclepius cult.

   Another complex intersection active in the *Hippolytus* and relevant for my
study concerns allusions in the drama to Athenian rites that were apotropaic
of plague and famine, *loimos* and *limos*, two disasters that were further
closely linked in Greek thought, as we have already seen, as early as Hesiod and at least through the time of Herodotus and Thucydides. These
rites in turn were associated with scapegoating rituals and ephebic initiatory patterns which are then part of the drama's architecture. There were
important connections in Athens among the main myths of Theseus' heroic
exploits, the Oschophoria and Pyanopsia, festivals which were celebrated
together during the fall month of Pyanopsion, and the Thargelia, the late
spring festival when the *pharmakos* ritual was observed.[10] The Thargelia,
while originally an agricultural festival under the aegis of Apollo, became
in the fifth century increasingly connected with dithyrhambic choral

---

[10] On the relationships among the myths of Theseus, initiatory rites and the *Hippolytus* see Mitchell-
Boyask 1999. Cairns 1997: 66–69 also discusses initiatory aspects in Hippolytus' speech about the
meadow of Artemis.

competitions held in honor of Dionysus.[11] I draw these connections from Claude Calame's recent work on the role of Theseus in the Athenian imagination, although Calame has left unexplored his work's implications for how we read specific Greek dramas (Calame 1990: 291–324). Calame, emphasizing the importance of agricultural cycles in the Athenian festival calendar, observes that the Pyanopsia and Thargelia occupy analogous positions and functions in the cycle. The Thargelia, situated at the end of May, two months after the City Dionysia, marked the beginning of summer when the first grains were harvested from the earth, while the Pyanopsia, along with the Oschophoria, ended the summer in October by celebrating the maturation of the final parts of the harvest, thus bifurcating the year according to the agricultural cycle. Recognizing this initial similarity allows others to emerge. For example, the Thargelia coincides with the presentation of the adopted son to the phratry of the father, which is distinguished from, yet parallel with, the similar registration of legitimate sons in the Apatouria during the month of Pyanopsion. Thus, like the Pyanopsia, the Thargelia concerns itself with the proper maturation and place of adolescents, which is further signified by the presence of Apollo overseeing the festival in both his *Pythios* and *Patroos* ("of the father") cult designations.[12]

Linked by the votive object, the *eiresiônê*, both the Pyanopsia and Thargelia are acts intended to drive away sterility from the land, and this fear of infertility and plague was attributed to the original cause of the tribute to the Minotaur that Minos demanded from Athens: the death of his son Androgeus in Athens. The son of Pasiphae and Minos (who were also the parents of Phaedra), Androgeus was killed in Attica either as a result of the jealousy aroused by his victory in the Panathenaic games or when Aegeus sent him out against the Marathonian bull. Enraged at his son's death, Minos attacked Attica and forced Athens to send annually its young to Crete as offerings to the Minotaur until Theseus arrived.[13] The legend is the beginning of the whole Cretan episode so important to Athenian festival life and Euripides' drama. The *pharmakos* ritual observed during the Thargelia was a ritual repetition of the purificatory measures undertaken after the epidemic and sterility sent by the gods to punish the city for the murder of Androgeus (Bremmer 1983; Calame 1990: 314–15). The Cretan episode in the heroic career of Theseus is thus essentially bound up with the seasonal cycle of the civilized production of human food, with

---

[11] Wilson 2000: 37. Wilson further notes the "intriguingly Dionysian overtones" of how an *aulos* (the oboe-like instrument which accompanied the tragic chorus) played while the scapegoats were expelled and the *sumbakkhoi* (fig-*bakkhoi*) given to the scapegoats themselves.

[12] Calame 1990: 322–23, with bibliography.   [13] Apollod. 3.15.7. Plu. *Thes.* 15.

the two festivals Pyanopsia and Thargelia functioning apotropaically for dispelling the risk of famine and plague. Thus we must pay close attention to a dramatic representation of a myth engaging part of this ritual network and featuring a figure who denies the course of nature, particularly since the Greeks frequently cast human development in terms of the growth of plants.

The relation of these festivals to each other is important for understanding the *Hippolytus*. Overseen by Apollo, the two festivals were each paired with one devoted to Dionysus, the Oschophoria and Anthesteria respectively, and both featured the rite of the *eirésiôné*, a branch or harvest wreath of olive or laurel wound round with wool that was borne at the Pyanopsia and Thargelia by singing boys and hung at the house's door, while offerings were made to Helios and the Hours.[14] The rite of *eirésiôné* functioned apotropaically against crop failure and epidemic, and as a propitiatory ritual for the beginning of the work in the fields. Pausanias further attributes the consecration of the *eirésiôné* to the myth of Theseus' victorious return to Athens, a legend commemorated in the Oschophoria with important ramifications for the *Hippolytus*.[15] Theseus' garlanded entrance in the drama could recall his return to Athens, commemorated in the Oschophoria, when victory mixes with lamentation on his learning of his father's death (Mitchell-Boyask 1999: 49–52). Given the obvious parallel between the first entrances of father and son where both come into the acting area bearing wreaths, it does not seem unreasonable to look for other similar resonances in the entry of Hippolytus. Because of the complex matrix of festival and mythical allusions active in Euripides' *Hippolytus*, I am inclined to believe that the drama's opening scene evokes the rite of the *eirésiôné* when the young man enters the stage singing and carrying a garland, placing it somewhere around the door of the palace, just as happens during the Pyanopsia and Thargelia. Hippolytus presents this garland to Artemis, one of whose important functions is to protect fertility, though typically outside in the open countryside, beyond settled agriculture. Artemis also likely had some kind of cultic healing function, as is witnessed by the presence of an Artemis temple in Asclepius' sanctuary in Epidaurus and by the evidence of healing prayers by Athenians at Brauron during the 420s in response to the plague.[16] By evoking rituals designed

---

[14] For sources and a brief account of the *eirésiôné* see Burkert 1979: 134.

[15] Calame 1990: 143–48 and 312–13, with the full range of sources.

[16] According to John Camp 2001: 125–26, the handsome buildings that one sees remains of today at the sanctuary of Artemis Brauron are dateable to the 420s BCE from unpublished inscriptions (*SEG* XL 91). This building was made as a thank-offering for saving the city from the plague because an

to ward off plague and famine, a purpose identical to the scapegoat rituals enacted around the same time, this gesture would thus prepare Hippolytus' transformation into a *pharmakos* (Mitchell 1991; Mitchell-Boyask 1999). A similar movement of thought in Aristophanes' *Knights* helps support my point here. Produced four years after the *Hippolytus*, this comedy, as Angus Bowie has argued, is full of ephebic themes, has a "hero," the Sausage-Seller, of the correct ephebic age and status, and a Chorus composed partially of young men. In the midst of the confrontation between the Sausage-Seller and the Paphlagonian slave (a thinly veiled caricature of the demagogue Cleon) over the affections of Demos (a character whose name means "the People"), Demos worries about the damage done to his *eiresiônê* (729), signaling a beginning to a kind of Thargelia, the festival where the *pharmakoi* were expelled (Bowie 1993: 45–77). After the Sausage-Seller has won and promised peace to the war-weary Demos, the latter calls the Paphlagonian/Cleon a *pharmakos* (1405), expelled from Athens. Further, Vernant's analysis of the *Oedipus Tyrannus* has shown how the suppliant branches and paeans sung in its opening scene are intended to recall the *eiresiônê* (Vernant 1988: 128–131). In Euripides' tragic drama, the wreath's placement at the palace door is thus a prelude to the ritual scapegoating of Hippolytus. Since the *Hippolytus* and *Oedipus Tyrannus* were produced in years quite close to one another (though we cannot be certain in what year for the latter), one scene could be evoking the other.

In the deployment of the young ephebic Theseus as a leading figure in these agricultural festivals, the Athenians seem to have built upon the traditional metaphor comparing the progress of humans and plants. James Redfield locates the equation of people and plants in myths of autochthony that maintain men are born from the earth (Redfield 2003: 123–24). Since Athenians believed themselves to be autochthonous, such equations must have been particularly suggestive to their social imagination. Prompted especially by the Sophists' questioning of the traditional attribution of goodness to nature (*phusis*) instead of convention (*nomos*), fifth-century thought drew comparisons between education and agriculture. In Euripides' *Hecuba*, after Polydorus compares his growth to a plant's (20), Priam's widow wonders (592–98) whether her daughter's capacity for virtue in the

unpublished inscription states that the buildings were dedicated to Artemis for the salvation (*sôtêria*) of the Athenian Demos. The purification of Delos in 426 was also likely a part of this effort; see Thucy. 3.104. The status of Artemis as a healing deity would receive further support in the light of the *parodos* of Sophocles' *Oedipus Tyrannus*, wherein the citizens of Thebes who suffer from plague call upon Delian Apollo (as Delian Paian), then Athena, then Artemis. Such a thank-offering to Artemis in the middle of the 420s would then correlate with the argument in Knox 1956 that the likely date of the production of the *Oedipus Tyrannus* is 426 or 425.

face of endless suffering and corruption comes from an innate, unchanging, nature, unlike how plants can thrive in bad earth as long as their needs are met, yet fail in good earth if untended.[17]

But a more general and fundamental form of this idea originally appears quite early, in one of the *Iliad*'s more memorable brief similes. Diomedes closes his questioning of the previously unknown Glaucus by defining humans as those who "eat the fruit of the field," as they so often are designated in Homer. Humans eat what grows and perishes, implying that they are like what they eat. Glaucus responds in kind (*Il.* 6.146–49):[18]

οἵη περ φύλλων γενεὴ τοίη δὲ καὶ ἀνδρῶν.
φύλλα τὰ μέν τ' ἄνεμος χαμάδις χέει, ἄλλα δέ θ' ὕλη
τηλεθόωσα φύει, ἔαρος δ' ἐπιγίγνεται ὥρη·
ὣς ἀνδρῶν γενεὴ ἡ μὲν φύει ἡ δ' ἀπολήγει.

As is the generation of leaves, so is that of men.
The wind blows the leaves earthward, but the flourishing forest
grows others, and the spring follows;
thus the generation of men grows and withers.

Glaucus perhaps reminds Diomedes of his relative youthfulness, something that Diomedes self-consciously asserts elsewhere. In any case, this becomes somewhat of a poetic commonplace – for example, Aristophanes uses it at *Birds* 685 – but I am not so sure that it becomes merely a poetic commonplace. In the light of later cultural developments, it seems noteworthy, if not potentially significant, that when this metaphor recurs in the *Iliad* the words come from the mouth of Apollo, the god of the Thargelia and Pyanopsia, the god who oversees ephebes and medicine. Apollo combines the words of both Glaucus and Diomedes in defining humans as those who die and return like leaves and eat the fruit of the field: οἳ φύλλοισιν ἐοικότες ἄλλοτε μέν τε / ζαφλεγέες τελέθουσιν ἀρούρης καρπὸν ἔδοντες, / ἄλλοτε δὲ φθινύθουσιν ἀκήριοι (21.463–65). The parallel between the two sets of remarks is strengthened by the similar thematic settings of the proper relationship between man and god. Diomedes asks Glaucus his identity because he does not want to fight a god, while Apollo distinguishes between mortal and immortal in claiming the impropriety of gods fighting among themselves over mere mortals.

---

[17] Depending on one's view of Hecuba's actions, this speech can be read as an ironic commentary on her revenge. See Mossman 1995: 120–21 and Nussbaum 1986: 399–401.

[18] On these lines and their implications, with a discussion of further related passages, see Nagy 1979: 178–79.

The Thargelia, Bremmer points out, was held in honor of Apollo Delius, whose primary festival, the Delia, was one of seasonal renewal strongly associated with adolescent development, as the Thargelia itself (Bremmer 1983: 319; Calame 1997: 104–10). The *eiresiônê*, carried by singing boys, was consecrated both in the sanctuary of Apollo and at the door of all houses to prevent famine and epidemic, a rite that thus integrated concerns with the young of Athens and the city's nascent crops. While the wreaths or branches were being hung, offerings were made to Helios and the Hours, signifying concern for the proper progress of time. The developmental rhythms of human existence are thus homologous with those in the wider natural world and with the results of agricultural labors. Disruption of the natural and agricultural cycles leads to disaster for humans, but, given these associations, what are the implications for the agricultural cycle of a myth where, unlike Theseus, a youth such as his son refuses his natural cycle by desiring to remain as he is forever (ἀεί, 80) and to end his life just as he began it (87)?[19] And Hippolytus' vision of an untouched meadow is fundamentally a world without agriculture. While in Hesiod's Golden Age and on the Islands of the Blessed (*Op.* 117–18, 172–73) crops grow without end and thus acyclically, in normal mortal parameters any interruption in the cycle yields disaster, as the *Hymn to Demeter* shows.

Hippolytus is not just a "Peter Pan" figure who refuses adulthood, but the son of the hero whose own youthful exploits stand at the center of two festivals dedicated to the sustenance of Athens. A human grows like a plant. The Athenians seem to have connected the fertility of their land to a myth where a young man passes to adulthood and takes his father's place in society. But that young man's own son resists the new social status that accompanies his biological development, and this refusal becomes expressed inversely as a desire to step out of the course of nature, with nature ultimately taking revenge in the form of the wild bull at the seashore. His refusal of Aphrodite engenders a *nosos* that permeates the drama's language. Given that the *pharmakos* ritual and rites of passage are built into the same cultural mythic matrix, both overseen by Apollo, I submit that, in Euripides' *Hippolytus*, plague, scapegoating and the trials of manhood are deeply interconnected. In the first scene of Euripides' drama, Hippolytus compares himself to a pure field uncut by iron blades, frozen outside of time – that is, a life beyond agriculture, without crops. Needless to say, he is oblivious to the larger implications of his remarks. Some caution

[handwritten margin note: ephebic rites]

---

[19] Cairns 1997: 57–58 observes of Hippolytus' dangerous anomalies: "The problem lies in his attitude to his *sophrosyne*; for even where that quality is expected, it is not envisaged as total and perpetual chastity."

is needed here: I am not arguing that Hippolytus risks bringing famine to Troezen or that he is some kind of Vegetation God, but that the life experience of the drama's poet and audience can structure the drama and our perception of it, and that the homologies among these different strands of Athenian culture are so strong that the breaking of one can suggest disaster in the other. Greek thought equates *limos* and *loimos*. Because of the plague, medical language in the Athenian Theater of Dionysus, especially in the early 420s, cannot be just medical language. We must take the situation of a drama's metaphorical structures at a level of complexity that approaches more completely relationships among the different discourses in Athenian culture. The *Hippolytus*, with its pestilential language and latent threats of famine, evokes the plague and Asclepius, and helps prepare the way for the god's entry into Athens, next to the Theater of Dionysus.

CHAPTER 5

Oedipus and the plague

No Greek drama is more instantly associated with plague, whether mythic or real, than Sophocles' *Oedipus Tyrannus*, and thus no Greek drama has received such scholarly attention in the context of the Athenian plague.[1] But failing to discuss the *Oedipus* in some sustained manner, however brief, might cause confusion and leave my picture incomplete. I shall therefore limit my discussion to supplementing a summary of Bernard Knox's perspicuous examinations of the plague and of medical language in the *Oedipus Tyrannus* (Knox 1956; 1957: 139–47), and this discussion is intended as an introduction to my subsequent analysis of the *Trachiniae* as a plague drama. My contribution will consist mainly of an interpretation of the circulation of nosological discourse throughout the text and a consideration of whether Sophocles' innovation of a plague at Thebes during the Athenian plague might have contributed to the second-place finish of the program that included the *Oedipus Tyrannus*. Knox (1957) discusses the image of Oedipus as a doctor and shows the role of various Hippocratic terms in the *Oedipus*, but he leaves Sophocles' means of the representation of the plague itself relatively unexplored; thus, while there are many Greek words in the index to Knox's *Oedipus at Thebes*, *nosos* is not one of them, nor, for that matter, is *loimos*. And, as with the case of other dramas I examine in this book, the deployment of *nosos* through the dramatic text is central to its meaning.

Scholars have not universally accepted that the production of the *Oedipus Tyrannus* was during the 420s, primarily because there is no secure external evidence as such, but Bernard Knox, in his 1956 article, submitted a series of arguments based on internal evidence that make a production date of 426 or

---

[1] For older bibliography see the works cited by Knox 1956: 133. Subsequent to Knox's two studies, the plague has received surprisingly little attention, aside from Ryzman 1992, who has little to add. Indeed, Winnington-Ingram 1980: 342 noted: "This important article has been unjustly neglected." Segal 1993: 73–77 provides a brief, but lucid, guide to the depiction of Oedipus' response to the plague in the prologue.

425, or perhaps slightly earlier, about as certain as one can determine based upon textual considerations that are supplemented by selected indirect external evidence such as that provided by Thucydides. Knox was careful to take into account arguments against his thesis, and nobody has since been able to mount a successful challenge to him.[2] While one could object that the plague depicted early in the drama owes much to the opening of the *Iliad*, Knox shows that a wealth of detail indicates that the Sophoclean plague both is comparable to and inspired by the actual plague, as described by Thucydides, and draws on traditional literary and religious thought (1956: 135–37). Moreover, the Chorus' prayer for the destruction of "raging Ares" (190) makes little sense for Thebes, which is at peace during the drama's action, but much for an Athens at war with Sparta (1956: 138–40). Details such as heat and blight and a reference to a previous visitation of the plague (164) in the *Oedipus Tyrannus* suggest the events of 427–426, again as described by Thucydides. As I observed in my previous chapter on Euripides' *Hippolytus*, archaeological discoveries at Brauron subsequent to Knox's article support Knox's linkage of the prayers to Artemis and Apollo in the *parodos* to the purification of Delos in 426–425 (Camp 2001: 125–26). Last, Knox argues (144–47) that Aristophanes' *Knights*, which was produced in 424 BCE, alludes to this drama, thus providing a possible *terminus ante quem*. Because Knox's initial thesis concerning Sophocles' innovation of a Theban plague is essential to a consideration of the drama's possible reception in Athens, I shall postpone my discussion of that part of his argument on the relationship between the Athenian plague and Sophocles' *Oedipus Tyrannus*.

First, I shall examine the circulation of disease language throughout the text, as it shows the rich Sophoclean mixture of the literal and the metaphorical and meaningfully joins together seemingly disparate elements. Before focusing on *nosos*, I turn to the verb *phthiein* or *phthinein*, which denotes passive destruction: to waste away, to wane, to pine or perish. This verb occurs six times in the *Oedipus Tyrannus*, initially to designate part of the effect of the plague on Thebes. Sophocles, in the Priest's long speech, unusually begins consecutive lines (25–26) with identical forms of this verb to describe the blight on the land of Thebes; the anaphoric repetition of *phthinousa* thus heightens the religious sense of doom. Then, as Oedipus' investigation into the plague's cause unexpectedly raises doubts about the

---

[2] Griffith 1996: 86 briefly attacks Knox's dates but errs in focusing totally on the coda to Knox's argument which examines echoes in Aristophanes' *Knights* and thus proposes 425 as one *possible* year for the *Oedipus*. Knox's other arguments, as well as the other years they support, are ignored. Müller 1984: 59 has argued against Knox's dating and for a production year of 433.

continuing power of the gods, the Chorus follows its doubts about the necessity of continuing to dance in the sacred chorus with a lament for "the ancient prophecies of Laius, which are wasting away" (φθίνοντα γὰρ Λαίου παλαιὰ / θέσφατ᾽, 906–07). Does the Chorus thus fear the plague is having some effect on the gods and their words? A few lines later Oedipus reacts to the news of the death of Polybus with the observation (962): "The wretch, as it appears, wasted away with disease." Now, while I am postponing discussion of *nosos* for a bit longer, it seems significant here that this line is so emphatically framed with such thematically important words; *nosois* (νόσοις) begins the line, which ends with *ephthito* (ἔφθιτο). This verb circulates through a small but significant network: first Thebes wastes away, then the oracles concerning Oedipus' father Laius, and it finally settles on the man whom Oedipus supposed, wrongly it will soon turn out, to be his father.

The other two uses of this verb are quite odd, but, I think, meaningfully so, for they both remarkably, in the context of their prominent use to describe the blight during the plague, convert a rather passive verb to an actively destructive one. First, the Chorus closes its singular, as Knox noted, prayer for help against "raging Ares" (190) with the plea: "O father Zeus, destroy him under your thunderbolt," ὦ Ζεῦ πάτερ, ὑπὸ σῷ φθίσον κεραυνῷ (202). Second, the Chorus later laments the fallen Oedipus as the one who "destroyed the maiden with the crooked talons who sang oracles," κατὰ μὲν φθίσας / τὰν γαμψώνυχα παρθένον / χρησμῳδόν (1198–200). This active use is extremely rare in tragedy and occurs even there only in lyric passages.[3] The audience is thus asked to hear the verb first mainly in its primary passive sense and then in these two extraordinary passages, an arrangement that suggests that Sophocles wants to link them to the effects of the plague. The Chorus' prayer against Ares would suggest a desire that the thunderbolt of Zeus bring plague against Ares, a somewhat startling idea which is supported by, in Parry's words, "the suppressed image" of Zeus' thunderbolt in the verb (σκήψας) in the Priest's lament, during the prologue, of the *loimos* that afflicts Thebes (Parry 1969: 114). The transfer by the Chorus of this unusual use of the verb to their recollection, just before the Messenger speech, of Oedipus' defeat of the Sphinx then alludes back to his earlier salvation of Thebes when he acted like a god, but also triggered the sequence of events that would eventually bring plague to Thebes. The mere presence of *skêpsas*, then, underscores the inevitable reversal of the

---

[3] A. *Eu.* 173, and, possibly, Soph. *El.* 1414.

victory of Oedipus over the Sphinx and perhaps even suggests that the plague, essentially, begins with this act.

A careful attention to the deployment of *nosos* in this text yields similar patterns. There are a total of fourteen instances of the noun *nosos*, its more abstract cognate *nosêma* and the verb *nosein*.[4] These are distributed unevenly, with nine in the drama's first half and five in its second; indeed, eight of the fourteen are clustered in the drama's first 307 lines. Those first nine denote literal sickness, while the later five are more, but not entirely, metaphorical. This compression, however, becomes even more pronounced in the light of the gradual focusing of the Theban crisis over the first few dozen lines. The scene of supplication that Oedipus first describes does not necessarily indicate that Thebes suffers from plague, and only the reference to paean songs (line 5) marks sickness at all. The Priest then further describes the nature of the suppliant crowd in front of the doors of the palace, before the repeated *phthinousa* that begins both lines 25 and 26 speaks of the blight. The speech thus carefully builds toward the climactic revelation of what is occurring: λοιμὸς ἔχθιστος, "most abominable plague" (28). As I argued earlier, *loimos* is an extremely rare word in the fifth century, and poets, especially after 430, avoid it to such an extent that one must conclude that there is some form of superstition driving its absence. Within the performative context of the Athenian plague, the effect of this word, coming from a character who is a religious authority and after Sophocles has so carefully built toward its enunciation, must have been quite shattering. Having made his point, Sophocles puts *loimos* away and returns to the more customary, more flexible, and safer, *nosos*.

Oedipus, who is responsible for the plague, is the center of talk about it. He speaks the word *nosos* eight times, more than any other character (60–61, 217, 303, 307, 960, 962), and is even responsible for its longest absence, the 329 lines after 307 when he is busy building his paranoid personal disputes with first Tiresias and then Creon. His increasing concern with himself is marked by Jocasta's first words, wherein she asks her brother and husband (635–36): "Aren't you ashamed for stirring private problems when the land is so sick (γῆς οὕτω νοσούσης)?" As the conversation between Jocasta and Oedipus suddenly turns to matters in the distant past, the language of disease naturally submerges, for 324 lines, until, somewhat surprisingly, it returns when Oedipus twice uses it in the discussion of the death of Polybus. The messenger from Corinth tells him that Polybus is dead. Oedipus wants to know how he died, and his questions show both the lingering effects of

---

[4] 60–61 (three times), 150, 169, 217, 303, 307, 636, 960, 962, 1054, 1293, 1455.

his suspicions about a plot by Tiresias and Creon and his concern with the plague, *nosos*, that he is attempting to stop (960–63):

> **Oedipus**
> Was it by treachery, or in contact with some disease (*nosou*).
> **Corinthian**
> A slight tip to the scales brings old bodies to their beds.
> **Oedipus**
> The wretch, as it seems, wasted away with disease (*nosois*).
> **Corinthian**
> And because he'd met the measure of his old age.

Much happens of significance in this simple exchange, but it is most important that its language returns to the plague even as it narrates events in Corinth. Given the prominence of *nosos* in the drama's language and themes, any instance simply cannot be explained away as disconnected from the rest of the text. I have already discussed how two words used earlier for the plague emphatically frame line 962, as it begins with *nosois* (νόσοις) and ends with *ephthito* (ἔφθιτο). Moreover, Oedipus' insistence on the role of *nosos*, a word Sophocles does not have to use here, marks a connection between the death of Polybus and the plague. Oedipus asks about *nosos* and the Corinthian stresses old age. Oedipus then ignores the Corinthian's response and insists, doubly, on *nosos*. That this insistence is a bit odd is marked by the Corinthian's return to old age as the primary cause of death. This exchange could have taken place with half the lines and without a return of the plague language from earlier in the drama. The strong echoes, at the beginning of this scene, of the opening tableau of the prologue in Jocasta's supplication of Apollo's altar prepare the reemergence of language from that earlier scene (Segal 1981: 236). This return is confirmed also by the last word in Oedipus' first question, ξυναλλαγῇ, which denotes dealings or exchanges and perhaps here personifies the dependent genitive *nosou* (νόσου). The word *synallagê* also was prominent in the prologue scene, and in exactly the same final location in the trimeter line, when the Priest, just after enunciating the taboo word *loimos* (28), warns Oedipus that he is not "equal to the gods" (31), but "first of men both in the chances of life and in dealings (συναλλαγαῖς)[5] with the gods" (34). These two lines mark the shift in Oedipus' status from being

---

[5] Jebb prints ξυναλλαγαῖς. His note on 960 points back to 34, almost as if to suggest a connection. Dawe and the OCTs of both Pearson and Lloyd-Jones print συναλλαγαῖς. Dawe in his note on 960 seems to follow Jebb in sensing there is some connection with line 34: "the same word as at 34, and as there clothing a matter of some solemnity with an expression whose meaning cannot be pinned down."

someone involved with the gods to someone involved with the plague, and together they suggest that the death of Polybus is not a coincidence with the plague but is in fact a manifestation of it – or rather, a manifestation of the gods' role in the plague. Polybus has died through contact with disease because his adopted son is first among men, for better and for worse, in contact with the gods.[6]

Jocasta twice speaks of disease, once in connection with the Theban plague and the second time in reference to herself; the plague seems to enter her as she realizes the truth about her second husband. In both places, Jocasta intervenes to stop her husband from a course of action, first, his violent quarrel with Creon and, second, his desire to interrogate the one person who might tell him the identity of his parents, the shepherd from the house of Laius:

> τί τὴν ἄβουλον, ὦ ταλαίπωροι, στάσιν
> γλώσσης ἐπήρασθ' οὐδ' ἐπαισχύνεσθε γῆς
> οὕτω νοσούσης ἴδια κινοῦντες κακα;

> Why, you miserable men, have you raised an ill-advised
> *stasis* of speech? Aren't you ashamed to stir up
> private troubles when the land is so sick?
>
> *OT* 634–36

> μὴ πρὸς θεῶν, εἴπερ τι τοῦ σαυτοῦ βίου
> κήδει, ματεύσῃς τοῦθ'· ἅλις νοσοῦσ' ἐγώ

> By the gods, don't seek this, if you care at all
> about your own life; I am sick enough already.
>
> *OT* 1060–61

That last line reaches back to two other key moments in the text. Her claim (1061), "I am sick enough already," first surely echoes Oedipus' early assertion, so pregnant with dramatic irony: εὖ γὰρ οἶδ' ὅτι / νοσεῖτε πάντες, καὶ νοσοῦντες, ὡς ἐγὼ /οὐκ ἔστιν ὑμῶν ὅστις ἐξ ἴσου νοσεῖ, "for I know well that you are all sick, and, although you are sick, none of you are as equally sick as I" (59–61). Note the shift from the plural collective participle for the citizens of Thebes to the emphatic singular pronoun (*egô*) with first Oedipus and then Jocasta, and in the same final position in the line; it is as if the plague has now focused on the one who is, in some ways, ultimately

---

[6] Peradotto 1992: 8 argues against the common acceptance of coincidence in the *Oedipus Tyrannus*, especially of the arrival of the plague "long after the fated pair have had time to breed four incestuous children, and precisely timed to coincide with the death of Polybus in such a way as to bring the announcement of his death to Thebes not twenty minutes too early or twenty minutes too late. Things like that do not appear to happen by accident."

responsible for it. Charles Segal, who is almost the only critic not to shrug off the imagery of this line silently, presumably as a dead metaphor (in a drama with a plague!), observes: "her metaphor of 'disease' contains a full recognition of what their life together means" (Segal 1993: 127). Rush Rehm adds: "The plague that afflicts Thebes now finds its source in Jocasta" (Rehm 1992: 117), a claim that finds further support in the second echo, from line 636. Both forms of the verb *nosein* in these two lines are feminine participles; the first modifies the land, *gê*, of Thebes, and the second the queen of that land. The morphological similarity of the two participles thus further strengthens the echo from the first to the second. Returning to the progress of *nosos* in the text of the *Oedipus Tyrannus*, I observe that the plague has moved fatally from the Theban populace to the king of Corinth, and now back to the Theban queen.

The plague will finally rest fully in Oedipus himself. While the Priest had articulated the plague, uniquely, as *loimos*, disease as *nosos* entered the drama's discourse first through the words of Oedipus (59–61), when his claims that acknowledge the suffering of Thebes, but also insist on his greater sickness, speak of it three times in three lines. "Nobody is as sick as I." This is, of course, one of the most poignant examples of irony not just in this text, but in all of Greek literature. Oedipus here seems to participate in modern scholarly arguments about the literal and metaphorical meanings of *nosos*, since he clearly does not believe he himself has the plague, yet he uses the language of such disease, which the text itself does repeatedly, to describe his own grief. Oedipus believes his emotions are an effect of the plague, just as Jocasta does at 1054, but really he himself is its cause. In the crisis of the *Oedipus Tyrannus* the distinctions between cause, effect and the plague itself blur and become meaningless.[7] Oedipus does not have the plague, but he does. Thus, the Messenger prepares his audiences, both those in the orchestra and in the theater, for the entrance of the blinded, bloody Oedipus in the climactic line that fulfills the nosological patterns of the drama: τὸ γὰρ νόσημα μεῖζον ἢ φέρειν, "his disease is greater than he can bear" (1293). Sophocles shifts his vocabulary slightly from the more common *nosos* to the more abstract and technical *nosêma*, a word which appears one other time in the text, line 307, when Oedipus describes to Tiresias the exact terms of Apollo's instructions for ridding Thebes of the plague.[8] At 1293 Sophocles seems to want to insist on the plague's transformation into Oedipus' personal catastrophe; the plague does

---

[7] On polarities and their inversion or reversal in the *Oedipus Tyrannus* see Vernant 1988: 113–40 and Segal 1993: 204–48.

[8] In the tragic corpus, five of the eleven uses of *nosêma* occur in Sophocles.

not disappear late in the drama, as some commentators suggest, but it moves into the body of Oedipus, mutating, to use the language of modern medicine. This mutation is what Sophocles' language tells us, for, as Page observed of Thucydides' terminology, "νόσος is, as a rule, a more general term than νόσημα, which is most often used when a particular malady is under consideration."[9] As Oedipus' suffering becomes physical and not just emotional, so the language surrounding his experience becomes more specifically medical and evocative of the plague.

Yet Oedipus rejects the judgment of the Messenger, not that he is sick, but that he is incapable of bearing its severity. His long speech after the *kommos* with the Chorus ends and climaxes almost exuberantly with his claim: τἀμὰ γὰρ κακὰ / οὐδεὶς οἷός τε πλὴν ἐμοῦ φέρειν βροτῶν, "There is nobody among mortals except for me who is able to bear my troubles" (1414–15). The assertion that he can bear (*pherein*) his troubles (*kaka*) echoes the Messenger's words that Oedipus cannot bear (φέρειν) his illness. While Oedipus, because he was offstage during the Messenger's speech, could not have heard the latter's assessment of what Oedipus can endure, the similarity of the phrasing suggests a rebuttal of the Messenger's judgment. Oedipus further glosses these two passages in his speech to Creon when, after requesting that he be led off to die on Mt. Cithaeron, he adds with sudden prophetic intuition that he is not destined to die now (1455–56): "And yet I know this, that neither disease (*noson*) nor anything else could ever destroy me." This is the fourteenth and final instance of *nosos* in the *Oedipus Tyrannus*, and its thirteen predecessors load a fairly simple statement with much more complex resonance than it would have in isolation. Yes, he can endure it. Oedipus only imagines things, not humans, animals or gods, threatening his life, and the only thing he specifies is *nosos*. Since he has already survived the great Theban *nosos*, in all of its forms, he cannot suffer it again. One is reminded here of Thucydides' observation (2.50.6) that the plague did not attack the same person twice with a fatal result. Thucydides here gropes in the direction of a concept of acquired immunity, and it would be foolish to see a direct connection between these two passages, especially since Oedipus here continues to intimate his new, almost god-like, status. And yet they resonate in each other. Oedipus cannot imagine meeting a greater *nosos* than the one he has just survived, and Sophocles hence closes the verbal path of the plague in his drama about Oedipus with a sickness that cannot kill.

---

[9] Page 1953: 100, also cited by Knox 1957: 249. Page continues: "It is noticeable that the word occurs in Thucydides only with reference to the plague."

What would the Athenians have made of this drama when they first saw it in the Theater of Dionysus? One can only speculate, but there are grounds, both in the language of the drama and its implied staging, for informed speculation. I shall deal with the latter aspect first. Following Gernet's lead, Vernant demonstrated how the prologue would have evoked the *pharmakos* ritual as well as other aspects of the festival of the Athenian Thargelia, sacred to Apollo, that were associated with the prevention of famine, *limos*, which, as we have seen, was closely connected with *loimos* (Vernant 1988: 125–38).[10] Various members of the throng seen before the palace of Thebes bear a suppliant branch, draped in wool (line 3), which was in form and function like the *eiresiônê*, a first-fruit offering at the Thargelia, and the paeans which are heard by Oedipus (line 5) were also purification songs sung during that same festival. The Athenian audience would thus be immediately confronted in this drama with a representation of the rituals designed to deal with the particular crises that have been afflicting them for the previous several years.

Sophocles explores the relationship between leader and community during a time of plague, in the process linking plague to the violation of the most fundamental customs of society, and this exploration represents the plague directly and in language that is not generally used in the theater. A century later, of course, Aristotle would elevate Sophocles' *Oedipus Tyrannus* to the highest rank of the tragedies he knew, which were many times more in number than what we have today. But at its first performance, the Second Hypothesis indicates, the reception was less enthusiastic: Sophocles was "beaten by Philocles, as Dikaiarkhos says." Philocles was a nephew of Sophocles' earlier rival Aeschylus. We know that he wrote a trilogy, the *Pandiotis*, and, at some point, an *Oedipus* of his own. He seems to have had little lasting impact on the Athenian theater, and yet he beat Sophocles in the year that Sophocles produced a drama which, in the fourth century, would be considered among his greatest and must have had a substantial, more immediate, impact because Sophocles felt impelled to return to its substance at the end of his life in his *Oedipus at Colonus*. Sophocles certainly did not win every year, though he did most of the time and he never finished third. Sophocles won first place eighteen times, and thus, since the victor at the Dionysia was recognized for his full slate of four plays, seventy-two of his dramas were judged to be worthy of the highest contemporary recognition. While not enough is known about the judging procedures and

---

[10] Against the widely held view that the *Oedipus Tyrannus* evokes scapegoating rituals see Griffith 1993. Foley 1993 offers a much more nuanced account of the complex relationship between *pharmakos* ritual and Sophocles' *Oedipus Tyrannus*.

criteria to explain why certain programs won and others failed, and little external evidence about the competition the year of the *Oedipus Tyrannus* survives, one can suggest a theory for Sophocles' defeat, based primarily on internal evidence.

My conclusion is that the direct, unmediated depiction in the Theater of Dionysus of a plague at a time when one was ravaging Athens, or had recently done so, made the relationship between the world of the stage and the world of the audience, in the words of Sourvinou-Inwood, "transgressive" (Sourvinou-Inwood 2003: 16). The two spheres simply became too similar. Again, Sophocles, early in the *Oedipus Tyrannus*, chooses to use the term for plague, *loimos*, that seems to have been otherwise under some kind of stricture during the fifth century, and I have already shown that he carefully builds toward its enunciation by a religious authority and does not use the word again. As Knox (1956) explains, many of the details of Theban suffering in the drama jibe with, or are only explainable by, reference to events during the plague that Thucydides records. Knox further demonstrates that Sophocles, based on the available evidence, seems to have invented the story of the Theban plague for this drama, since no extant source composed before the *Oedipus Tyrannus* mentions it, and even later works that cover some of the same events, such as Euripides' *Phoenissae*, fail to mention a plague at Thebes (Knox 1956: 134–36). The sheer size of the *Oedipus* prologue, its 150 lines being the longest in the surviving plays of Sophocles, indicates that it carries a far greater narrative burden than is normal for Sophoclean drama.[11] Thus, in terms of content, diction and form, Sophocles still signals that he here deals with unusual and, in some sense, dangerous material.

Sophocles did not suffer the fate of Phrynicus, fined heavily after his historical drama *The Sack of Miletus* early in the fifth century (Hdt. 6.21), but a second-place finish for a program that crossed an unspoken line despite its artistic merits, if not superiority, might have been deemed sufficient punishment. Moreover, Sophocles, the most successful playwright of his era, who had also served as a general during the Samian War and who would again take important roles in the government of Athens, was perhaps unpunishable in this context. It is possible that other surviving dramas from the plague years, such as the *Hippolytus*, thus succeeded, in the literal sense, more fully because they avoided *loimos* and kept their depictions of *nosos* to a more metaphorical range while still harnessing the plague's social and emotional energies. In the succeeding chapter, I shall argue that the

---

[11] Prologue line counts for Sophocles: *Aj.* 133, *El.* 120, *OT* 150, *Ant.* 99, *Tr.* 93, *Ph.* 134, *OC* 116.

Trachiniae, while its year of production and immediate level of success is unknown, belongs among the group of tragic dramas that directly engage the plague but filter it through a metaphorical structure. The *Oedipus Tyrannus*, despite its obvious virtues, failed to win the highest acclaim at the City Dionysia, I believe, because its depiction of a plague simply scraped violently at emotional wounds that had barely had the time to form scabs.

CHAPTER 6

The Trachiniae *and the plague*

"People who confidently claim to know the date of Sophocles' *Electra* or *Trachiniae* are living in a private world."[1]

H. Lloyd-Jones

In this chapter I explore the reasons for placing the composition and production of Sophocles' *Trachiniae* during the plague years and the implications of such a situation for understanding this tragic drama about the circumstances of the death of Heracles. Since the production of only two extant Sophoclean dramas, the *Oedipus at Colonus*, staged posthumously in 401 BCE, and the *Philoctetes* of 409, can be fixed to definite years, most scholars generally rely on internal, stylistic, criteria to date the other five with some hope of accuracy. Yet studies of the *Trachiniae* on such grounds have been inconclusive, not least because they contradict one another. Moreover, this drama seems to lack completely any secure reference to external events, which thus enables a startlingly large range of possible dates; anywhere from 457 to 410 has been proposed at one time or another. It is, I suggest, at the very least a worthwhile intellectual enterprise to examine the reasons for accepting the later (though not the latest) part of this range and why Sophocles might have composed such a work during the 420s. But I also more fundamentally propose to change the way we ask this question: let us accept, for the moment, that Sophocles composed the *Trachiniae* sometime between 430 and 425, and then consider what would happen to our understanding of it in such a context. The *Trachiniae*, I shall thus argue, is a plague drama, and viewing it as a response to the plague should change the way we read it, namely as a drama engaged with the worship of Heracles and as a Sophoclean reaction, not just to the plague, but to the concurrent Peloponnesian War as well.

The thematic significance of the prevalence of *nosos* in the heroes of Sophoclean drama has long been recognized (Biggs 1966; Segal 1995: 35–37;

---

[1] As quoted in Winnington-Ingram 1980: 182.

Knox 1957: 139–47), and Heracles certainly resembles other male Sophoclean protagonists in his illness and its disruptive affects on his relationship
with his community.[2] Heracles first suffers from the disease of an excessive
amount of *eros*, as Deianira describes it (443, 491, 544), and then from the
effects of a poisonous mixture spread on his clothing, which is narrated in
similar language. Years before, Heracles had shot the Centaur Nessus with
his arrows, dipped in the venom of the Hydra, after Nessus had attempted
to rape Deianira while ferrying her across a river. Nessus had promised her at
his death that the mixture of his blood and the poison would form a magical
drug that could keep Heracles from ever loving any woman other than her.
During Sophocles' drama, then, Deianira, terrified of losing her husband
to the captive Iole, sends Heracles clothing smeared with this potion, and
Heracles, after donning the gift, feels the poison start to work, activated
by fire, in the midst of a sacrificial offering to Zeus. He thus suffers *nosos*
before and during the drama. In suffering a *nosos* Heracles is not unique
among Sophoclean heroes. The madness of Ajax is a *nosos*, Oedipus is, in
his own words, sicker that the entire plague-ridden city of Thebes (though
he does not, of course, realize he is the illness itself), and the festering
wound on Philoctetes' foot causes his expulsion from the Greek army on
its way to Troy. Yet Heracles' *nosos* is in some sense unique in that his is
the only one of this group that is, during the first half of the *Trachiniae*,
clearly metaphorical as the disease of *eros* (443, 491, 544), not literal, and
it is the only one, except the *nosos* of Oedipus, that endures through the
whole sequence of scenes with no hope of a cure save death. Indeed the
shift here of disease from metaphorical to literal mirrors the movement in
the *Oedipus Tyrannus* from metaphorical to actual blindness. The death
of Ajax removes all talk of illness from the drama that bears his name; no
instances of *nosos* occur after line 635, which is even before his "deception
speech." Philoctetes, on the other hand, leaves Lemnos still diseased but
with the assurance from the divinized Heracles that Asclepius will heal him
at Troy. Only Heracles and Oedipus enter and leave the stage diseased, and
this itself might point to a closer chronological relationship between the
two dramas than has traditionally been suspected. Disease in the *Trachiniae*
is thus different from that in the other extant dramas of Sophocles, so a
return to basic questions such as its production date seems warranted in
order to understand how and why it is different.

---

[2] It is interesting, and might be significant, that the only Sophoclean protagonists to lack *nosos*, Antigone
and Electra, are female. However, as the deuteragonist, or tritagonist, Jocasta begins to realize the
truth about her husband Oedipus, she ends her second attempt to stop his pursuit with the claim
(*OT* 1061) ἅλις νοσοῦσ᾽ ἐγώ – "I am sick enough already."

DATING PROBLEMS

First, I should explain why the various attempts to date this tragic drama have proven unsuccessful, or at least not completely convincing, whether scholars have focused on influential links with other texts, as German scholars tended to do in the first half of the twentieth century, or on style, as American and British scholars did during the subsequent decades.[3] Wilamowitz believed the sleeping Heracles in the exodus to have been modeled on Euripides' treatment in his own *Heracles* and thus assigned the *Trachiniae* to sometime between 420 and 410 BCE, much later than almost anyone.[4] Pohlenz, then, following the lead of Johanna Heinz, argued that, no, the main influence was Euripides' *Alcestis*, and thus assigned the date to sometime soon after 438. Next, Reinhardt compared the *Trachiniae* to the rest of Sophocles and concluded, on the basis of form and content, that it must have come during the 440s, after the *Ajax* but before the *Antigone*.

The focus then shifted to form and style, with similarly mixed results. Webster supported Reinhardt's date with the argument that the "diptych" style of the *Trachiniae* was the mark of relatively early Sophocles (Webster 1969: 54); this approach, however, ignores how the extremely small sample of Sophoclean tragedy still surviving makes it difficult to generalize so, as well as the fact that Euripides wrote dramas structured in such a way (e.g. the *Hecuba*) well into the 420s. On the other hand, studies of lyric meters in the *Trachiniae* have concluded that it was likely composed close to the date of Sophocles' *Oedipus Tyrannus* (Pohslander 1963; Raven 1965). Stinton, on the other hand, examined the avoidance of hiatus between verses in the dialogue trimeters and deduced that this drama must be very early, if not the earliest, in the extant work of Sophocles (Stinton 1977). Different features of Sophocles' style thus mark different possible ranges of dates; Raven even noted that one aspect of the metrics of the *Trachiniae*, free responsion, only occurs otherwise in dramas composed later than 424 BCE (Raven 1965: 228), and almost nobody, aside from Wilamowitz, has ever placed this drama that late. Style can help establish general parameters and hinder us from assigning the *Trachiniae* to, say, the same year as the

---

[3] For a concise account of such efforts among German scholars see Schwinge 1962: 11–14. Easterling's summary (1982: 19–22) of the controversies surrounding the date of production is even-handed and judicious, coming down, ultimately and tentatively, on a date sometime in the late 430s. There have been no substantial attempts to tackle this problem since the publication of Easterling's commentary. Segal 1995: 28–29 briefly argues for a date in the 430s.

[4] Schwinge 1962: 14 summarizes critically the claims of Wilamowitz, who then also seems to have been the unacknowledged source for the similar dating of 410 by Pickard-Cambridge 1946: 47, which, read by itself, is somewhat startling.

Philoctetes, but, when the results are mixed, if not contradictory of one another, then one must be, at least, extremely careful, especially heeding the example of Aeschylus' *Suppliant Women*, which, for half of the twentieth century, scholars thought to be a relatively early product of the creator of the *Oresteia*, until a papyrus publication in 1951 showed it to be, in fact, a relatively late play.[5] Until then, everything about the text had pointed to it being a relatively early drama, but the papyrus showed that, the same year as its production, Sophocles took second prize, and he debuted at the City Dionysia with a victory in 468, so Aeschylus must have composed his *Suppliant Women* sometime during the final fifteen years of his life. Podlecki's work on the political background of the *Suppliant Women*, in which the new later date supplies the basis to consider the drama's political language in the light of the Argive reception of the ostracized Themistocles, provides us with an example of how a shift in the time of production can allow for a paradigm shift in interpretation (Podlecki 1966: 42–62). We thus must consider that there is even less evidence to date the *Trachiniae* relatively early in Sophocles' output than there was for the *Suppliant Women* when it was still believed to be an early work of Aeschylus. Hammond, considering these changes to the dating of the *Suppliant Women*, observed in terms that are useful to the study of the *Trachiniae*: "The style of any one play cannot be used by itself to put a date on that play either within a series of plays or in absolute terms" (Hammond 1988: 13).[6] Raven and Pohslander both dated the *Trachiniae*, based on style, to sometime close to the *Oedipus Tyrannus*, and, as I shall argue later, important shared themes, actions and concerns strongly link these two dramas.

The most widely accepted *terminus ante quem* date of 430 seems generated more by the desire to have the *Trachiniae* before the *Oedipus Tyrannus* than any other factor and thus assumes a date of 429 for the latter, but since, as Knox demonstrated (1956), the production of the *Oedipus* could have been as late as 425, the *Trachiniae* could thus move easily into the 420s,

---

[5] The redating of the *Suppliants* was based on *P.Oxy* XX 2256, fr. 3. The discussion by Jones 1962: 67–72, in a section with the title "The Matter of a Date," lucidly shows the dangers of making large assumptions about an author based upon a small part of a huge body of work. Podlecki 1966: 42–45 further summarizes the stylistic evidence and then demonstrates how a date late in the 460s makes coherent the political context of the suppliant drama in terms of the Argive reception of Themistocles following his ostracism. More recently, however, Scullion 2002 has cast doubt on the later dating of the *Suppliant Women* and advocated a return to the 470s, but, in order to argue this in the face of the information about Sophocles in the papyrus fragment, he must argue that Sophocles debuted at the City Dionysia in 477, and was thus granted one of the three choruses by the archon, at the very tender age of nineteen.

[6] This is part of Hammond's defense of the Aeschylean authorship of the *Prometheus Bound*, and, while I increasingly find that specific position harder to justify, I am in sympathy with the statement I just quoted and with his general observation in these pages that the dating of the *Suppliant Women* shows that great poets can escape stylometric analyses.

and into the years of the Athenian plague. It seems that the sole scholar to link the *Trachiniae* to the plague has been Marsh McCall, who, in 1972, having accepted Knox's arguments concerning the possible years of the *Oedipus Tyrannus*, made this observation to close a more general study of the *Trachiniae* (McCall 1972: 163):

> The mood of darkness, the prevalent language and imagery of sickness, and many other factors, seem in fact to support the thesis that, like the *Oedipus Tyrannus*, the *Trachiniae* derives from the first years of the Peloponnesian War and has the Athenian plague in the background of its conception.

This comment, placed at the end of a substantial article and disconnected from the rest of the subject of its examination, attracted very little notice from subsequent scholars for whom the date of the production was a more pressing issue. My concern in the following pages will be to give life to and flesh out McCall's skeletal comments, since his intuition was, I believe, correct. Since nobody has tackled the date of the *Trachiniae* for over two decades, and the general study of Athenian drama has changed much since 1980, a fresh approach and a greater concern with context might yield new findings.

"The *Trachiniae* has no references to outside events and is quoted by no comedy." So wrote once T. B. L. Webster on the difficulty of locating this work in history (Webster 1969: 4). I hope to show now that both assertions were misplaced. The *Trachiniae* refers to the Athenian plague of the early 420s and Aristophanes' *Clouds* engages in a parody of its exodus, and both support a production date in the 420s. I shall deal with the *Clouds* first and the plague reaction second.

A PARODY OF HERACLES IN THE *CLOUDS*

In placing the date of the *Trachiniae* in the 420s, and perhaps even the mid-420s, there is an unexpected ally: the scene in Aristophanes' *Clouds* when Strepsiades must lie on a couch in order to think deeply about his problems.[7] In brief, Strepsiades and Heracles both lie on couches screaming in pain at the assaults on their bodies from hostile forces, the latter from the deadly poisons from Nessus the Centaur and the former from bed-bugs.[8] Dover, in his commentary on the *Clouds*, observes that the scene is a parody

---

[7] Kirk Ormand first pointed out to me the resemblances between the two scenes. I have developed and elaborated his basic idea that Strepsiades on the philosophic couch is a parody of the exodus of Heracles, but the idea still remains Ormand's. I am extremely grateful to him for this generous donation.

[8] Vickers 1991 argues on the basis of a comparison of Thucydides' plague narrative and this scene that Strepsiades' sufferings evoke those of plague victims. I shall argue below that Heracles' own distress is

of tragedy, but does not elaborate at all.[9] Here is the heart of that scene (707–16).

Στρεψιάδης
ἀτταταῖ ἀτταταῖ.
Χορός
τί πάσχεις; τί κάμνεις;
Στρεψιάδης
ἀπόλλυμαι δείλαιος· ἐκ τοῦ σκίμποδος
δάκνουσί μ' ἐξέρποντες οἱ Κορίνθιοι,
καὶ τὰς πλευρὰς δαρδάπτουσιν
καὶ τὴν ψυχὴν ἐκπίνουσιν
καὶ τοὺς ὄρχεις ἐξέλκουσιν
καὶ τὸν πρωκτὸν διορύττουσιν,
καί μ' ἀπολοῦσιν.
Χορός
μή νυν βαρέως ἄλγει λίαν.

Strepsiades
Ow! Ow!
Chorus
What do you suffer? What ails you?
Strepsiades
I'm being destroyed wretchedly! In this little bed
some Corinthian bugs are biting me,
and they chew my sides,
and drink down my life,
and drag out my balls,
and dig through my rump
and they will destroy me!
Chorus
Don't be aggrieved so mightily!

Strepsiades does use language suggestive of tragic lament in his initial cries of *attatai attatai* (707), and then by opening and closing his first extended lament with "I am being destroyed wretchedly! (*apollumai deilaios*, 709) and "they [the bed-bugs] will destroy me" (*m' apolousin*, 715); the ring composition of the two forms of *apollunai* underscores the tragic parody. Indeed, while such language is fairly generic, Heracles himself does cry out, in response to attempts to adjust his position on his couch, ἀπολεῖς μ', ἀπολεῖς (*Tr.* 1008). Both scenes open with references to the sleep of the

---

modeled on the experiences of plague victims, and Strepsiades' pains could thus be *indirectly* evocative of the plague; I am hesitant to believe that the plague would be a direct source for comedy.
[9] Dover 1968: 188 simply observes on these lines in the *Clouds*: "There may be a parody here of a tragic hero expressing his agony in anapestic verse."

heroes (in Strepsiades' case, his wakefulness) and both open and close with verses in the anapestic meter. Strepsiades focuses on the pains to his sides (*pleuras*, 711), seemingly echoing the prime location of Heracles' agony (*Tr.* 1053, 1081). His laments of the bugs biting and "drinking" him could play off the repeated imagery of the poison afflicting Heracles as a wild beast devouring him. The Chorus then instructs him to cover his head (726), and the play with his covers that ensues might echo the horrific unveiling of Heracles as he puts his condition on display for all to see and pity.

That Aristophanes frequently returned to Heracles as a source for comedy strengthens the case that this scene is a deliberate parody of the *Trachiniae*. The gustatory and sexual gluttony of Heracles, his general excessiveness in all matters make him rich fodder for the comic stage. The particular Athenian concern with his divinization then likely turned him into a large and inviting target for Aristophanes, who thus ridiculed the logical consequences of the divinization of the gluttonous, violent Heracles in the *Birds*, where Heracles participates in the divine embassy to negotiate with the upstart Athenian (only to be quickly outwitted with the prospect of a barbeque meal), and who then played off Heracles' many descents to Hades by having him advise Dionysus how to go there in the *Frogs*. But Heracles, while not appearing himself in the *Clouds*, still serves as a named source for its comedy, for the Unjust Argument opens its attack on how the Just Argument moralizes to Strepsiades' son Pheidippides with an appeal to the valor of Heracles.[10] The Just Argument has scorned the modern preference for warm baths, so the Unjust Argument, after the Just concedes that there was "no better man than Heracles" (1050), points out that natural hot springs are called "Heraclean baths" because the gods had made them for Heracles during his travels, with the implication that the hero himself was no softy. Heracles thus serves as the first, and thus foremost, weapon in the Unjust Argument's arsenal and Aristophanes coopts the bravery of Heracles for comedy, just as he had earlier during Strepsiades' time on the couch.[11]

There are certainly important thematic connections between these dramas of Aristophanes and Sophocles here as well. Both works involve the problem of the intelligibility of the will of the gods and then reassert traditional Olympian religion in the face of skeptics, but, more importantly,

---

[10] While the debate between the two Arguments is believed to have been added during Aristophanes' revision of the *Clouds*, nonetheless there would have been some kind of debate in the first version, which might have contained the same joke about Heraclean baths. See Dover 1968: lxxx–xcviii.

[11] If the *Trachiniae* is in fact in the background earlier, this scene could be connected to the lament on the couch, since Heraclean baths had associations with healing due to Heracles' role as healing deity; see Farnell 1921: 151 on Heraclean baths and healing.

both depict the attempts by a father to enforce his will on his recalcitrant son. Now, while the prospect of Pheidippides beating his father does not obviously resemble the recalcitrance of Hyllus when ordered by his father to marry Iole, his father's concubine, and to immolate Heracles himself (thus committing patricide), both dramas still struggle to assert that filial obedience is essential and even natural by presenting extreme examples of the consequences of filial disobedience and paternal demands. Heracles commands his son himself to follow willingly, "having discovered the finest law, to obey [his] father," νόμον κάλλιστον ἐξευρόντα, πειθαρχεῖν πατρί (1177–78). This is the very *nomos* that Pheidippides rejects after his time in the Thinkery. In the end both Heracles and Strepsiades insist that their sons must obey them, and the rebellion of sons against their fathers was a much greater issue after 430 than before it, given the acceleration of social changes by the initiation of the Peloponnesian War.[12]

If the *Trachiniae* does play a role in shaping the *Clouds*, then one would expect them to be reasonably near to one another in their years of initial performance. The *Clouds* (that is, the first version of it) we can date with confidence to 423 BCE, so, assuming that Aristophanes does want his audience to recognize the appearance of the distressed Strepsiades on the couch as based on the exodus of Sophocles' *Trachiniae*, one would have to put the production of the latter no more than a few years before that of the *Clouds*; the scene is not a generic parody of tragedy but of a particular tragic drama. While in the *Frogs* Aristophanes could play off a range of dramas from Euripides, he generally chose ones of recent vintage or others which were more remote but also had particularly notorious aspects, such as the infamous line from the *Hippolytus* (612), heard over twenty years before the *Frogs*, "My tongue has sworn but my mind is unsworn," or the extended parody of Euripides' *Telephus* over a decade later in the *Acharnians*.[13] If the parodies of the *Oedipus Tyrannus* in Aristophanes' *Knights* and of Euripides' *Helen* in the *Thesmophoriazousae* are useful in establishing the years of those tragic dramas (Knox 1956), then it would seem that, in order to establish the date of the *Trachiniae*, one would be wise to consider the evidence presented by the *Clouds*, which seems to suggest a date of around 425 or 426, two strong candidates for when the *Oedipus Tyrannus* was first produced.

---

[12] See Strauss 1993 generally on this problem in the last part of the fifth century in Athens.

[13] I think, moreover, that the comedy in the *Acharnians* relied as much as on generic associations of Euripides with rag-clad heroes as it did on *Telephus* in particular. Foley 1988: 42–43, on the other hand, argues that Aristophanes intentionally divides his audience into those who recognize the *Telephus* allusions and their function and those who do not, which would suggest that the thirteen-year gap between the two productions plays a role in its meaning.

HERACLES AS PLAGUE VICTIM

The Heracles described by Hyllus to his mother as the Centaur's poisonous potion begins to take effect and physically presented in the acting area during the exodus resembles the plague victims described by Thucydides in his gripping narrative (2.49) enough to warrant examination at the very least. Yet, indeed, I shall also argue that Sophocles is intending his audience to see Heracles as experiencing not only a fatal contact with a magical potion that ravages the inside and outside of his body but also the same symptoms as many in the audience had recently witnessed or even had themselves. His implied divinization pursuant to his bout with the plague, I shall argue later, thus increases the religious and emotional power of the exodus of the *Trachiniae*.

Comparison of the language of Thucydides to describe the effects of the plague with Sophocles' depiction of the effects of the poisonous concoction of the Centaur Nessus on Heracles shows strong correspondences. For the sake of efficiency and clarity, I shall first sketch out the plague symptoms as summarized by Rusten in his commentary on Thucydides 2.49 and then list those of Heracles, before focusing on specific Greek words.

Thucydides

49.2 heat in the head; inflammation of eyes; suffusion with blood of tongue and throat; fetid breath

49.3 hoarseness and violent coughing and sneezing; vomiting of bile

49.4 retching and convulsion

49.5 pustular and ulcerating skin eruptions; total body hyperesthesia and restlessness; irresistible thirst and desire for immersion to alleviate body heat

49.6 terminal exhaustion, apparently produced by diarrhea

49.8 loss of toes, fingers and genitalia; destruction of eyes; convalescent amnesia

Sophocles

767 sweat covers entire body; clothes cling; sweat must start on head as it is visible; flesh erupts

770 spasms; convulsions (repeated 770, 786, 805, 1082, 1254)

972–82 sleep through exhaustion; disorientation at awakening

1007–10 pain is exacerbated through touch and movement

1053–55 sarcal dissolution passes inside, including bronchial tubes

1070–73 heightened emotions; loss of control; comparison of self to female

1082–83, 1089 burning pangs

1103 paralysis.

Considering that Sophocles, of course, did not have the text of the Athenian historian in front of him and was not intending to match the descriptions we read in Thucydides (though Thucydides, while writing, could have had the text of Sophocles at his side), the number and types of correspondences are startling; Sophocles' descriptions display heightened and intensified symptoms compared to Thucydides, but that intensification is due to the magical qualities of their cause and the narrative need to communicate quickly the scope of Heracles' disaster. Even the course of the trauma is roughly similar, and I now thus combine the discourse of both Thucydides and Sophocles. Heracles breaks out in sweat under the sensation of intense heat; his skin erupts in ulcerations and sores and begins to dissolve; the poison descends into his body and penetrates it, affecting his lungs and bronchial tubes; he experiences convulsions or spasms; his clothing is intensely uncomfortable; he has burning sensations all over his body; he sleeps as the result of sheer exhaustion; he is temporarily unaware of his surroundings when he awakes and he may have suffered the loss of his genitalia. And, to move further into Thucydides, the extent of his suffering leads to a disruption of burial practices in the form of an abuse of funeral pyres (2.52.4), and it causes those around him, here in the form of Hyllus in the final lines, to doubt the gods (2.52.3–4). While Sophocles returns several times to brief indications of each symptom, having no need to explore the cataclysm in particularly great medical detail (and, more practically, under a time constraint unknown to the historian), Thucydides tersely and exactly itemizes them. But we wind up with, essentially, the same description cast in extremely similar language. Sweat induced by heat is specified by Sophocles and implied by Thucydides. Spasms mark both texts (*Tr.* 770, 786, 805, 1082, 1254) as do massive disruptions to the external flesh and burning sensations inside and outside the body. Indeed adjectives and verbs based on words for fire are the dominant descriptions in both narratives. The Athenians would shed their clothing and plunge into water, while Heracles cannot take his off and, when he attempts to uncloak his body, finds the pain forces him to recover himself as quickly as possible. Both plagues are animated, represented as living beings that attack their victims. Sophocles presents Heracles' *nosos*, as he will later depict that of Philoctetes, as a wild beast that launches itself savagely against its victim (e.g. 730, 1084) (Sorum 1978; Biggs 1966; Segal 1995). Thucydides animates the plague in a personification, Parry observed, as a hostile enemy warring against Athens: "Much of the language of the description of the Plague, in fact, suggests that it comes as a military attack; verbs like ἐπιπίπτειν, ἐσπίπτειν, νικᾶν, ξυναιρεῖν" (Parry 1969: 116).

The plague-like suffering of Heracles might also explain why Sophocles has Heracles speak of himself in starkly feminine terms, a passage that bears examining in some detail in the light of Thucydides. I shall attempt to link Heracles' concerns about his sudden femininity to the attack of the plague on male genitals. I thus now ask my readers for some patience in an argument that will take some time to develop fully and that will also, at times, go further out on a limb than may be comfortable for some, but, then again, the scene it examines is remarkably uncomfortable in itself. I shall first examine the gendered self-display of Heracles; second the importance of Heracles' lungs, with a necessary excursus into the anatomy of the Centaur; and, third, the implied destruction of the sexual organs of three characters in this drama's story, set in the context of Thucydides' description of the final symptom of the Athenian plague. All point to the emasculation of Heracles as a plague victim. The emotional apex of Heracles' lament for himself lies in his commands to Hyllus to pity his ravaged body (1070–79):

> ἴθ', ὦ τέκνον, τόλμησον· οἴκτιρόν τέ με
> πολλοῖσιν οἰκτρόν, ὅστις ὥστε παρθένος
> βέβρυχα κλαίων, καὶ τόδ' οὐδ' ἂν εἷς ποτε
> τόνδ' ἄνδρα φαίη πρόσθ' ἰδεῖν δεδρακότα,
> ἀλλ' ἀστένακτος αἰὲν εἱπόμην κακοῖς.
> νῦν δ' ἐκ τοιούτου θῆλυς ηὕρημαι τάλας.
> καὶ νῦν προσελθὼν στῆθι πλησίον πατρός,
> σκέψαι θ' ὁποίας ταῦτα συμφορᾶς ὕπο
> πέπονθα· δείξω γὰρ τάδ' ἐκ καλυμμάτων.
> ἰδού, θεᾶσθε πάντες ἄθλιον δέμας,

> Son, have courage, pity me, I who am
> pitiable to many, who, like an unwed girl,
> have roared in my weeping, and this nobody
> ever could say he has seen *this man* do before,
> but I always followed my troubles without a groan.
> But now, after being such a man, I am found a wretched woman.
> Come now and stand near your father,
> and examine these things I have suffered by such a disaster.
> For I shall reveal these things out from under their covers.
> Look, behold, everyone, my wretched body.

Heracles compares himself in his crying to a maiden (*parthenos*, 1071) and he adds that, despite his heroic achievements, "I am discovered to be a female" (*thêlus*, 1075), before uncovering his body for all to see.[14] Now the

---

[14] See Ormand 1999: 59 on Heracles' claim to be a *parthenos*, as well as Segal 1995: 84–85. Loraux 1993: 40–41 argues, on the other hand, that Heracles' suffering in general is symptomatic of a woman in childbirth.

gender dynamics in this passage can be read on a number of levels (one of which I shall reserve for a later portion of my argument), all of which are significant for the themes of the drama as a whole, and their narrative sequence is particularly important in signaling to us how to read these words. On the one hand, Heracles has been made to feel like the young, agitated members of the female Chorus, and, more tellingly, like his victim Iole herself (and, by extension, his dead wife). On the other, this thought works with his display of his ravaged body to the assembled crowd, a gesture Seaford sees as an allusion to the bride's unveiling of herself in the ritual of the *anakaluptêria*, which thus extends the theme of incomplete marriage begun by Deianira's early anxiety about her marital status (Seaford 1986: 58–59; Segal 1995: 84–86). But Heracles wants all to see the damage done to his male body in the context of his concerns about his masculinity: "this man," τόνδ' ἄνδρα. And *anêr*, the first word of Homer's *Odyssey* (also in the accusative, ἄνδρα), is not a neutral word in the signification of gender in Greek literature, but speaks directly to male heroism. The unveiling seems to be part of Heracles' concern about his masculinity, and the placement of the unveiling after the strongly gendered lament suggests as much, but why? It could be that Heracles is referring not just to his loss of emotional control but also to the mutilation of his male organs by the poisonous ointment. At least one scholar has suspected as much, for Bruce Heiden, after somewhat strangely accusing Heracles of exaggerating his distress, speculates: "Perhaps we should suppose that Heracles' genitals have been mutilated. His description of the robe's effect on his skin is such that his genitals could hardly have been left intact." But Heiden leaves a more clinching support to this speculation buried in a footnote, where he points out that the mutilation of Heracles' genitals "would also prevent Heracles from loving any woman besides Deianira, which Nessus predicted would be the effect of the drug" (μήτιν' εἰσιδὼν / στέρξει γυναῖκα κεῖνος ἀντὶ σοῦ πλέον, 576–77) (Heiden 1989: 139–40; 187). Only genital mutilation would fulfill the promise of the potion's effect made by the Centaur Nessus to Deianira at his own death.

At this point I should consider two arguments that might be raised against this reading: a similar verbal emasculation in the *Ajax* and the difficulty of representing the castration in the theater. In the famous "deception speech" in Sophocles' earlier work, Ajax comments, "I am made female with respect to my mouth by this woman," ἐθηλύνθην στόμα / πρὸς τῆσδε τῆς γυναικός (651–52), a comment which thus creates the possibility that being feminized is just a trope, a turn of phrase for these hyper-masculine heroes.[15] Yet Heracles' speech displays this concern with gender throughout its course, while that of Ajax is restricted to this one comment (though one should allow for the phallic symbolism of the insistence on burying his sword); indeed, one can imagine Sophocles remembering Ajax's line and redeploying its thought here because it could now be used in a more thematically integral way. Ajax also shows no interest in the display of his body as Heracles does. That brings us to the staging. I am not at all implying a realistic depiction of a Heracles with bloody thighs, as there is simply no reason in the text to think that way, and Greek scenic conventions do not demand that level of verisimilitude; neither the groin of Heracles, nor the wound on the foot of Philoctetes mean much from several hundred feet away in the audience. Yet both are there in the language of the dramas, projected toward the audience's imagination, and the language is the world that Sophocles creates.

And closer attention to Sophocles' language yields more support for this reading of the *Trachiniae*. The specific attacks by the poison on Heracles' lungs could also be an appropriate response to his overly charged libido and thus, essentially, serve as a displaced form of emasculation and so further ground what is implied by Heracles' gendered lament. Both Hyllus' narration of his father's initial seizures (778) and Heracles' own laments (1054) specify the tremendous distress that Heracles' lungs experience: σπαραγμὸς αὐτοῦ πλευμόνων ἀνθήψατο, "a spasm grabbed his lungs" (778). But πλεύμων can designate not just the specific lungs but also the most vital inner part of a person (LSJ s.v.). The lungs also happen to be where Heracles wounded the Centaur Nessus many years ago when the latter attempted to rape Deianira while carrying her across a river. Heracles readied an arrow from the river's far side and "it sped to the lungs through his chest," ἐς δὲ πλεύμονας στέρνων διερροίζησεν (567–68). Now, two questions arise here: first, why specify the lungs as the arrow's target, and, second, where are a Centaur's chest and lungs? It would seem more appropriate that Heracles launch his unerring arrows against some part of the Centaur that has something more directly to do with sexual passion, such as his loins, but in fact we do have a fragment of another Sophoclean drama that locates the power of *eros* in the lungs themselves: "Aphrodite has complete power over ('tyrannizes') the lungs of Zeus," [Κύπρις] Διὸς τυραννεῖ πλευμόνων

---

[15] Comparable here is the last part of Hector's speech to himself while awaiting Achilles. After first considering a negotiation with his enemy, he scorns such conversations as like those between a boy and a *parthenos* (*Il.* 22.126–28). His scorn of himself here suggests he imagines himself as the *parthenos*.

(S. Fr. 941.15). A line from Aristophanes' comedy of libido, *Lysistrata*, might further support this point. As the semi-choruses of men and women square off against each other after the women have seized the Acropolis, they menace each other with violence. Shortly after the women threaten to bite the men's testicles "like a bitch dog" (363), they then attempt to terrorize with what is, I think, a similar threat, βρύκουσά σου τοὺς πλεύμονας καὶ τἄντερ' ἐξαμήσω, "I'll devour your lungs and cut out your innards" (367). That English rendition reflects the common consensus of translators who see these organs as lacking a visibly euphemistic role in comedy. But any word, especially an anatomical term, can, with the right spoken tone, become innuendo, and since lungs have an aphrodisiac association, balls, which come in pairs like lungs, have just been mentioned, biting has just been threatened, and devouring (*brukousa*) is an extreme intensification of biting, I would suggest that the threat here is to the men's genitalia.[16] The final verb here, *examan*, does not mean "cut out" as much as "cut off," "mow down" or "reap," an activity which cannot be directed to objects that are completely inside a person; indeed, it is a verb which can be used for sexual sowing and reaping, and, as chance would have it, it appears thus in the *Trachiniae* when Deianira describes her absent husband who sows and reaps his children like a farmer his crops (33). So, in order words, "lungs" can mean something other than just lungs. The Centaur thus takes his proper full vengeance against his killer when his toxin concentrates part of its effect on Heracles' lungs, the very organ struck by Heracles' arrow, and the erotic excess of Heracles is appropriately punished, as are the eyes of Oedipus which have seen his mother as they should have not.

Thus, the anatomy of a Centaur now comes into play since it has two different chest cavities that could house the essential organs, and this ambiguity, combined with the repetition of certain anatomical terms from one character's suffering to another, further suggests a displacement of sexual language. A Centaur sometimes appears earlier in Greek art with a complete man at the front and a horse, minus the front quarter, stuck on to the rear, but, more frequently, as a human torso emerging from a horse's body which is itself complete save for its head and neck. Nessus himself appears thus, with four horse legs, in one Attic vase (Louvre E 803) from the mid-sixth century, and similarly on another (Boston 00.345) from the last quarter of the fifth century. Such is the way Athenians would have imagined their

---

[16] Indeed the combination of the verb *brukô* and the noun *pleumôn* are strangely evocative of the exodus of the *Trachiniae*.

Centaurs, an impression no doubt confirmed by the metopes on the Parthenon which displayed the battle of the Lapiths and the Centaurs. The Roman Ovid shows us that questions occurred concerning their doubled anatomical areas to at least one poet in antiquity, as, in the Centauromachy in Book 12 of the *Metamorphoses*, Peleus manages, after firing an arrow into Centaur Demoleon's lungs (as in the *Trachiniae* Heracles does to Nessus), to strike first the human torso and then the equine one together when the Centaur Demoleon rears up quickly: *uno duo pectora perforat ictu,* "with one blow he pierces two breasts" (12.377).[17] The Centaur's human torso stops just north of where his sexual organs should be; unlike the satyrs, bipeds who are half goat and half human, and who are at least just as sexually excitable as the Centaurs, in Greek art the Centaurs never actively display their genitalia, which remain where a horse's would be, and horses frequently appear as symbols of male sexuality in particular. If the Greek imagination associated lungs with sexual desire, it makes more sense, I suggest, that the Greeks would have imagined them in the equine thoracic cavity, not the human one, and thus closer to the horse's genitals. As noted earlier, Greek tragedy does not refer openly to sexual anatomy and shies away from bare references to sexual activity, save for *topoi* such as the plowing of fields,[18] and it might be thus significant that Sophocles omits from Nessus' recipe the Centaur's own sperm, which we see preserved in the account of Nessus' death in Apollodorus, which itself seems largely modeled on Sophocles (2.7.6).[19] I shall return to this absence momentarily. But there appears to be a certain amount of significant inference and metonymy operative at least in the *Trachiniae.*

This inferential tendency is confirmed, I think, in Deianira's speeches, first when she describes Nessus' gift of the potion as he dies, and then when, after realizing the true destructive power of his concoction, she describes how he gave it to her:

---

[17] I am grateful to Dunstan Lowe for this reference. The presence of Nessus (*Met.* 12.308) here might also be a nod that Ovid is self-consciously playing off Sophocles' text.

[18] E.g. *Tr.* 33, *Ant.* 569, *OT* 1210, 1403, 1497. Oedipus in the last example cited imagines the plowing of the mother as a taunt his daughters could hear in the future, which might suggest that even the euphemism could be recognized as a coarse image for tragic diction; in each of these Sophoclean examples, Creon's rejection of the importance of Antigone in particular, the image does not suggest pleasant images of procreation. In general on the agricultural commonplace of intercourse as the sowing of crops, especially in the *OT*, see Goldhill 1986: 207–08 and Knox 1957: 144.

[19] Segal 1995: 222 notes that Sophocles has omitted the Centaur's semen but he does not ponder on the implications of his observation. Kamerbeek 1970: 133–34 on line 580 records and dismisses the scholiast's comment that "according to the instruction of Nessus she also mixed in some other things," which implies the semen. The scholiast's comment, though, indicates that the drama's early readers were very much aware that there is something odd about the specific formula here in Sophocles.

ἐκθνῄσκων δ' ὁ θὴρ
τοσοῦτον εἶπε· παῖ γέροντος Οἰνέως,
τοσόνδ' ὀνήσει τῶν ἐμῶν, ἐὰν πίθῃ,
πορθμῶν, ὁθούνεχ' ὑστάτην σ' ἔπεμψ' ἐγώ·
ἐὰν γὰρ ἀμφίθρεπτον αἷμα τῶν ἐμῶν
σφαγῶν ἐνέγκῃ χερσίν, ᾗ μελαγχόλους
ἔβαψεν ἰοὺς θρέμμα Λερναίας ὕδρας,
ἔσται φρενός σοι τοῦτο κηλητήριον
τῆς Ἡρακλείας, ὥστε μήτιν' εἰσιδὼν
στέρξει γυναῖκα κεῖνος ἀντὶ σοῦ πλέον.

And the beast, dying, said this:
"O child of old Oineus,
so much you will gain from my portage,
if you should comply, since I sent you across last of all.
For if you should bear in your hands the blood which clotted around
my wounds, where the Hydra, Lerna's monstrous beast, dipped the arrows with
   black gall, then you will have a love-charm
for the heart of Heracles, so that he will never see and love another woman more
   instead of you.

Tr. 568–77

ἐγὼ γὰρ ὢν ὁ θὴρ με Κένταυρος, πονῶν
πλευρὰν πικρᾷ γλωχῖνι, προυδιδάξατο
παρῆκα θεσμῶν οὐδέν,

For I neglected none of the edicts which the beast Centaur
taught me while he was suffering in his side from the bitter arrow point.

Tr. 680–82

If we imagine the arrow as having struck the equine chest of Nessus, much closer to his sexual organs, then both the elision of the semen and the creation of the love-charm from these fluids make more sense. With the blood emerging from a wound near his genitals there is no need to mention semen (a word not high on anyone's frequency list for Greek tragedy) because it is obviously, though implicitly, there. Hydra's venom and Centaur's blood do not sound like much of a love-charm, but mixing in the sperm of a Centaur, a proverbially randy creature, certainly would create at least the appearance of one. Deianira would understand that her husband knows Centaurs and they know him, and that Centaurs are much like one another; it is no accident that, as soon as Hyllus says the name "Nessus" to his dying father, Heracles comprehends all. Now, here I can note that Deianira's second reference to the wound of Nessus introduces a more general anatomical term, *pleura*, which allows for a reconsideration of the wound's location but also binds together the suffering of all the characters in the drama.

Pleura, "side," is used by Sophocles to designate the flanks of Nessus (*Tr.* 681), Heracles (768, 1053, 1083), and Deianira (926, 931, 938–39); in that last instance Hyllus flings his side at his mother's, so her wound becomes his. Sophocles in this drama only deploys *pleura* when violent acts occur to the bodies of the characters. Easterling (1982), in a note on line 938, comments on how "the word play draws attention to a detail which links the deaths of Heracles and D[eianira]," yet a closer examination yields that this detail links together also Nessus and Hyllus with Heracles and Deianira. But Sophocles, by continuing to use vague anatomical language,[20] can direct our attention further down the bodies of his characters once we pay full attention to the language that surrounds the individual words. After tearing open her gown past her breasts Deianira plunges a sword into her "side struck under the liver and her heart," πλευρὰν ὑφ' ἧπαρ καὶ φρένας πεπληγμένην (931). *Phrên* designates the general area of the chest where the heart resides and is, for the Greeks, the seat of general consciousness, for both cognition and emotion. The specificity of her driving the blade below the chest and liver suggests her midriff. Sophocles could have Deianira stab herself in her chest, and might even intend us to expect that – after all, she does bear her breasts first – but instead this mother kills herself in the area where her son once grew for eight or nine months, the son whose bitter accusation drove her to suicide. The site of her destruction is her womb, her sexual reproductive organs, broadly considered. She destroys herself thus as a mother and as a possible productive bed partner of any male.[21] The Centaur's sexualized death hence passes to her before it reaches Heracles fully. Sophocles' language carefully yet powerfully designates the shared destruction of the reproductive functions of the three. Let us examine the further consequences of this realization.

Recognizing the disasters as punishment for first Nessus' and then Heracles' excessive sexuality helps explain the repeated references to the work of an Erinys, or Fury, after Heracles receives the poisoned garment.[22] First, Hyllus concludes his denunciation of his mother after his report of the poison's effect with his wish, "May Justice and an Erinys punish you in return for these things" (ὧν σε ποίνιμος Δίκη / τείσαιτ' Ἐρινύς τ', 808–09). Second, the Chorus imagines the effect of Iole herself as an Erinys (893–95):

[20] Easterling's commentary observes of line 931: "poetic descriptions of anatomy tend to be vague." Here it is useful to note that, in comedy at least, *pleura* can be used as a euphemism for intercourse in the idiom "to shake sides"; see Henderson 1991: 161.

[21] Loraux 1995: 42, who abstracts the play's language too much from its inner systems, observes that Deianira stabs herself where Homeric heroes are often fatally struck and a woman carries her child.

[22] I am grateful to Malcolm Heath and Fiona McHardy for this suggestion.

ἔτεκεν ἔτεκε δὴ μεγάλαν
ἀνέορτος ἅδε νύμφα
δόμοισι τοῖσδ' Ἐρινύν.

This bride without marriage ceremony gave birth
to a great Erinys for this house.

The larger point here, of course, is that Iole will give birth to no child
through Heracles, though she will for Hyllus in a new house outside of
Trachis. For Deianira and Heracles, however, Iole only engenders destruction. Third, Heracles describes the cloth sent by Deianira as "a woven net
of the Erinyes," Ἐρινύων / ὑφαντὸν ἀμφίβληστρον (1051–52).[23] Why the
Furies keep appearing in this drama is linked to the origins of the Erinyes
in the castration of Ouranos in Hesiod's *Theogony*. Gaia, angered because
Ouranos will not allow her children to be born, while he still engages in
intercourse with her nightly, arranges for her son Kronos to castrate his
father, and the genitals, after Kronos flings them into the sea, produce the
Giants, the Erinyes and Aphrodite (*Th.* 176–99). Not coincidentally, the
power of Aphrodite, as Kypris, is also acknowledged three times in the *Trachiniae* (497, 515, 860), and the word "Kypris" itself would be a reminder of
her birth since it denotes Cyprus, where she emerged from the sea.[24] In the
first two instances, the Chorus invokes the power of Aphrodite just after
it and Deianira have learned the truth about the intentions of Heracles
with regards to Iole, and, in the third, the Chorus reacts to Hyllus' report
about his father's anguish with the observation that "unspeaking (ἄναυδος)
Kypris is clearly the creator of these things." The silence of first Iole and
then Deianira is thus transformed into the workings of the goddess of *eros*
herself. The Chorus later shifts the silence to Heracles who, it observes,
enters (969) "unspeaking," ἀναύδατος, thus further linking the characters.
Aphrodite here is twinned with the dark forces that were born with her
in the castration of Ouranos. References to the Erinyes and to Aphrodite,
therefore, further support the reading that Heracles, whose unrestrained
sexuality evokes early deities such as Ouranos, suffers emasculation.

   The chemical castration of Heracles would thus also complete the gender
reversal of Deianira's phallic masculine suicide by sword. And, if we are to
imagine his weeping like a maiden and being found to be a woman, the
imagined blood on his loins would be the sign of the loss of his virginity,

---

[23] In each of their commentaries, Easterling and Davies note that these lines strongly echo Aeschylus'
Agamemnon 1382 and 1580 in depicting the vehicle of the death of Agamemnon.
[24] Parry 1986: 108 briefly discusses the links between the *Trachiniae* and Hesiod, but does not mention
the births of Aphrodite and the Furies.

proven as he uncovers himself in a grim parody of the Greek wedding (Seaford 1986). As Ormand observes (Ormand 1999: 52–53), Deianira's tale of the *deltos* inscribed with the instructions of Nessus figures her pubic area as penetrated by the Centaur (682–83). Her *deltos* thus now is inscribed on the body of Heracles. There is no exact reference here in the text to his castration because tragedy, unlike comedy, does not refer explicitly or even with relatively clear implication to *phalloi*; that is the province of comedy. My argument is now ready to return to Thucydides.

If Heracles' symptoms are intended to suggest those of the plague victims in Athens, then we should consider his chemical castration in the light of the penultimate effect described by Thucydides: κατέσκηπτε γὰρ ἐς αἰδοῖα καὶ ἐς ἄκρας χεῖρας καὶ πόδας, καὶ πολλοὶ στερισκόμενοι τούτων διέφευγον, εἰσὶ δ' οἳ καὶ τῶν ὀφθαλμῶν, "For it was blasting its way down into the genitals and to the fingers and toes, and many, deprived of these things [or "depriving themselves"], survived, and others, though deprived of their eyes, did as well" (2.49.8). The thought here is somewhat elliptical and its compression can lead to several different readings. First, however, no matter how we read these lines, it is clear that the plague did attack the genitals, resulting in their loss, but how the loss occurred, whether passively or actively, has been debated. Lucretius' transformation of Thucydides in his own plague narrative in *De rerum natura* (6.1205–12) implies self-mutilation, which some scholars have seen as an indication that Thucydides, who does not specify the manner of castration, should be read thus. Rhodes, in his edition of Book 2, does not comment, but his translation shows that he thinks that the plague, not its sufferers, performed the emasculations, an assessment with which I agree.[25]

As Adam Parry observed, Thucydides often puts metaphors into his verbs, and the verb in this sentence, *kateskêpte*, is pregnant with associations and forms an important link to the *Trachiniae* and to tragedy in general (Parry 1969: 114). Commenting on a slightly different form of this verb at 2.47.3 when Thucydides first describes the outbreak of the plague, Parry pointed out that *enkataskêpsai* contained a "suppressed image" of Zeus' thunderbolt which thus struck Athens in the form of the plague. Parry noted that the exact same verb is used for Zeus' punishment of the Persians in Aeschylus (*Per.* 514) and a slightly different version in the *Oedipus Tyrannus*

---

[25] The translation of Rhodes 1988: "It attacked the privy parts, and the fingers and toes, and many people survived but lost these, while others lost their eyes." Gomme in his commentary reports the Lucretian-influenced readings but replies: "I do not believe this," while Rusten in his, more recent, edition, repeats the Lucretius passage, allowing its authority but still adding that the participle is "vague."

to describe the plague sent by the gods against Thebes (27–28); we should remember here that this is the only instance in the *Oedipus* where *loimos* occurs, thus further marking this passage as significant.[26] The third example Parry chooses is at *Trachiniae* 1087, where the desperate Heracles longs for Zeus' thunderbolt to strike him to relieve his agony,[27] which, of course, tradition says does happen after the drama concludes, and which, I shall argue below, is clearly intended here as it is part of his apotheosis. Translators of Thucydides tend to back away from the full force of this verb; Crawley's classic rendition meekly has "it settled in the privy parts," while Blanco's much more recent English Norton Critical Edition of Thucydides translates it "spreading down" into the extremities. Settling and spreading are certainly not the same sorts of actions as blasting and striking with the thunder. Now, Thucydides may have meant merely to personify the plague in yet another way, or this may be one of those instances where some version of Cornford's "Mythohistoricus" Thucydides shows his face.[28] Either way, the language of this passage suggests that the plague smites the sexual organs of the Athenians as if the thunder of Zeus were striking them in anger, and so, if our passage from the *Trachiniae* does itself suggest a similar event, then the two passages do seem linked, since, as Hyllus (or the Chorus) tells us at the end of the *Trachiniae*, there is nothing in the drama that is not Zeus. The plans of Zeus bring Heracles to such a level of torment that only the lightning of Zeus can "heal" Heracles and produce his apotheosis, which, as it happens, will be the next step in this study.

But before moving on to the implied apotheosis of Heracles, I would like to close this section with a reiteration and an expansion of a thread that has run throughout this part of my argument, that Sophocles links the deaths of Deianira and Heracles, and sometimes Nessus as well, with shared language, imagery and gesture. Many works in Greek literature, through common acts, images and words, relate the deaths of their major characters as part of the structural building blocks of their systems of meaning. For example, the *Iliad* associates the deaths of Sarpedon, Patroclus, Hector and, by extension, Achilles through shared actions, words and, for the latter three, the armor of Achilles itself. The *Oresteia* powerfully associates the murderous actions of Clytemnestra and Orestes by creating tableaux

---

[26] ἐν δ' ὁ πυρφόρος θεὸς / σκήψας ἐλαύνει, λοιμὸς ἔχθιστος, πόλιν, "The fire-bearing god, detested plague, drives against the city."

[27] ἐγκατάσκηψον βέλος, / πάτερ, κεραυνοῦ·, "Father, hurl down your weapon of lightning."

[28] See Hornblower 1991 on the several different authorial personae visible in Thucydides' plague narrative in 2.49.

wherein the killer stands over two victims at the close of each of the first two parts, which are perhaps then reversed by the more chaotic events in the doorway of the Pythia's temple at the opening of the third. In the *Trachiniae*, characters are joined by their silence, by damage done to their sexual organs, by specific anatomical terms, and, last, by the word *nosos*. While the *nosos* of Heracles, both metaphorical and real, has received much attention, both in previous scholarship and in this chapter, little attention has been paid to its echo in Deianira. At the start of the same antistrophe which closes when the Chorus recognizes what is happening as the working of "unspeaking Aphrodite," the Chorus laments the *nosos* which is "poured over" Heracles (852). Then, a few brief moments later, the Chorus reacts in horror to the announcement of Deianira's suicide, which has occurred while the Chorus sang of Heracles' *nosos*, by asking the Nurse "what passion (*thumos*), what illness" (the plural *tines nosoi*, 882) drove Deianira to such an act.[29] Deianira, they imply, has lost control of her *thumos*, the seat of her emotions, much as Heracles is prone to. The illness of Heracles has passed over to his wife at her death, but the same linguistic "contagion" occurs at a roughly similar moment in the *Oedipus Tyrannus*, as I observed in the previous chapter, when Jocasta responds to her realization of the truth with a plea that Oedipus cease from his inquiry (1061): "I am sick enough already." In my chapters on Euripides' *Hippolytus* and Sophocles' *Oedipus* I studied the movement of *nosos* among characters and, in the case of the latter, between *polis* and individuals, and in subsequent chapters I shall show this circulation operative in Euripides' *Heracles* and *Phoenissae*, and even in Sophocles' *Philoctetes*. Despite Thucydides' acute observations neither he nor any contemporary medical observer developed a real theory of contagion, yet what I see here in Sophocles, and earlier in Euripides, seems remarkably like an intuition of contagious disease for dramas written during the plague years and a decade later.[30] The infections enter and circulate through the discourses of the *Trachiniae* and the *Oedipus Tyrannus*, destroying both male hero and wife in each text. Plague catalyzes and is the vehicle of the crisis in these two Sophoclean tragic dramas, yet in the *Trachiniae* Sophocles imagines another stage in his response to the plague as he prepares his audience for the transfiguration of Heracles after the performance of the drama ends.

---

[29] Easterling 1982 comments on line 882: "[Deianira's] *nosoi* have been prompted by the *nosos* at 852."

[30] Thucy. 2.50.1 shows that animals which touched the corpses died themselves; in 2.50.4–6 men catch it through nursing each other.

THE PLAGUE AND THE APOTHEOSIS OF HERACLES

Whether Heracles exits the acting area on his way to Mt. Oeta simply to die or to be transfigured into a divinity on the pyre has long been one of the main controversies, aside from the production date, for scholarship on the *Trachiniae*. The argument has concerned whether the popular Athenian tradition of his divinization would weigh more than the absence of clear references to his apotheosis in the body of the drama. Perhaps now it is more accurate to write it "was" one of the main controversies, since Philip Holt (1989) laid down an almost unimpeachable brief for a Sophoclean intention of a Heraclean apotheosis with the fullest case possible, which consists of the popularity of the divine Heracles in Athenian art, the importance of Heracles to the cultic life of Athens, and, most tellingly, the ritual acts established by Heracles during the exodus which do not make any sense unless they are a preparation for his cult. Subsequently, Finkelberg (1996), in further support of Holt's case, showed how the second stasimon of the *Trachiniae* refers to the fire-festival in honor of Heracles on Mt. Oeta that dated from the archaic period but whose evidence was only discovered by modern researchers in 1920; the events implied by the exodus are the etiological myth for that festival.[31] With references to the apotheosis thus established in more than one part of the drama, the divinization of Heracles seems fundamental to its action and meaning. The question, I submit, should now shift from *whether* Sophocles composed a drama about the circumstances of the divinization of Heracles to *why* he did so, and I shall argue that he did so as a response to the crisis of the plague and, possibly, the turmoil caused by the early years of the Peloponnesian War. I shall thus try to avoid the tendency, which Holt faulted, of advocates of the implied Heraclean exaltation at the close of the *Trachiniae* to fail "to explain how their position on the question affects the interpretation of the play" (Holt 1989: 69). Holt keeps away from the question of the production date of the drama, but his analysis does fit well with seeing the *Trachiniae* as a response to the plague of the 420s in Athens. In the course of my argument, I shall bring in other new evidence to support the case for Heracles' incipient divinity during the exodus.

---

[31] Finkelberg, after assessing the scholarly resistance to the importance of the divinization of Heracles to the *Trachiniae*, concludes (1996: 143), "it is imperative to recognize that the *Trachiniae* has been misinterpreted for centuries." Holt 1989: 69–70 provides a full bibliography on both sides of the controversy, including those who, like Hoey 1977, argue that the end of the *Trachiniae* is intentionally ambiguous with regards to the final death or apotheosis of Heracles. Since the publication of Holt, Segal 1995: 53–54 has further explored the case for Sophocles' intended implication of an apotheosis.

The people of Athens seem to have taken a much greater interest than any other early Greek society in the afterlife of Heracles, and this interest also appears to have taken wing at an earlier date than elsewhere, but it likely further intensified during the plague, a shift that Sophocles involves at the end of the *Trachiniae*. In his recent overview of the archaeology of Athens, Camp demonstrates that, already in the middle of the sixth century BCE, the Athenians had constructed a small building on the Acropolis whose pediments depicted the heroic deeds of Heracles as well as his introduction to Olympus (Camp 2001: 22–23). In his study of the Hesiodic *Catalogue of Women*, M. L. West concludes that the tradition of Heracles' apotheosis originated in Athens during the sixth century (West 1985: 130,169). This tradition thus had deep and wide roots by the time the Peloponnesian War had commenced and the plague had begun to rage in 430. In the deep despair of the plague crisis, it would be natural to turn to the superhuman, divinized Heracles who had saved their imagined ancestors from countless monsters and beasts. *Nosos,* imagined by Sophocles in both the *Trachiniae* and *Philoctetes* as an attacking wild animal, would thus be his next bestial opponent, one that initially masters him, only to be defeated finally by Heracles' godlike capacity to endure.[32]

Heracles, like his half-brother Apollo, came to be worshipped as *Alexikakos,* "Averter of evil," and strongly associated with healing, especially during the plague years (Woodford 1976; Kearns 1989: 14–15; Parker 1996: 175, 186). A scholiast to Aristophanes' *Frogs* line 501 reports that the shrine of Heracles Alexikakos at Melite, one of the demes of Athens contained entirely within the city walls, received a new statue during the plague. This sanctuary appears to have been important at one time, but either fell into disuse or was destroyed before Pausanias could visit and record his impressions. There has been some controversy about whether this was an entirely new statue, since known dates of the named sculptor cannot be right, or a statue rededicated because of the plague.[33] We do not need proof of an entirely new statue to show that Heracles Alexikakos became newly and urgently important during the plague, since the evidence simply shows that something substantial was happening in that sanctuary at that time. The associations, moreover, in Athens between Heracles and healing, and Heracles and Asclepius, would become even stronger if Woodford's suggestion is correct that a sanctuary of Heracles was likely on the south slope of

---

[32] See thus Burkert's chapter "Heracles and the Master of Animals," 1979: 78–98.

[33] See Kearns 1989: 14 and Woodford 1971 on the inscription and the statue in general. Parker 1996: 186 doubts the dating of the sculptor to the plague. Woodford 1971: 218–19 suggests the statue was made earlier and then associated with the Athenian plague of the 420s, or was rededicated then.

the Acropolis, near the Asklepieion (Woodford 1971: 220). It is moreover, I submit, significant here that Euripides' *Heraclidae*, in which a messenger reports that the divine Heracles and his wife Hebe miraculously rejuvenate his nephew Iolaus in order to protect Heracles' children, is believed to have been produced between 430 and 427 BCE, roughly the time I am arguing for the *Trachiniae* (Wilkins 1993: xxxiii–iv).

Having composed at least two tragic dramas involving the divinization of Heracles, Sophocles appears to have been particularly interested in the worship of this hero. There is no surviving information concerning the treatment of Heracles in other Sophoclean tragedies,[34] and thus it could be that the presence of the popular great hero in the *Trachiniae* and *Philoctetes* played a role in their preservation when the current seven dramas were culled for use in education. And Aristotle did observe in the *Poetics* that the varied, disunified, nature of Heraclean myth made him a difficult subject for the tragedians (1451a). While the biographical tradition, which I discuss in detail in the next chapter, of Sophocles' role in the introduction of the Asclepius cult to Athens has received much attention, for better or for worse, over the years, little notice has been paid to his alleged role in the creation of a shrine to Heracles. The ancient *Life of Sophocles* (12) records that Heracles appeared to the poet in a dream and informed him of the whereabouts of a golden crown that had been stolen from the Acropolis. After Sophocles recovered the crown, he used the reward from this discovery to institute the shrine of Heracles Menytes, "Heracles the Informer." This anecdote does not seem to be modeled on an episode from Sophoclean drama as much as was the story of the reception of Asclepius in his house, but still should be treated with caution.[35] Ultimately, it does signify the close associations among Sophocles, the Acropolis and the worship of Heracles, and it thus buttresses the case that Sophocles would have chosen Heracles as his subject during the crisis of the plague, just as he later evokes him to save Philoctetes and the Greek cause at Troy during the final years of the Peloponnesian War, a relationship I shall explore in a subsequent chapter.

MUSIC, CLOSURE AND CULT

The exodus of the *Trachiniae*, as we have begun to see, is extraordinary on many levels, and becomes even more remarkable when we consider the role of music and poetic form, and what they can signal. The unseemliness

---

[34] No such evidence exists in *TGF* or in (the more accessible) Sutton 1984. Of course, it is always possible that Heracles appeared in dramas about which we now know nothing.

[35] Lefkowitz 1981: 83 does not seem very troubled by this anecdote.

of Heracles' character in much of this scene and his unrelentingly harsh demands on Hyllus have bothered critics for over 200 years, and the form of the exodus has more recently been debated at length. Aside from the controversy over whether the exodus does imply the apotheosis of Heracles, scholars are unsure whether Hyllus or the Chorus speaks the last lines, since the Chorus goes silent at the arrival of Heracles.[36] I have come to believe that their stunned inarticulateness, combined with the scene's music and its use of anapests in particular, is extremely important to the meaning of the exodus and helps justify an argument that Hyllus speaks the chilling assertion that "there is nothing in these matters that is not Zeus."

The entry of the ruined Heracles drives the Chorus into a speechlessness, the effect of which is only paralleled perhaps by the more famous silent exit of the Chorus members at the end of Aeschylus' *Agamemnon*, where their failure to speak symbolizes the incipient tyranny in the collapsed *polis* to be ruled now by Clytemnestra and Aegisthus. The muting of the young maidens is part of the great structural rhythm of the drama, as it balances and echoes first Iole's silent entrance and presence and then Deianira's final wordless departure from the theater after her son blasts her with responsibility for the destruction of her husband. The music of this Chorus thus dies, only to be replaced by the anapests of the procession. While it is often difficult for a modern reader to notice major interruptions of the musical flow of a Greek tragedy, there have been several acknowledgments by scholars that something extraordinary is happening as the procession which carries the sleeping Heracles enters the acting area. William Scott, in his study of the musical structure of Sophoclean drama, observes: "the women fall into such confusion at the entrance of Heracles that the rhythms of Sophocles' universe must be reestablished with new music from the singers." Similarly, Easterling comments: "Moments of high tension – the death of Deianira, the arrival of Heracles – are marked as such by their distinctive metrical form" (Scott 1996: 120; Easterling 1982: 14). That new music and, in the case of the arrival, that metrical form are the anapests accompanying Heracles' arrival (971–1003), which come less expectedly in Sophocles than one might otherwise think, and the anapests which are deployed here will thus be an important part of the meaning of the last scene and signal to us, perhaps, how to read it.

Anapests appear here to an extent atypical of Sophocles. Sylvia Brown, in her revelatory study of the anapestic meter in Greek tragic drama that will

---

[36] On who speaks the final lines see the commentaries of Davies and Easterling, and then Lloyd-Jones and Wilson 1990: 177–78.

inform much of my subsequent discussion, shows how much more rarely Sophocles deploys anapests compared to Euripides or Aeschylus: 3.8% of Sophocles is anapestic, Aeschylus 8.6% and Euripides 5.5% (Brown 1977: 47).[37] Thus, the substantial anapestic sections surrounding the preparations for the funeral pyre become more significant both because, in the dramas we still have, Sophocles tends not to use this meter, and because he does also deploy it elsewhere in extraordinary ways. In the *Oedipus Tyrannus*, for example, Sophocles keeps his poetry free of anapests in order to maximize their impact when they do appear late in the action; when the bloodied, blinded Oedipus staggers back into the theater to the horror of all around him, his bewildered cries of pain to the gods are chanted in anapests (1307–11). Oedipus laments himself and addresses the gods here in anapests (Brown 1977: 56–57; Scott 1996: 144). Following the anapestic beginning of this scene then, Oedipus engages, or tries to engage, those around him in a *kommos* with the Chorus, yet he gradually appropriates its role, much as the lamentations of Heracles take over from the silent Chorus of the *Trachiniae*; in the first the Chorus of Thebans refuses to engage responsively with the blind Oedipus and in the second the Chorus of young women seems unable or perhaps also unwilling to answer the mutilated hero.[38] In the *Trachiniae*, as in the *Oedipus Tyrannus*, Sophocles withholds the anapestic meter until very late; before the exodus begins, it appears in only a few odd lyrics sung by the Chorus (497/507, 959/968) and Sophocles further pushes its use in new directions, as we shall see shortly later in this discussion. During a lengthy anapestic entrance such as Heracles' one would expect the Chorus to play a role, yet here the opposite occurs and the actors completely take over (Burton 1980: 79). As the Chorus falls silent, Hyllus emerges from the *skênê* and initiates a substantial anapestic section of thirty-two lines (971–1003) with the Old Man as the cortege brings in the sleeping Heracles, followed by two anapestic cries by Heracles during the *kommos* (1081, 1095–96), and then the drama closes, as do many other Greek dramas, with several lines of anapests, 1269–78, though this last run is slightly longer than typical and is further marked by its almost unique bleakness. Most commentators assign these anapests to the basic category of the meter used for processions and entrances.[39] But this is an awfully long anapestic section for an entrance, and

---

[37] Also, Webster 1969: 140 notes: "Trochaics and anapests are perhaps the least common of the Sophoclean meters, and both are used less by him than by the other two tragedians."

[38] Scott 1996: 144–48 on the *Oedipus Tyrannus* and 113–14 on the *Trachiniae*. Scott, however, does not connect these two similar movements.

[39] So Scott 1996: 107 on lines 971–1003. For a typical overview of the use of anapests in tragedy see Pickard-Cambridge 1968: 160–62.

more than just entering is occurring, as the Old Man in brief conversation advises Hyllus as to the proper course of action and Heracles begins to awaken. What else then could be happening at the opening of the exodus and in the drama's final lines other than generic entrances and exits?

Here is where Brown's work on anapests becomes particularly useful for it shows how the tragedians actually used anapests, as opposed to what the handbooks tell us they are. While anapests do in fact accompany entrances and exits, there are a number of instances where they also appear when an already present character is completely stationary, as when the distraught Hecuba lies on the ground (Eur. *Tr.* 98–100) or when the chained Prometheus chants his great lament (*Pr.* 93–100). Anapests often signal events other than simply entrances and exits as they frequently are the form of laments or prayers, a context which thus that there is a potentially significant religious aspect to the anapests. But these anapests also surround lyrics, and thus one of their main functions is as emotional "gateways" between spoken sections of dramas and lyric passages where emotions are often much heightened; they typically serve as an emotional crescendo into a lyric ode or a diminuendo out of it. However, they do not always accompany lyrics and the appearance of tragic anapests before and after lyrics is always "the marked case and is significant; their absence is apparently not" (Brown 1977: 51). In other words, anapests tend to be a signal by the poet that something significant is occurring or being said, especially when they appear in an unusual place or sequence.

As the *Trachiniae* moves from the Chorus' confused final lyrics into anapests one might expect an emotional diminuendo,[40] perhaps even leading to an ending; Heracles, after all, could simply be carried into the house to await death without the long series of orders and instructions we see next. Yet the anapestic section in between the end of the fourth stasimon and Heracles' song functions oppositely, and Sophocles actually escalates the tension through the course of Hyllus' anxious questions, the Old Man's terse admonitory responses and Heracles' initial confused, interrogative prayers to his divine father Zeus. The anapestic section, as it were, displaces the energy lost from the last confused choral ode. Much that is without parallel and musically remarkable happens in the exodus of the *Trachiniae*. Sophocles expresses the tension of this scene by the use of *antilabê*, as Hyllus interrupts the Old Man three times in the space of fourteen lines (977, 981,

---

[40] On the flat, often unstable, lyrics of the Chorus of the *Trachiniae*, especially as symptoms of first their naivety and then utter bewilderment, see Scott 1996: 102–114, with a summary of all the lyric odes at 121. Henrichs 1995: 85 comments on the effect of the aftermath of line 970: "when the pipe falls silent, the chorus stops dancing, 12 lines before Heracles enters and 300 lines from the end."

991), and while *antilabê* is by no means uncommon in Greek tragedy, its use here inside anapestic lines is completely unique (Davies 1991: 225). The lyric songs further unusually incorporate two blocks of hexameters (1010–14, 1031–40), the meter of heroic epic poetry, within the dominant lines of dochmaic verses, which traditionally accompany songs of great passion suffering, but the songs also contain four lines of anapests which further heighten the emotions (1007–08, 1028–29). Dale notes thus: "When a character sings (or recites) melic anapests in contrast to the recitative systems of the Chorus . . . the effect is to isolate the melic singer on a high emotional level" (Dale 1948: 52). Heracles himself, after he shifts from lyric meters to trimeters, still prays to Zeus in anapests (1081, 1095–96). Brown categorizes these lines as taking place within a "sacral context of prayer"; as Heracles begs for death, "[t]he meter used is non-lyric anapests. After each outburst he is subsiding into normal speech and the meter moves from anapests back to conventional iambic trimeters" (Brown 1977: 73). In comparing the placement of anapests in the work of the three tragedians, Brown further notices that Sophocles generally reserves them for relatively late in each relevant drama, "when the entire spectrum of feeling is organized into a crescendo" (Brown 1977: 56). In other words, the anapests are a key part of Sophocles' poetic tools in orchestrating the emotional impact of his craft.

Nineteenth-century commentators such as Schlegel were embarrassed by the *Trachiniae* and regarded it as primitive, a bias that persisted into the twentieth century when scholars tried to assign it, on the basis of some of the allegedly more unsophisticated aspects of its style, to relatively early in Sophocles' career. However, more recent critics have been inclined to appreciate the subject matter of this drama, and unprejudiced analyses of its choral odes, such as Scott's, show the art in their seeming artlessness as the relative emotional flatness of the odes reflects the inexperience and naivety of the young maidens rather than any poetic failing on the part of Sophocles; indeed, in such matters as the withholding and then deployment of anapests to certain effects, the *Trachiniae* resembles the more acclaimed *Oedipus Tyrannus* to a startling degree. The anapests are the "new music" required once the Chorus stops singing only to be replaced, again as in the *Oedipus*, by the lyric voice of the hero (Scott 1996: 113–14, 142–48).[41] The raging, arrogant, worldly Heracles subsumes the role of the naive young maidens of the Chorus, who cannot respond in song to the catastrophe they

---

[41] Despite sketching out how the two dramas both have a decomposition of musical forms succeeded by unusually placed anapests, Scott does not draw a connection and see a pattern.

see, and this hence forms part of the motivation for Heracles' lament that he is "weeping like a maiden" (*parthenos*, 1071); he thus identifies, during the trimeter section of the exodus, the unusual shift in lamentation from the Chorus to himself. The anapests that introduce and close the exodus form part of a rich orchestration of moods by Sophocles that point, I submit, to the approaching apotheosis of Heracles on Mt. Oeta because anapests can mark contact with divinity. Brown's work on anapests says very little about the *Trachiniae*, so let us explore their possibilities further now.

The anapests in the *Trachiniae* signal the operation of rituals, particularly rituals of lamentation and communication with the gods. Hyllus speaks in anapests, but he is not part of the entrance procession, since he moves toward it after he enters through the *skênê* door (Winnington-Ingram 1969: 44–47). But also he is engaging in lament, which Brown identifies as an important aspect of the anapest, perhaps even as an original source for lamentation ritual itself (Brown 1977: 48). Lamentation ritual here moves us closer to a broader connection between anapests and the gods that might further support arguments concerning the implied divinization of Heracles after the drama itself concludes. Again, Brown identifies the dramatic contexts of anapests, all of which are applicable to the exodus of the *Trachiniae*: "processions which often portray regal or divine pomp; religious rituals such as prayer, incantation or lamentation; and finally overt references to the play's actual production which endanger the suspension of disbelief required of the audience for the drama" (Brown 1977: 48). Anapests, since they typically accompany the procession of actors and chorus from the theater, thus signal to the audience the ending of the drama as an act of mimesis, yet, in the *Trachiniae*, Hyllus' insistence on the gods, to the very last line and word of the drama, "Zeus," fights against the mimetic closure as long as possible, maintaining the closing anapests as reminders of religious rituals; after all, Hyllus' own instructions to the Chorus (and, possibly, Iole) are part of the religious rituals, they believe, of the death of Heracles which will actually lead to his apotheosis, his immortality. Brown concludes her argument thus (Brown 1977: 71):

For reasons long since lost to us, the anapestic rhythm was felt to be particularly suited to signal mimesis and so this meter was used regularly for the rituals portrayed within a play and also for the ritual of a play itself. A mimetic religious rite usually has a conflict built into its very core: the action pretends to be the real event in question and so accomplishes the desired goal; at the same time there is an acknowledgement that the action is a mere substitute operating at one remove. In Greek tragedy the anapestic meter, which marks both the entry into the divine realm and the spectator's presence at a dramatic production, fulfilled both functions.

The musical metamorphosis of the *Trachiniae* that begins with the silence of the maidens of the Chorus continues through the subsequent anapests and then into the lyrics of Heracles signals the shifts in Heracles' being from hero, to suffering "girl," back to a hero who begins to act like a god in his imperiousness and indifference to the human consequences of his demands (Winnington-Ingram 1980: 215). The shock of the plague-like sufferings of Heracles and the defamiliarization wrought by the musical experimentation here likely induced the audience members, I suggest, to think about the hero Heracles as being simultaneously like themselves (that is, those who had survived the plague) and like the god to whom they prayed for help during the plague itself. The mimetic rite they experience here, with the expectation that this ruined human will soon become a god, thus would ameliorate their own suffering.

Not that, for the human characters left after Heracles, this is any consolation, and, indeed, the emotional wreckage and sheer despair of the end of the *Trachiniae* have been used as a major argument against an implied apotheosis; how could Heracles get his wish and achieve bliss amidst such sadness? Yet we would thus confuse the achieved goals of a single character with their impact on his immediate *philoi*, much as in the later *Oedipus at Colonus*, which presents an important model for viewing retrospectively the ending of the earlier drama about Heracles. Oedipus arrives at the outskirts of Athens only to realize the convergence of his life with an older prophecy about his death, and he immediately begins preparations for his own transfiguration, and, in the process, he begins to act like the god that he will soon become. Oedipus ascends (or descends) to the gods, yet one son leaves to go and kill the other, and his daughters, desiring to stop the mutual slaughter, prepare to return to Thebes where, the audience knows (having seen the *Antigone*), they will all, save Ismene, die. Oedipus achieves bliss as a reward for his suffering, yet the outcome for everyone else is extraordinarily bleak. Thus, an implied apotheosis in the *Trachiniae* is not inconsistent with the decidedly depressing human scene before the audience. Hyllus correctly assesses that everything here is Zeus, but he does so, ultimately, in a form of dramatic irony: Hyllus believes his impending orphancy comes from the will of his indifferent, to a cruel extent, divine paternal grandfather, but, in a pattern reiterated throughout the drama, he speaks wrongly because he speaks in ignorance of the larger unfoldings of destiny. Indeed, placed in the context of the other works of Sophocles, the last line of the *Trachiniae* is unique neither in form nor content since Hyllus' lament, κοὐδὲν τούτων ὅ τι μὴ Ζεύς, "and nothing of these matters is not Zeus" (1278), bears a striking resemblance in language and tone to Oedipus' mantic cries to the

Chorus' question of what god had driven him to blind himself: Ἀπόλλων τάδ' ἦν, Ἀπόλλων, φίλοι, "Apollo, these things were Apollo, friends" (*OT* 1329).

The destruction of the human Heracles is not a random event, but part of a larger structure unapparent to the youthful characters in this play, Hyllus and the Chorus of young women. Thus, one might recall the wise words of Easterling that the last line of the *Trachiniae* is "an assertion that the universe is orderly, not chaotic: you have to take the consequences for what you do, and Zeus has not restricted his son in allowing the natural laws to take their course" (Easterling 1968: 60). The audience members know, and have been reminded of during the exodus, the larger destiny of the hero and now view "their" Heracles, who during the exodus suffered as they do (or did) during the plague, the god they worship in cult, leaving the acting area to initiate his own ascendancy to divinity. The bitterness in Hyllus' final lines surely is driven by the recognition that his parents' deaths served no purpose, and they had no redemptive function. And Hyllus is wrong. Yet, I suggest, because of the particular nature of Heracles' torment and the circumstances of Athens during the years of the *Trachiniae*'s production, the redemptive suffering is not for the benefit of any member of the stage community, but for another community entirely: for Athens.

SOPHOCLES, HERACLES AND ATHENIAN IMPERIALISM

If Heracles replicates something that Athens has experienced, then perhaps the relationship, in the *Trachiniae*, between Heracles and Athens runs particularly deep, but nowhere near the surface since the drama is set in Trachis and does not seem to refer overtly to Athenian institutions. That distance throws us back on the language and themes of the text. As noted earlier, Heracles is unique among tragic heroes in moving from displaying a metaphorical *nosos*, in the form of *eros*, to a real one, though the arc of this passage resembles the reification of the blindness of Oedipus. The metaphorical illness manifested itself in the form of the desire for a woman so strong that he was willing to go to war and destroy another city to fulfill it. As an ultimate, if indirect, result of this war, he finds his flesh dissolving, his body wracked with unbearable pain. To return to the Greek formula I discussed much earlier, this is *nosos kai polemos*, the proverbial conjunctive combination of disease and war seen first in the *Iliad* and thematized by Hesiod, and then articulated anew for the fifth century by Thucydides. At the opening of the *Trachiniae*, Deianira laments her husband's repeated extended absences, many of which would have involved wars of conquest.

Moreover, the first hint of Heracles' current whereabouts, given by Hyllus, is that he is campaigning in Euboea (74–75). The desires of Heracles both generate his greatness and create difficulties for all around him. One recent commentator has described the reputation of one of the primary agents of discomfort in this region during antiquity as "a kind of monstrosity, even a threat to civilization: too big, too rich, too powerful, too permissive in its social and political life" (Redfield 2003: ix). The subject there is Athens, but these words could also apply to Heracles. Suddenly, Heracles begins to look much like Athens itself.

This is not Heracles the Panhellenic hero, but Heracles the Athenian.[42] Bernard Knox's classic examination of the *Oedipus Tyrannus* showed Oedipus to embody both the virtues of Athens as a society at the beginning of the Peloponnesian War and its vices as an imperial power and, I suggest, Sophocles presents Heracles as an analogous, though darker, figure (Knox 1957).[43] In essence, Heracles represents the drive of Athens to dominance that pushes it to disaster. If the *Oedipus Tyrannus*, as Knox and Ehrenberg suggested, was generated in part by Sophocles' uneasiness with modernist rationalism and political imperialism of Pericles, then the *Trachiniae*, if it was produced in the 420s, shows an analogous, distinct discomfort with the consequences of Pericles' empire because of the plague-like consequences of the greed of Heracles.

Sophocles and Pericles, we know, were members of the Athenian elite and partook of the same intellectual and social circles, yet, despite Sophocles' popular reputation for social ease and grace, there is also evidence for tension between these two Athenians.[44] In 441/0 Sophocles was elected to serve as one of the generals alongside Pericles, after having worked prominently in the government only two years previously, and participated in the campaign to suppress the rebellion of the inhabitants of Samos from the Delian League. He thus had direct first-hand experience with the consequences of the imperial policies of Pericles. Plutarch records several anecdotes that indicate tension between Sophocles and Pericles or events that could not have sat well with Sophocles if his dramas reflect his personal beliefs at all. Other sources record that Sophocles, during a sojourn en route to this conflict, used an elaborate ruse to get a beautiful young boy to kiss him

---

[42] One can compare here the pains Sophocles takes in the *Ajax* to link its hero, even though he is a Salaminian fighting at Troy in the mythical past, to Athens, to the point where he is virtually called an Athenian; see Ormand 1999: 104–05.

[43] Scodel 2003: 41 also argues that Sophocles' dramas show that the poet was concerned about the negative consequences of Athenian imperialism.

[44] On the relationship between Sophocles and Pericles in general see Ehrenberg 1954 and Podlecki 1998: 121–25.

and exclaimed: "I am interested in strategy [*stratêgein*, being a general], gentlemen, although Pericles said I can write poetry, but don't understand strategy; but now didn't that strategy of mine work out perfectly?"[45] A charming anecdote and possibly innocuous, yet it could be that Sophocles, who, as the stereotype fostered by Aristophanes' *Frogs* shows, was renowned for his easy social deportment, was here suggesting that there were other models of actions possible than the one imagined by his colleague. Plutarch records that Pericles responded in kind (*Per.* 8.8): "a *stratêgos* must not only have clean hands but also a clean mind." Now, while this typifies the moral rectitude of Pericles, it also signals the possibility of some sort of larger tension that the outcome of the Samian War could have greatly exacerbated. Here we are intrigued yet hindered by our sources, for Plutarch seems skeptical of his own source, Douris the Samian, who accused Pericles of torture, mutilations and the exposure of corpses (26.2–3). While charges of war atrocities have always been hurled recklessly throughout recorded human history, one could easily imagine that something less than wholesome could have emerged at the end of so heated a conflict and that the smoke of the allegations could be signaling a fire, though perhaps a smaller one than Douris would have wanted it to appear, and modern scholarship has tended to support some form of the contentions of Douris, and not Plutarch's squeamishness.[46]

We have no clear, direct idea how Sophocles reacted to the end of the Samian War, but if there were in fact atrocities committed, it does not sound likely that the author of the *Antigone*, if that drama reflects its author's real beliefs, would have been too pleased with what he witnessed; I shall have more to say on the *Antigone* shortly. Ehrenberg, however, after commenting on the disagreement between Sophocles and Pericles on sexual *mores*, observed: "There is, on the other hand, not the slightest indication that he ever objected to Pericles' imperialism and his treatment of the allies" (Ehrenberg 1954: 119). There is no evidence, but there is certainly much room for reasonably informed speculation. Moreover, Ehrenberg here was concerned with the immediate aftermath of the Samian War, and he left the Peloponnesian War of a decade later, which has much more direct consequences for Sophocles' Athens, as an open question, and, indeed, Ehrenberg himself did propose that Sophocles composed the *Oedipus Tyrannus* in part as a warning to Pericles, not about imperialism, but about the consequences

---

[45] T75 = *FGrH* 392F6, translated by Lefkowitz 1981: 81. See Ehrenberg 1954: 119.

[46] Podlecki 1998: 125 is particularly skeptical about the reports of atrocities at Samos. However, Meiggs 1972: 191–94 supports Douris' concept that Pericles did commit atrocities at Samos, as does Lewis 1988: 46–47.

of the excessive rationalism of his intellectual circle; and with its insistence on the truth of oracles, the *Trachiniae* seems cut largely from the same cloth.

But that there were certain strains among the members of the aristocracy over Pericles' conduct of an imperialist policy is shown by another anecdote from the Samian War. Pericles returned from the war triumphant, gave a great oration at the funeral of the fallen warriors and was then lauded and festooned with garlands and wreaths, Plutarch says, "like some victorious athlete." Elpinice, the sister of Cimon, Pericles' bitter rival from earlier in his career, approached him with a different tone and assessment (*Per.* 28.4): "These things are amazing, and worthy of crowns, that you have for us killed so many good citizens by warring not with the Phoenicians nor the Medes, as my brother Cimon did, but by subjugating an allied and kindred city." Cimon, a great, aristocratic general, is likely to have been close with Sophocles before his ostracism; he even was an impromptu judge on the occasion of Sophocles' first victory at the City Dionysia and was allegedly able, through his popular authority, to calm the angry audience after the young playwright defeated the crowd-favorite Aeschylus (*Cim.* 8.7).

Recent scholarship has reconnected the Samian War to Sophocles and his dramas in arguing that Sophocles likely produced the *Antigone* after the Samian War in 438 BCE and not before it in 442. The case, briefly, is: in 443/2 he would have been too busy with his important work as *hellênotamias*; we know that Euripides won first prize in 441, Sophocles served as a general in the Samian campaign in 441/0 and 440/39, but won first prize in 438, with a program of which we know nothing.[47] Moreover, in order to discourage domestic attacks against Pericles over Samos there was a ban on comic drama between 440 and 438, which would thus have increased the need for some other outlet for political dissent at a mass gathering of the citizenry of Athens. A production of the *Antigone* in 438 would have provided such an outlet, and its depiction of the necessity of traditional burial rites even in the face of a bitter war, if 438 indeed is the correct year, surely must have been directed as a criticism of the aftermath

---

[47] On all of these matters Lewis 1988 is most convincing to me. Scholars have placed far too much weight on the passage in the *Vita* (9) which purports Sophocles was given his generalship after the *Antigone*; this passage, Lewis stresses (35–36), is textually unstable and "over-emended." He is particularly effective against Ehrenberg's (1954: 38) somewhat strange undervaluing of Sophocles' duties as a *hellênotamias*, concluding that "he would be a rash archon who 'assigned a chorus' to a poet who was an elected *hellênotamias*, and a rash *hellênotamias* who applied for one." Subsequently, Tyrrell and Bennett 1998: 1–5 further examine the debate over the date of the *Antigone*, and the implications for its relationship to Samos, and they build a reading of Sophocles as a response to the moral issues raised by Athenian conduct there.

of Pericles' punishment of the Samians. Thus, we now have an example, in the *Antigone*, of Sophocles incorporating a debate over Athenian policy as part of his task as a dramatic poet. We really have little idea what Sophocles might have thought of the origins and conduct of the Peloponnesian War, since there is no hard proof that any of his dramas were produced in the 420s. Moreover, for the next decade, there is perhaps only the *Electra*, which seems to depict a world of brutalized youths, and then, after the oligarchic revolution of 411, the *Philoctetes*, which seems itself, as I shall discuss in the next chapter, to have something to do with Athens late in the Peloponnesian War, and the *Oedipus at Colonus*, composed at the end of Sophocles' life as a celebratory lament for an Athens that was dying, if not already dead. But my working assumption throughout this chapter has been that the *Oedipus Tyrannus* belongs to the 420s, and my working hypothesis that the *Trachiniae* belongs close to it there, so let us see further how they relate to Athens early in the Peloponnesian War.

If the plague-like suffering of Heracles, combined with the signals of his approaching apotheosis, has religious implications for the Athenian audience, so too, I suggest, Heracles might be a darker version of the *polis tyrannus* delineated by Bernard Knox (1957: 60–67, 100–05). While Heracles displays in the exodus the qualities that make him like the divinity he will become after the end of the drama, he has reached that point through his activities as a human which are dangerous to both friend and foe; it is thus not a self-contradiction to argue that Sophocles depicts the incipient apotheosis of Heracles while using the same hero as a vehicle to connect the disasters afflicting Athens with the behavior of Athens itself. Heracles, essentially, embodies the imperial program of Pericles through his journeys of conquest throughout the Mediterranean, and in the process of his heroic career he lays the seeds of his own destruction through the need to satisfy the demands of his excessive individualism. To an even greater extent than Oedipus, Heracles pushes the limits of what it means to be human. Knox skirted the trap of simplistically aligning another relentless hero, Oedipus, with Pericles by envisioning the character of Oedipus modeled not so much on Pericles as on that of the Athenian people as a whole, for better and for worse. He sums up his argument thus (Knox 1957: 105):

. . .the play is a tragic vision of Athens' splendor, vigor, and inevitable defeat which contemplates no possibility of escape – the defeat is immanent in the splendor. The mantic vision of the poet penetrates through the appearances of Athenian power to the reality of the tragic reversal, the Fall towards which Athens is forcing its way with all the fierce, creative energy, the uncompromising logic, the initiative and daring which have brought her to the pinnacle of worldly power.

If, as Knox argues, Sophocles senses that the tyrannical power of Athens
with respect to its empire is linked to its initial fall through the plague, and
if Sophocles composed the *Trachiniae* at least in part as a response to the
plague, then what could have brought about the plague-like symptoms of
Heracles in the *Trachiniae*? The answer lies in the character and conduct of
Heracles, whose main flaw, as Deianira asserts several times, is his excessive
devotion to *eros*, which acts like, or is, a disease. That *eros* manifests itself
in a desire for more, a greed for sexual conquest and for a dominance over
the male relatives of his desired women.[48] Not content just with his wife,
he would install Iole in his house as well. His desire for mastery over others,
ultimately, is his real sickness as *eros* is just a manifestation of that. In a
nutshell, the downfall of Heracles is caused by *pleonexia*, the term given by
Thucydides to mark the dark side of Athenian energy and ambition.

   Pleonexia characterizes no other Greek tragic hero more thoroughly than
Heracles, and *pleonexia* came to describe Athens especially during the middle of the 420s in Thucydides' *History*.[49] *Pleonexia* is the desire to acquire
more wealth, more territory, more glory and connotes the particularly Athenian sort of self-aggrandizement that made its neighbors so uneasy. Ryan
Balot, in his study of greed in Athens, observes that, after the competition between elites and the demos of Athens had been ameliorated by
the development of democracy in the fifth century, "[t]he greed that has
once characterized competing groups within Athens now became the pre-
vailing attribute of the city as a whole."[50] Already in the Corcyrean *stasis*,
Thucydides designates *pleonexia*, along with *philotimia* (ambition), as one
of the root causes of the turmoil outside of Athens (3.82.8), and in Book
4 he describes the Athenians' reaction to their unexpected good fortune
(*eutuchia*) at Pylos in 424 BCE as desiring more (4.65.4). In the following
year, Nicias bases his plans for negotiations in part on the need for Athens
to avoid *pleonexia* (5.13.2) (Connor 1984: 141). "Grasping for more" seems
in Thucydides to be a pathology that worsens considerably during the
420s, to the extent that Hornblower deems it a "thoroughly Thucydidean
preoccupation" (Hornblower 1987: 119). As Hornblower further contends,
pleonexia really was a larger Athenian problem, antedating not just 425 but

---

[48] Ormand 1999: 48 observes: "The *defining* object of desire for Heracles is not Iole herself (however
   much he may lust after her), but mastery over his rival."
[49] On *pleonexia* in Thucydides see Connor 1984: 120–21, Hornblower 1987: 174–78 and Balot 2001:
   136–78. On the role of *eros* in the politics of Athens see now Wohl 2002, who discusses its relation
   to Athenian imperialism (171–214) by focusing on Thucydides' narrative of the Sicilian expedition.
[50] Balot 2001: 5. Balot's work is an important contribution to this subject, but he does not discuss
   Athenian tragic drama at all. I hope that the following paragraphs form a useful supplement to that
   study.

the entire Peloponnesian War, back through the rule of Pericles and even to Cimon and Themistocles, but Thucydides' nostalgia for the Athens of his youth and his distaste for the generation of Cleon prevented him from associating it with earlier Periclean rule (Hornblower 1987: 174–78). The impulse of Athens to expand, to grasp more and more, is inseparable from its empire. Heracles, the hero of enormous appetites, is the fitting symbol for that regime as much as the intelligent, caring, Oedipus so devoted to the common good is for democratic Athens. In the next century, Plato would pick up these metaphorical strands from Sophocles and Thucydides and repeatedly assert that *pleonexia* is a form of *nosos*, and that *pleonexia* is *eros*. Plato thus reiterates the triangulation of the two legs of *eros* and *nosos* stated by Sophocles with the third implied leg of *pleonexia*.[51]

Ultimately, the hardest to answer question one might ask of a text is why the author wrote it, or, in a formulation less redolent of the Intentional Fallacy, what forces brought about its particular construction. If the answer is compelling and true to the internal dynamics of the text we should find it inside of the text, not artificially imposed from the outside. I hope I have shown that the language, structure and imagery of the *Trachiniae* is consistent with a reading that has it produced in the 420s and as a response to the great plague of Athens. The erotic *pleonexia* of Heracles destroys him, in proof of the oracles of old, long dormant through Heracles' life. The vehicle of his destruction is a poisonous concoction the effects of which resemble the symptoms of the plague as described by Thucydides. Sophocles thus depicts the suffering Heracles on his way to becoming the god who might assist Athens in its own crisis, as well as a Heracles whose misconduct has itself provoked this crisis in himself. The responses to the plague and the early years of the Peloponnesian War form a significant, though by no means total, part of the meaning of the *Trachiniae*, which can be read productively in several ways without reference to historical context. Writing of how Victor Ehrenberg conceived of the relationship between Oedipus and Pericles in Sophoclean drama, James Redfield commented that Oedipus is like Pericles not "because Sophokles intended a point about Perikles, but rather (I am suggesting) because he relied on his audience's understanding of Perikles to create for them a believable Oidipous" (Redfield 1990: 325). Now, while I do in fact believe Sophocles was intending a point (or several) about Pericles, recognizing the reverse, in Redfield's formula, is helpful for understanding the economy of meaning in the *Trachiniae*,

---

[51] Plato represents *pleonexia* as *nosos* at *Laws* 906c, *Republic* 609 and *Symposium* 188a. *Pleonexia* is *eros* at *Republic* 572e4–573a2. On these passages see Chapter V of Balot 2001.

wherein the audience's own experience of the plague was essential, and our understanding of that experience is essential, for creating a Heracles who suffers on such a scale believably. That audience's experience, plus their religious reaction to the plague, must be taken into account in figuring out what Sophocles was attempting when he created this drama.

The *Trachiniae* resembles the *Oedipus Tyrannus*, as I have shown, in so many ways: from their problematic protagonists, to the silent exits, to suicides of the heroes' wives, to the language of disease, to the concern with the proof of ancient oracles, to the collapse of choral singing in the face of the hero's disaster after which the hero assumes the Chorus' role. We do not know enough about Sophocles' other dramas during these years to say how many of these similarities were in fact prevalent throughout Sophoclean drama then, or whether there is a deep, indelible connection between these tragedies about Heracles and Oedipus. My final sense is that either the *Trachiniae* was a dry run, one year before, for the *Oedipus*, or, more radically, that they were performed on the same program sometime between 429 and 425 BCE.[52] My argument thus points to a possible solution of the two most vexed questions of the *Trachiniae*: whether it alludes to the divinization of Heracles and when it was produced.

But Sophocles' tragic drama was not the last instance where the Theater of Dionysus witnessed such language attached to Heracles, and I will thus turn to Euripides' *Heracles*, which was produced roughly one decade after the *Trachiniae*, and in an environment newly receptive to the language of disease, but with new semantic ranges. Before returning to Euripidean drama, however, I shall discuss what enabled the new semantic ranges: the construction of the Athenian Asklepieion. ✓

---

[52] Padilla 2002: 142 speculates: "it is an interesting exercise to wonder if the *Women of Trachis* was produced in the same program with the *Oedipus the King*. The two plays serve as ideal complements on several thematic levels."

CHAPTER 7

Materials II: The cult of Asclepius and the Theater of Dionysus

Why should the Athenians, as a response to the waves of plague that struck their city during the first half of the 420s, have placed, six or seven years later, their new Asklepieion on the south slope of the Acropolis, as Figure 1 shows, below the Parthenon, the temple dedicated to Athena, and above the Theater, part of the sanctuary dedicated to Dionysus? Does Asclepius have some connection with drama, or was the shrine location purely coincidental? I have demonstrated that drama shows a persistent, though undeveloped, interest in disease imagery that becomes especially strong after the plague's onset, and this interest opens the door to the arrival of Asclepius near and in the Theater of Dionysus. The development of the cult of Asclepius in Athens and the range of myths involving him both associate him with Dionysus, the Greek god of, among other things, theater. Thus, on the levels of theme, ritual and performance Asclepius is important to Greek drama in the last quarter of the fifth century and beyond. Here I should make it clear, however, that I am not positing Asclepius as a god who appears as an overseer of the action in tragic plots, for he is far too benign and helpful a figure to play the same part as the more ambivalent gods Apollo and Dionysus.[1] In fact, the only extant drama in which Asclepius intercedes beneficially and directly is Aristophanes' late comedy, the *Wealth*; the *Alcestis* opens with Apollo's account of Asclepius' earlier disastrous attempts at resurrection that ultimately resulted in Apollo's own servitude, while in Sophocles' *Philoctetes* his healing of that hero is promised for when Philoctetes reaches Troy, well after the ending of the stage action. Indeed, Asclepius' role in tragic plots and myths as a mortal differs sharply from his divine nature in cult, but such myths and dramas can help us understand the function of the cult as it stands adjacent to the theater.

---

[1] I am grateful to Albert Henrichs for reminding me of this. On the decidedly "unclassical" beneficence of Asclepius see the sensible comments of Parker 1996: 184–85.

Hence, my concern here is with Asclepius' role in the performative context of the Theater of Dionysus.[2] In this chapter I shall examine the relationship between Asclepius, theater and Dionysus, and then pursue how the unique-ness of the Athenian Asklepieion further suggests that its relationship to the Theater of Dionysus is significant.

The principal sanctuary of Asclepius was in his legendary birthplace of Epidaurus, most famous today for its theater (which is, as I shall discuss later, located in the Asclepius sanctuary itself), and his cult was brought to Athens anywhere from one to nine years after the first outbreak of the great plague, although myths about him, as the *Oresteia*, *Alcestis* and *Pythian* 3 show, were sufficiently well known to allow poets to refer to it in passing with the assurance that their audiences understood the allusion's function. Our sources on his arrival in Athens are uncertain and the date remains somewhat controversial. Some scholars, particularly the Edelsteins, have hesitated to locate Asclepius' arrival during and as a result of the plague, presumably because it makes the mighty Athenians seem weak and irrational. However, a consensus appears to have emerged that the cult of Asclepius was introduced at least to Attica in the Piraeus, if not in central Athens itself, shortly after the outbreak of the plague.[3] The date matters in that it indicates the extent to which the plague affected the practices – religious and otherwise – and institutions in Athens. So even if we were finally to ascertain that there was no sustained cultic activity in Athens until 420 BCE, this delayed construction in itself would still indicate the lasting impact of the plague on the Athenian imagination. But given the relative renown of the myth of Asclepius and the extensive medical crisis in Athens, private religious activity for the god of healing before 420 seems plausible, if not probable. A fourth-century inscription indicates that before an Athenian named Telemachus established the shrine to Asclepius, the Asklepieion, on the south slope of the Acropolis, the cult of Asclepius first came to Piraeus, the Athenian port which Thucydides

---

[2] Wiles 1997: 43–44 notes the proximity of Asclepius sanctuaries and theaters, yet makes much of neither the Athenian configuration nor the possible meaning of such a relationship. Wiles' generally insightful reading appeared well after the development of my thesis.

[3] On an early date as a reaction to the plague see Burford 1969: 20–21, Padel 1992: 145, Mikalson 1984, Parker 1983: 275, and Garland 1992: 130–32. Against the Edelsteins, Burford argues: "The cult's advance to international status was most likely a direct result of the great plague in Athens. The two visitations of 430 and 427 gave rise to exactly that state of depression compounded of loneliness, terror and despair in which one would turn to any new source of healing." On the introduction of the cult of Asclepius to the Acropolis of Athens during the Peloponnesian War see Camp 2001: 122–27.

designates as the site of the first outbreak of the plague (2.48.2).[4] It may have also been the case that the year 420 was the Athenians' first opportunity, when the Peace of Nicias temporarily slowed the Peloponnesian War, to bring Asclepius fully to Athens (Mikalson 1984: 220). It does seem that Asclepius entered the plans of Athens quite early, for, soon after the initial outbreak of the plague, the Athenians, as Thucydides records (2.56.4), tried to take Epidaurus militarily, perhaps with the goal of acquiring the help of Asclepius for their domestic medical crisis; Thucydides adds (2.57) that during this campaign the plague was laying waste to both the Athenians at home and those attacking Epidaurus, among other cities. Plutarch's mistake in mixing up the chronological sequence so that he attributes the plague to this attack shows at least the later power of the belief in Asclepius, as well as the further associations between plague and war (*Per.* 35.3). One extant tragic drama, Euripides' *Hippolytus*, involves, directly and indirectly, both these cities and Asclepius, and it might also be the earliest surviving literary response to the great plague of Athens.

ASCLEPIUS AND THE GOD OF THEATER

My working hypothesis, again, is that the Athenians' decision to locate their Asklepieion arose not from the coincidence of the availability of a nice piece of real estate, but from deeper associations among drama, healing and the Athenian *polis*. Expanding now my focus from Asclepius and one drama to Asclepius and the god of drama, I can observe that Asclepius and Dionysus appear to cooperate or resemble each other on several levels. The first, as we have seen, is in the Eleusinian Mysteries, a festival where Dionysus plays a key role. Asclepius also mediates between Dionysus and more ascetic gods such as Apollo and Artemis. The myth of Asclepius' birth, which the Edelsteins believed was unique (Edelstein and Edelstein 1945: 1.136), actually possesses a remarkable homology with that of Dionysus. As Pindar tells the story in *Pythian* 3, Coronis lay with Apollo and conceived Asclepius, but she then bedded a mortal, without proper wedding rituals and in secret from her divine lover. For this betrayal, Artemis killed Coronis and Apollo snatched the fetus from the pyre before it was consumed. This structure strongly resembles two myths of Dionysus: his birth and the destruction of Ariadne. Like Asclepius, Dionysus was saved by his divine father from the burning corpse of his mother, and Dionysus himself later killed his mortal

---

[4] *IG* II² 4960. On the Telemachus monument see Garland 1992: 118–20 and Camp 2001: 122.

lover Ariadne for betraying him with Theseus. A schematic representation can help clarify the structure:

Pattern	Semele	Coronis	Ariadne
woman loves god	Semele loves Zeus	Coronis loves Apollo	Ariadne loves Dionysus
woman betrays god	Semele asks to see real Zeus	Coronis beds a man	Ariadne loves Theseus
god kills woman	Semele immolated by the lightning of Zeus	Artemis kills Coronis	Artemis kills Ariadne
god's son saved from fire	Dionysus sewn in Zeus' thigh	Apollo snatches fetus of Asclepius	(Ariadne dies giving birth)
son has special powers	Dionysus born a god	Asclepius a healer	

The chart helps show how the Asclepius legend takes over the form of two strands of the Dionysus myth, thus elevating Asclepius in stature by making him correspond to certain patterns of heroic divinity; the purifying fire of Zeus/Apollo burns away the mortality of Dionysus/Asclepius so the would-be mortal can become a god.[5] We also might add the association of the snake with both Dionysus and Asclepius, and that Dionysus had healing powers, especially ascribed to him through wine;[6] the Chorus in Sophocles' *Antigone* asks Dionysus to come with his "purifying foot (καθαρσίῳ ποδί, 1144) since the city is held by a violent disease." Homer tells how Ariadne died from the arrows of Artemis after Dionysus gave witness of her betrayal of him when she ran off with Theseus, much like Coronis who died at Apollo's hands (*Od.* 11.325), and another tradition, recorded by Plutarch, tells that Ariadne died at Cyprus in childbirth (*Thes.* 20), but the two myths are essentially the same since childbirth is the province of Artemis; either way, Artemis kills her. Like her brother Apollo, who can both bring plague and cure it, Artemis assists or kills mothers in birth.[7] Here we might also notice a confluence of the supposed opposites Artemis and Aphrodite analogous to the cultic cooperation of Apollo and Dionysus. Cyprus, the

---

[5] Burgess 2001 discusses structural resemblances between the labors of Semele and Coronis and the association of the female with mortality. See also Currie 2005: 360–68 on the parallels with the Dionysus myth and the theme of immortalization by fire. Destruction by fire would be seen, as with the death of Heracles, as a means to heroization or apotheosis.

[6] Eur. *Ba.* 280–82, 772. See Cordes 1994: 44–45. But see Scullion 1998 on how one must be careful about ascribing healing powers to Dionysus.

[7] Otto 1933: 55: "Artemis ist bekanntlich die Göttin, die den gebärenden Weibern den Tod bringt."

other death site of Ariadne, is one of the places sacred to Aphrodite, and Plutarch further reports that in a sacred rite in Ariadne's honor "one of the young men lies down and cries, and acts like women in the pain of childbirth; and they call the grove of Amathousius, in which they show her tomb, that of Ariadne of Aphrodite." Kerényi concludes from this story that, because the young man essentially takes the birth pangs over from Ariadne in his mimesis of her, he becomes a Zeus to her Semele. This might be stretching the structural correspondences a bit, but it is worth keeping in mind. Noting the concinnity of the three narratives, Kerényi adds: "Koronis proves to be a repetition not only of Semele, but of Ariadne . . . The story of Koronis in death bearing Apollo a son resembling him, Asklepios, may be later than the story of Ariadne, whom Dionysos made into a mother bearing in death; but it is the same pre-Hellenic sacred narrative" (Kerényi 1959: xix–xx).

The involvement of Asclepius and Dionysus in the Mysteries and their similar birth legends are part of a greater set of shared rites and functions that culminate in the installation of the Asklepieion next to the Theater of Dionysus. With the overlap between the myths of Dionysus and Asclepius and their participation in similar rituals, we can see one of the most pronounced examples of the cooperation between Apollo and Dionysus. Throughout the important shrines of Apollo in Greece, especially Delphi, Dionysus plays an important part in cultic activity (Burkert 1985: 223–25). The two gods are often set in relation to each other iconographically, and the tragedians tend to associate Dionysus with Delphi as well, as is seen particularly in Euripides' *Ion* (216–18), a drama about another son of Apollo. A fourth-century paean by Philodamus for the Dionysian festival at Delphi even attributes to Dionysus paeanic cries, thus directly equating the two gods. In sum, their complementarity necessitates each other's existence. Des Bouvrie further suggests that in order for Dionysus to have boundaries to dissolve Apollo must first provide and then restore them in Dionysus' wake: "The god supervising the boundaries and categories in the world at times gives way to the god obliterating those boundaries, in order to revitalize society and its hierarchies" (Des Bouvrie 1993: 109).

With these associations in mind, I suggest again that the placement of the Asklepieion immediately above the Theater of Dionysus is not a mere coincidence, but rather it arises first from archaic associations between poetry and healing that became more urgent because of the plague. This interpretation of the meaning of shrine location is in line with recent developments in archaeology that have offered "radically new insight into the significance of where the gods were worshipped."[8] Apollo and his healer son are at times interchangeable and, through the spatial semantics of the shrines on the south slope of the Acropolis, Apollo has access to the tragic festival. The popular tradition that arose soon after Sophocles' death that he was the one who introduced Asclepius to Athens signals the deeper relationship between the City Dionysia, Apollo and the tragic poet most closely associated with civic norms.[9]

This link between Asclepius and poetry is by no means unique, for he seems to have quickly developed strong associations with the arts in general, as a brief survey of the evidence from throughout antiquity shows. At the beginning of Plato's *Ion*, Socrates meets the rhapsode Ion shortly after the latter has come from a rhapsodic competition in Epidaurus in honor of Asclepius. A fragment of Aelian preserves a story about Aristarchus, a fifth-century tragic poet:[10]

Aristarchus of Tegea, a poet of tragedies, had some sort of illness. Then Asclepius cured him and ordered thank-offerings in exchange for his health. The poet offered a drama named after the god.

Suidas' *Lexicon* records a story about Theopompus, a poet of the Old Comedy, and one of Aristophanes' rivals:[11]

[It is evident] that Asclepius was also a protector of those people in culture: at least when Theopompus was worn down and wasting away with consumption, he cured him and raised him up to produce comedies again, making him whole and safe and sound.

Similarly, Libianius, an orator from late antiquity, writes in one of his letters:[12]

"And he not without the aid of the gods," says Homer, nor do you write these words without the affect of Asclepius, for clearly he himself joined with you in writing. It is fitting for him, as the son of Apollo, that he has something of the poetic art (*mousikês*) of his father and that he apportions it to whomever he desires. How then would he not assist you in composing these discourses concerning himself?

---

[8] Osborne, in Alcock and Osborne 1994: 1. The collected essays in this volume follow the lead of Polignac 1995 [French original published 1984], whose latest ideas form that book's first chapter.

[9] On the tradition of linking Sophocles and Asclepius see Aleshire 1989: 9–11. I discuss the credibility of this story later. Aristophanes' *Frogs*, composed almost immediately after the deaths of Euripides and Sophocles, provides the clearest indication of the common reputation, however stereotypical, of each.

[10] Aelianus, *Fragmenta* 101. Testimony 455 in Edelstein and Edelstein 1945: 1. This passage, and those subsequent, I have translated anew based on the texts provided in Edelstein.

[11] Testimony 456 in Edelstein and Edelstein 1945: 1.

[12] Libianius, *Epistulae* 695.1–2. Testimony 610 in Edelstein and Edelstein 1945: 1.

Thus Asclepius is represented as a patron of the arts of the word. Aristides extends the link even further:[13]

> To us, however, [Asclepius has given] knowledge and melodies and the subjects of speeches and in addition to these the concepts themselves and the wording, just like those who give basic education to children . . . To me, O Lord Asclepius, many and things of all sort, indeed, as I have said before, have come from you and your love of men, the greatest of all, however, and most worthy of gratitude, and, so to speak, closest to home, are my speeches. For you have reversed that which was Pindar's lot: Pan danced his paean, as the story goes, but I – if divine law allows me to say so – I am the performer [of that which you yourself have taught me].

Asclepius thus takes over artistic associations and functions from his father Apollo.

But the specific god more directly associated with tragedy was not Apollo but Dionysus, and Asclepius also has strong ties in Athenian festival life to the god of wine and theater. Not only was the Asklepieion strongly connected to the Eleusinian Mysteries (Aleshire 1989: 8; Parke 1977: 25; Currie 2005: 385–405), but Asclepius also played a part in the other festival of importance for Dionysus in Athens, the City Dionysia itself.[14] Aristotle's *Constitution of Athens* (56.4) records that the archon supervised one procession for the celebration of Asclepius when initiates held a night vigil, and another one for the City Dionysia. And from at least 420 BCE the Asklepieia, the feast for Asclepius, was held on the 8th of the spring month of Elaphebolion, and this was the day before the City Dionysia began and the very day of the Proagon itself (Pickard-Cambridge 1968: 64–67). The Proagon was literally "the ceremony preliminary to the contest," where each of the competing dramatic poets would stand with their actors on a temporary platform in the Odeion of Pericles and announce the subjects of the dramas he was about to stage on one of the succeeding three days. It was at the Proagon in 406 that Sophocles allegedly dressed his chorus in black to announce the death of Euripides, and, if this actually happened, that day's Asklepieia must have had a particular significance. While the addition of Asclepius to the Eleusinian Mysteries acquired a ready explanation of his own initiation into them, we are left guessing as to why the Athenians chose

---

[13] Aristides, *Orations* 42.11–12. Testimony 317 in Edelstein and Edelstein 1945: 1.

[14] Parke 1977: 135 lays out the information on the connections between Asclepius and the Dionysia in Athens and senses its possibilities, but does not draw the connections: "[Asclepius] was housed in a sanctuary above the Dionysiac theatre on the higher slopes of the Acropolis under the cliff wall . . . The annual festival of his arrival in Athens was celebrated at the time of the Eleusinian Mysteries. His other festival called the Asclepieia was held on the day of the Preliminary to the Contest . . . There is no usual connection between him and Dionysus, but it may be more than a coincidence that one of the Athenians most prominent in introducing this new god was Sophocles."

the day of the Proagon, which dates back at least to the construction of the Odeion by Pericles in 444, to honor Asclepius. Unless these dates were an amazing coincidence, and Athenians tended not to leave such coincidences completely unmotivated, we are bound to ask what prompted them to honor the healing god as they were preparing in the theater to celebrate Dionysus, another god with curative powers, and I do not think we can avoid here Apollo's function as leader of the Muses and the associations in Greek culture between music and healing that were so strong that Sophocles came to be seen as Asclepius' sponsor in Athens. Festivals devoted to Asclepius thus became linked closely to two of the most important festivals in Athens, and, as Parke observes, "[t]he whole arrangement suggests the conscious planning of a careful priesthood working in harmony with the authorities of Athens" (Parke 1977: 65).

Let us pause now for a moment over the alleged role of Sophocles in the cult of Asclepius, as this story either indicates the power of the associations between poetry and healing, or they in turn explain why the story arose. One always needs to be careful with traditional information about the lives of the Greek poets; Mary Lefkowitz (1981) has shown how the biographies attributed to the ancient Greek poets developed in the Hellenistic era either from misinterpreted information in the poets' works or from jokes comic writers like Aristophanes made about them, however improbable they might have been.[15] As these traditions developed, scholars would then turn to Aristophanes' comedies in a bit of circular argumentation to support the biography. Thus, Euripides was a misogynist as we can see from the wanton women in his plays and from what Aristophanes says; Sophocles was pious because he depicted pious people. One anecdote reports that Sophocles "gave hospitality to Asclepius," by receiving him in his house (T67; the *Life of Sophocles* 11), and thus Sophocles later was worshipped as *Dexion*, "Receiver." Moreover, Sophocles even wrote a paean to Asclepius. This all sounds nicely convenient, but, as Lefkowitz observes, the latter story too strongly resembles other misattributions based on personal information in an ode, like Pindar's *Hymn to Demeter*, and the former anecdote seems inspired more by the plot of the *Oedipus at Colonus*, where Oedipus receives a hero's grave, than anything else (Lefkowitz 1981: 84). Lefkowitz does not suggest, however, that tradition may have made Sophocles Asclepius' patron because of the prominence of disease in dramas

---

[15] For the skeptical tradition about Sophocles' role in the Asclepius cult see also Garland 1992: 125, Parker 1996: 184–85 and Connolly 1998. Connolly's analysis of this story in the context of the (false) tradition of the heroization of Sophocles should be conclusive. Lloyd 2003: 85 resurrects the connection, though without indicating that it had been mortally wounded.

such as the *Oedipus Tyrannus* and *Philoctetes* and because at least two of his plays, including the *Philoctetes* and the now lost *Phineus*, alter traditional myth to incorporate Asclepius. Thus, according to one of these Sophoclean dramas, Philoctetes will be healed not by one of Asclepius' sons, as was the traditional story, but by Asclepius himself, and in the other Asclepius, not Jason, cures Phineus' blind eyes.[16] While the construction of the Asklepieion, I argue later in this study, influenced the end of Sophocles' *Philoctetes*, the date of Sophocles' *Phineus* is unknown and thus any possible relationship between cult and drama there remains untenable. Connolly has more recently reexamined the evidence and concluded that Sophocles certainly was not heroized before the 330s and that the story of his reception of Asclepius was surely a Hellenistic invention (Connolly 1998). Despite such doubts, it is entirely possible, indeed it is very plausible, that Sophocles participated in some way in the beginning of the Asclepius cult in Athens, but the traditional story need not be taken fully at face value. Although Asclepius and disease figure at least as strongly in Euripidean as in Sophoclean drama, the biographical tradition would not have made Euripides Asclepius' patron because it had already declared Euripides an atheist.[17] Commenting on the "extraordinary 'friendliness to man'" of Asclepius, Robert Parker further trenchantly notes that, although Euripides received the charge of destroying the spirit of tragedy, it would actually be Sophocles who did so because he "received this harbinger of the Hellenistic age into his house" (Parker 1996: 184–85). In addition to the undependability of ancient biographical traditions clear evidence exists that a man named Telemachus founded the City Asklepieion, whose construction of a dedicatory monument with his own name may have been prompted by the flourishing of the posthumous story attributing the Asklepieion to the tragic poet (Aleshire 1989: 9–11). Finally, given the proximity of the Asklepieion to the Theater of Dionysus and the sense of loss in Athens after the deaths of Sophocles and Euripides, so palpable in Aristophanes' *Frogs*, it seems natural that some Athenians would have wanted Sophocles to have some large role in the cult that was becoming so important in the city, even if that role was fictive.

If the adjacency of the healing shrine and the theater is actually significant and meaningful, then one would expect to see some kind of further replication and extension of this organizing concept in or around the Theater, and in fact the spatial relation between Asklepieion and Theater of Dionysus

---

[16] On the *Phineus* and Asclepius see Vojatzi 1982: 80–82.

[17] Lefkowitz 1989 and Sourvinou-Inwood 2003 present arguments in favor of a Euripides whose dramas more closely adhere to traditional religion.

recurs in the seating arrangement of the Prohedria inside the Theater itself. The Prohedria, literally "the seats in front," located at the bottom of the Theater, in between the benches and the orchestra, was where important public officials such as priests and generals sat. As Goldhill and others have recently stressed, processional display and public ceremony were important components of the City Dionysia (Goldhill 1990; Ober and Strauss 1990). The audience's hemispherical seating arrangement in turn was visibly divided into wedges, corresponding to the customary order of the ten tribes, with the central wedge occupied by the Boule (Council) and the outer two by non-citizens (Winkler 1990: 37–42). Given this structural template, it should not seem unreasonable to suggest that the seating plan in the Prohedria did not lack meaning, and, given the patterns elucidated thus far, it seems meaningful that the extant array places the chair of the priest of Asclepius immediately adjacent to that of the priest of the Muses.[18] The remaining Prohedria has a series of stone thrones, and the inscription identifying their assigned occupants dates from an Imperial era reworking of the Prohedria, but it appears that the later reconstructions were based ultimately on a fifth-century Prohedria, and the inscription itself is likely copied from a throne of the fourth century (Maass 1972: 44, 133; Aleshire 1989: 83). Maass observes also that the Athenian inscription of the office titles on the thrones is unique among Greek theaters (Maass 1972: 33), and that the actual recipients of such honored seats were doubly blessed since the number of honorable theatergoers in Athens outnumbered the possible quantity of designated seats in the Prohedria (Maass 1972: 1). Obviously, with such evidence I cannot prove that in the last quarter of the fifth century the two priests of Asclepius and of the Muses, or even of Dionysus, sat together, but the order is consistent with the patterns observed thus far and with the more general associations that I am attempting to establish here.[19] If nothing else, the adjacency of the Asklepieion to the Theater of Dionysus and the growth of nosological language in Athenian drama during the last third of the fifth century likely influenced this arrangement in the fourth century. Given the rapid growth of the cult of Asclepius in Athens after the plague, and the deeper connections in traditional Greek thought

---

[18] See Maass' seating plan, 1972: 141–44, which follows Fiechter's work. Maass (1972: 79) notes that the practice of Prohedria dates from Archaic times. See also Pickard-Cambridge 1946: 19–21.

[19] Maass 1972: 18 notes that the office of the occupants probably changed over the course of time, especially during the Roman Empire, and in fact Asclepius was important during the Hellenistic and Imperial eras. However, Asclepius rapidly grew in importance during the last quarter of the fifth century, so we should not exclude either possibility. Aleshire 1989: 82, citing *IG* II² 354.15–17, notes that "the priest in 328/7 B.C. was honored for having joined with the *epimeletai* in preserving *eukosmia* in the theatre."

between music and therapy, the juxtaposition of the priests of Asclepius and the Muses in the Theater does not seem accidental, and reduplicates and reinforces the significance of the larger juxtaposition of the Theater of Dionysus and the Asklepieion.

THE UNIQUENESS OF THE ATHENIAN ASKLEPIEION

Another aspect of the Athenian City Asklepieion that suggests some kind of significant relationship with the Theater of Dionysus below it is that the Athenian shrine resembles no other Asclepius sanctuary in form and function, a uniqueness that raises the question of its specifically Athenian nature. Even after its completion, as Aleshire observes, "it was neither an international colonizing sanctuary as was the Asklepieion at Epidaurus, nor the site of a great medical school as was that on Kos, nor the cult focus of a major Hellenizing monarchy as was the Pergamene Asklepieion" (Aleshire 1989: 4). Why then, I believe we must ask, did the Athenians build this temple where they did? This temple had a particularly local origin and importance, I argue, because it arose in response to a specific event, the plague of 430–426, which struck a fairly complex urbanized environment. Because of unsanitary conditions associated with urban crowding, Asclepius sanctuaries tended to be extra-urban, if not rural, in location. The common belief among sick people that a more strenuous effort to reach a holy place will lead to greater reward further motivated the typically remote location of healing sanctuaries; in other words, sanctuaries need to be separated from everyday life to preserve their sanctity and enhance the experience and status of the worshipper. The Athenian Asklepieion, positioned on the slope of the Acropolis and within the city walls, does not fit this pattern.[20] If, as Fritz Graf claims, Asclepius has strong associations with the forest and the wild (Graf 1992: 184), then the Athenian location is even more remarkable, but Graf, in my view, seems to overplay the binary opposition between city and country when he insists that the Athenian Asklepieion lies "in a liminal space between city and town", with distinctly rural associations.[21] The Theater of Dionysus was definitely part of the Athenian civic space, both physical and conceptual, and the Asklepieion stands even closer to the Parthenon than the lower Theater. A brief glance at the opening of Plato's *Phaedrus* shows that the important conceptual (if not actual) demarcation was not the Acropolis but the larger city walls. The Athenian temple was

---

[20] On the typically extra-urban or liminal siting of Asklepieia see Graf 1992: 168–72.
[21] My translation of "in einem liminalen Raum zwischen Stadt und Burg," Graf 1992: 170.

called the City Asklepieion, with all connotations of such a designation, as was the case with the festival of the City Dionysia.

Because the idea that one needs to separate oneself from the *polis* for health depends on the very existence of the *polis*, it would seem that the growth of the Asclepius cult is tied intimately to the city-state's development. Even excavations at Epidaurus, the center of the worship of Asclepius, date the cult there only to the end of the sixth century (Edelstein and Edelstein 1945: 1.243). With the growth of complexity and size of cities, and the concomitant multiplied risk of contagion, illness became a problem of civilization and society, not just an individual concern, and thus, Krug remarks, "care for health or care for the sick arose as in the original sense a political problem, as the appointment of the city doctor shows" (Krug 1993: 120).[22] Already the *Acharnians* of 425 refers to a public doctor (1030–32). For Athens, a city overcrowded by the design of its leaders during the Peloponnesian War, where a quarter to a third of the population perished from the plague, disease became very much a civic problem, and while the Asclepius cult there may have been founded by private citizens, within a relatively short space of time the *polis* took over its administration. The tendency among scholars of the cult of Asclepius has been to assign this divinity to the function of meeting the needs of private individuals, while gods such as Dionysus and Athena watch over the city as a whole, but the picture I have just sketched suggests that the Athenian cult at least had a different purpose. Moreover, on the Athenian Acropolis Athena had been worshipped, before the arrival of Asclepius, as Athena Hygieia, "Athena of Health," and her function as goddess of health was directed to the well-being of the community as a whole (Garland 1992: 132; Parker 1996: 175); I discuss Athena Hygieia further in my chapter on the *Philoctetes*. It is also unlikely, as Parker suggests, that Telemachus could have acquired such a sizable portion of land on the crowded slope of the Acropolis without at least the consent of the *polis* (Parker 1996: 180–81). Aristophanes' *Wealth* shows that the sanctuary in Piraeus, the port of Athens, featured the traditional water cures and incubations, but this practice would have been more difficult – though not prohibitive, given the existence of a spring on the site – on the more arid south slope of the Acropolis. Therefore, the untraditional placement of the Athenian Asklepieion within the city and its proximity to the Theater points to a distinctly motivated connection here between healing sanctuary and theater, which itself is part of the sanctuary of Dionysus, and between the two sanctuaries and the *polis*. The roles

---

[22] The translation is mine.

that Asclepius played in the Eleusinian Mysteries and the Proagon of the City Dionysia further this relationship between sanctuary and city. These connections and others indicate that the propinquity of the Asklepieion to the Theater of Dionysus turns the latter into a symbolic place of healing for the *polis*, an aspect which will become much more fully recognizable once I turn to the discussion of some specific dramas which were produced after its construction. Thus, theaters do not stand next to Asclepius shrines so that sick people can catch a play during their cures; the drama is part of the cure, and in Athens, at least, the remedy is not just for the individual, but for the city itself as a whole.

ASKLEPIEION–THEATER CONFIGURATIONS IN OTHER *POLEIS*

While I have noted the singularity of the Athenian temple's placement, the situation of an Asklepieion near a theater, following the model of Athens, is so common, surprisingly so, that the relationship between healing, music and theater becomes all the more apparent, and Asclepius himself begins to resemble something like a theater god. Here I shall include some post-classical theaters, since, as I argue below, these later developments merely bring fully to the surface and develop conceptual structures that are more latent, yet active, in the fifth century. I begin with late examples. The Messenians incorporated their Hellenistic theater into the side of an Asklepieion founded in the fourth century,[23] and at Pergamon another Hellenistic theater lies near an Asklepieion dating back to 400 BCE. In Dion a third-century theater overlooks a sanctuary of Asclepius approximately 300 meters downhill; the latter is itself close to a Demeter sanctuary. At Corinth, the theater lies closer (350 meters) to the Asklepieion than any other of the major civic structures, and the two buildings are considered to be in the same quarter of the city; in fact, at 500 meters distance even the theater at Epidaurus is further from its Asklepieion than the Corinthian theater.[24] Moreover, in order to reach this Asklepieion from the agora one had to travel a road running alongside the theater. The shrine began as one for Apollo and was converted to Asclepius' sometime in the last quarter of the fifth century, as was a typical pattern then as Asclepius grew in importance, and this occurred at roughly the same time as the Corinthians

---

[23] Given th   .ation between Hippolytus and Asclepius it is interesting to note that a temple to Artemis (.a is part of the Epidaurian Asklepieion.

[24] See Roebuck 1951: 1, who adds that the proximity of the temple to other shrines and recreational structures made such elaborate arrangements as those at Epidaurus and Pergamon unnecessary in Corinth. On the topography of Epidaurus see Käppel 1989.

built their theater (Stillwell 1952: 5). At this point in my argument I hope I can say with some justification that the site and time of the constructions were not merely coincidental. This is not unlike the situation in Athens, where the Theater of Dionysus may have received extensive reconstruction during the Peace of Nicias (421–416 BCE), which was also the time of the Athenian Asklepieion's construction, but I would be hesitant to draw many inferences from this (much as I would like to).[25]

The orientation of the *cavea* or *theatron* (seating area) of the Athenian Theater of Dionysus toward the Temple of Dionysus so that the spectators can always see the god's shrine further suggests an analogous relationship between the Corinthian theater and the Asklepieion, as the latter pair's orientation directed the spectators' attention beyond the orchestra and stage, toward the temple. The approximate contemporaneity of the two theatrical structures, and the possibility that the Corinthian theater was inspired by rivalry with the Athenian reconstruction during the Peace of Nicias (Stillwell 1952: 131),[26] may indicate that the orientation of the *cavea* toward a temple was intentional practice. It certainly seems to have been customary to situate thus the *cavea* of a theater at a shrine. For example, the *cavea* of the fourth-century theater at Epidaurus, situated in the Asclepius sanctuary, also was oriented toward the temple, and the theater at Delphi sits just above and thus situates its audience's gaze toward the Temple of Apollo, with the Delphic Asklepieion slightly further down the slope.

The most well-known and clearly visible relationship between an Asklepieion and a theater is at Epidaurus, the international center of the Asclepius cult, and this site could explain the relationship between the other temple–theater configurations, as it brings to completion features partial or latent in the other theaters, especially the Athenian one. By evoking the idea of completion I do not assume some kind of Aristotelian teleology of medical theater, but I would like to suggest that the theater at Epidaurus, far from inventing its Pythagorean, therapeutic symmetries out of thin air, built on the implications both of the Asklepieion–Theater configuration in Athens and of the prominence of nosological imagery from the texts of Athenian drama which were exported throughout the Greek world, not least to Epidaurus. The striking geometrical plan of the theater, responsible for its visual beauty and auditory clarity, may or may not have been integral to its original design, and so scholars range its construction date sometime around 350 or 330 BCE, the likely era of the composition of Aristotle's *Poetics*.

---

[25] Pickard-Cambridge 1946: 17. Dinsmoor 1950: 208–09 argues that the lower part of the theater during these years was transformed from wood to stone, although most of the seats were still made of wood.

[26] I should stress here that, in actuality, the temple is oriented to the hillside *cavea* and not the opposite!

According to Lutz Käppel, the theater at Epidaurus was in fact conceived as a whole as it currently stands (as opposed to being constructed over time and in stages) and around a geometrical figure in the orchestra, the pentagram, that, Käppel hypothesizes, had specific mystical connotations for Pythagoreans. Käppel relates an account by Lucian that the Pythagoreans called the pentagram "Health" (*Hygieia*) and used the geometric figure as a symbol for it (Käppel 1989: 102–03).[27] Along with the mathematically balanced proportions of the number of rows and sections, the pentagram forms part of the mathematical harmonies of the theater as a whole. Käppel concludes that *Hygieia* is the fundamental concept (*Grundidee*) of the theater of Asclepius, an idea that partakes of the healing powers the Pythagoreans attributed to music. And because the stair flights and stage front proceed out from the points of the pentagram, "the principle of the Golden Mean, which controls the pentagram, continues into the seats . . . With this unity the *Hygieia* symbolized in the pentagram over the Golden Mean becomes effective to the last row and to the last spectator" (Käppel 1989: 104–05).[28] Just as the famous acoustics of this theater allow the slightest sound to be audible in the back of the *cavea*, so too does the member of the audience who is less fortunate in seating receive the full healing power of the artistic event. The theater itself can cure, just as songs have been thought to heal from at least the time of Homer.

By this point, I have moved far afield from the specific dramas of Aeschylus, Euripides and Sophocles, but this extended detour was important for ascertaining the interrelationships of health, disease metaphors and the performative context of drama. If I am correct in linking the Athenian Asklepieion and nosological language in Athenian drama with the construction of the theater in Epidaurus, then there certainly was a dynamically interactive relationship, starting in the late fifth century, between the texts of Athenian drama and their performative contexts, at least in terms of the discourses of healing. While the Theater of Dionysus developed architecturally over time and thus lacked the original unifying idea of the theater at Epidaurus, I believe that the latter merely brings to the surface concepts latent in the performative semantics of the Athenian theater.

Having addressed the relationships between Asclepius and Dionysus and between healing and drama, here I should address what in some ways is a fundamental question for this topic: why should the construction of new buildings on the Acropolis have anything to do with how the Athenians

---

[27] The date of construction around 350, however, is contested. See Wiles 1997: 39–40. The controversy does not affect my basic points here.

[28] The translation is mine.

received, and we understand, the dramas performed in the Theater of Dionysus? In previous eras of criticism, scholars focused on the text as a self-contained object, with often merely a passing nod at the particularities of the relationship between text and context. Over the last thirty years, however, scholars such as Vernant and Loraux have taught us how to read the congruencies and homologies among the civic, mental and emotional spaces of Athens. More recently, David Wiles has provocatively reexamined the performative space of Athenian tragedy. Thanks to the work of such scholars, we now understand more than ever about the workings of tragic drama in the *polis* and on the Acropolis of Athens. More specifically, some studies have seen the possible influence of developments in architecture on the Acropolis on specific dramas. But such thoughts have occurred long before to other scholars and critics, though in a less sustained or systematic manner. For example, Jebb, in his note on the *Oedipus Tyrannus*, line 20 (πρός τε παλλάδος διπλοῖς ναοῖς, "by the two temples of Pallas"), suggests succinctly, "[i]t was enough for Sophocles that his Athenian hearers would think of the Erechtheum and the Parthenon – the shrines of the Polias and the Parthenos – above them on the Acropolis." However, Jebb does not connect this situation of "Thebes" back to the plague of Athens which the audience below Athena's shrines had been suffering. More recently, Paul Cartledge observes that even the temple ruins wrought by the Persians during their invasion in 480 and 479 would have produced a powerful political effect on the theater audience who looked over their shoulders during the performance of Aeschylus' *Persians* in 472 (Cartledge 1997: 19). Wiles sees a persistent association of the hillside Athenian *theatron* with Mt. Cithaeron near Thebes, the site of so many disasters in Athenian tragic drama. The lost Euripidean drama *Erechtheus* seems to have been inspired by the construction of the Erechtheum on the top of the Acropolis beginning probably sometime between 423 and 421.[29] Loraux further connects the completion of the Erechtheum to the production of Aristophanes' *Lysistrata* in 411, though the question of the completeness of the Erechtheum at that time remains open to question (Loraux 1993: 172). Thus, there is ample precedent in seeing a meaningful relationship between the topography and architecture of the Athenian Acropolis and the dramas produced in the Athenian Theater of Dionysus, and it is further noteworthy that the Erechtheum paradigm is formed roughly at the time when the dramas that we are about to examine were produced.

[29] On the dating of the *Erechtheus* and its relationship to the Erechtheum see Calder 1969, Loraux 1993: 37–71, Sourvinou-Inwood 2003: 25–31.

With the ideas always in mind, first, that there is an increase in the frequency and intensity of disease metaphors in the years of the plague, and, second, that the Asklepieion was under construction between 420 and 416 and in an area immediately overlooking the shoulders of the spectators of the tragic theater, let us return to Athenian tragic drama. Asclepius and his cult afford deep, strong connections to Dionysus and drama, so, given the paradigm of just the Erechtheum, which had little to do with tragedy *per se* and which was on the opposite side of the top of the Acropolis, rereading tragic drama in the light of these associations will yield new insights. I shall now proceed chronologically through another set of dramas in the order in which they were produced. I examine the texts of Euripides' *Heracles* and *Phoenissae*, and finally Sophocles' *Philoctetes*, in terms of their disease imagery and the historical function of that imagery in the context of the topography of the Acropolis.

CHAPTER 8

Disease and stasis *in Euripidean drama: Tragic pharmacology on the south slope of the Acropolis*

I earlier suggested how Euripides' *Hippolytus*, read as a plague drama rife with disease metaphors, rituals designed to ward off plague and famine, and allusions to Asclepius, emerges as a more topically significant and historically richer drama. The *Oedipus Tyrannus* of Sophocles and the *Trachiniae* were likely composed during or soon after the last attacks of the plague, the influence of which we see throughout both. These dramas are in the first wave of the plague's effect, with the second wave coming roughly a decade later because of the new Asklepieion next to the theater and because political conditions in Athens lent themselves to a revivification of the metaphor of the sick city. After the construction of the Asklepieion gets underway around 420 BCE, patterns of nosological imagery and civic *stasis* intensify in Euripidean drama, and they continue through the subsequent decade. In this chapter I shall focus primarily on two Euripidean tragedies that are broadly concerned with nosological discourse, the *Heracles* and the *Phoenissae*, though I shall also be bringing to my study, as needed, other tragedies which survive both complete and in fragments. My discussion will be somewhat circuitous, as I internally frame a broader examination of the *Heracles* with an analysis of aspects of the *Phoenissae* and other dramas composed during the same period (including ones that only survive in fragments), but this path will enable a clearer understanding of the nosological dynamics in the *Heracles*.

SICKNESS AND *STASIS* IN EURIPIDES' *HERACLES*

The *Heracles* in particular engages the full scope of my concerns here: combined images of disease and political strife, the theme of mortality, Asclepius, the paean and the return from the dead. Like Asclepius, Heracles serves a double role in myth and cult as hero and god. However, in general, literary treatments of Heracles most often stress his mortality.[1]

---

[1] For a concise treatment of the problems raised by Heracles' dual nature as man and god see Silk 1985.

Indeed, as Justina Gregory observes, Heracles is "a hero whose experience summarizes the poignancy of the human condition" (Gregory 1991: 122). In the *Heracles*, and in the *Phoenissae*, the medical metaphor for political turmoil suggests that only the destruction of the royal household and its aristocratic ethos can cure the city of the disease of civic strife, *stasis*, afflicting it. My inquiry here finds support in Seaford's recent formulations (1993, 1994) on Dionysus' role in Athenian tragic drama as destroyer of the royal household to preserve the *polis*. Given the homologies between Dionysus and Asclepius that I observe earlier in my argument, the medical metaphorical structure and the Dionysiac patterns may be part of the same process.

Behind the immediately pressing concern of the drama's plot, the fate of Heracles' family, is the political crisis afflicting Thebes, described persistently as *stasis*; indeed, as Kosak notes, this term occurs more frequently in Euripides' *Heracles* than in any other extant tragic drama (Kosak 2004: 153). I shall first briefly summarize this crisis and the play's action. Heracles had earlier left his wife Megara and children in Thebes, along with his mortal father Amphitryon, while he journeyed to Hades to fetch the three-headed dog Cerberus in the last of his twelve labors for Eurystheus; Euripides restructures the sequence of labors to stress Heracles' violation of the boundaries of Hades. While he is away, the city falls into *stasis*, Lycus overthrows Megara's father Creon, and then persecutes Heracles' family. Threatened with death, Amphitryon, Megara and the children claim suppliancy at the altar of Zeus Soter, "Zeus the Savior." Amphitryon and Lycus debate the relative merits of Heracles' heroic activities. Heracles returns in the nick of time to save them, but, as he enters his house for a celebratory sacrifice after killing Lycus, the goddesses Iris and Lyssa (Madness) appear, and on Hera's instructions they drive him insane, so that he kills his own entire family while mistaking them for his enemy, leaving only his mortal father Amphitryon alive because Athena intervenes and knocks out Heracles. As he regains consciousness, the horror of his deeds moves him to consider suicide, but his friend Theseus unexpectedly appears and consoles him, convincing the shattered hero not to kill himself but to journey to Athens and become a part of Athenian society. At first glance, the plot in itself does not seem remotely connected to disease imagery, or to the topography of the Athenian Acropolis, but a closer examination of the drama's language yields a constant concern with disease and its cure, and the production of the *Heracles* shortly after the construction of the Asklepieion just above the Theater of Dionysus lends added meaning to its nosological concerns.

The city falls ill with dissension and then Heracles goes mad, an internal discord, and this sequence, combined with the identical language used for each, suggests some relationship between the hero's health and the body politic. Euripides connects the city's political crisis with Heracles' madness through nosological imagery.[2] In the prologue Heracles' mortal father Amphitryon describes Thebes at Lycus' attack as "this city sick with civil strife" (στάσει νοσοῦσαν τήνδ' . . . πόλιν, 34). While we should keep in mind warnings that in Greek tragic drama illness can be used to describe anything in general that goes wrong, it appears that here at least the text does not engage the metaphor casually, as it deploys the image in this specific form alone two other times in the play before Heracles becomes ill himself. From the later passages it appears that Lycus did not come when the city was sick with strife but that he brought this disease to Thebes. After Lycus leaves the stage, the Chorus closes an unusually long (for a chorus)[3] speech to Megara and Lycus with this metaphor: οὐ γὰρ εὖ φρονεῖ πόλις / στάσει νοσοῦσα καὶ κακοῖς βουλεύμασιν, "for the city does not think well, being sick with *stasis* and with evil purposes" (272–73). When Heracles finally appears, he asks Megara how Lycus managed to gain control from Heracles' father-in-law Creon (541–43):

> Μεγάρα
> Λύκος σφ᾽ ὁ καινὸς γῆς ἄναξ διώλεσεν.
> Ἡρακλῆς
> ὅπλοις ἀπαντῶν ἢ νοσησάσης χθονός;
> Μεγάρα
> στάσει· τὸ Κάδμου δ᾽ ἑπτάπυλον ἔχει κράτος.

> **Megara**
> Lycus the land's new ruler killed him.
> **Heracles**
> By confronting him with weapons, or was the land sick?
> **Megara**
> Sick with *stasis*: he holds the seven-gated power of Cadmus.

This triple occurrence of the same metaphor, split among three different speakers and subtly amplified each time, surely indicates a significant role in the drama's structures of meaning. In these passages Euripides takes over the image of the sick city of Thebes from Sophocles' *Antigone* and *Oedipus*

---

[2] Kosak 2000: 48–49 notices that similar language is used for both the city and Heracles, but not that *stasis* is transferred to Heracles, as I shall argue here. More recently see Kosak 2004: 151–74. On the causation and typology of Heracles' madness see Papadopoulou 2005: 58–84.

[3] Note Bond 1981: 133 here: "These lines, assigned to Amphitryon in L, are given to the chorus by modern editors."

Tyrannus, yet he then also makes it his own. In his commentary on these lines, Bond observes that this is "a rare and bold metaphor", since, while in fifth-century Athens writers commonly cast *stasis* as a *nosos* for the *polis*, they always combine it with descriptions of rebellion, not leaving *nosos* as a straight equivalent for *stasis* as is the case here. In Thucydides' description of the Corcyrean civil war (3.82), for example, the historian hammers away at the term *stasis*, and a couple of times makes nods toward calling it a medical condition for the *polis*, yet even Thucydides never makes the direct equation. Clearly, I do agree that the Euripidean metaphor is bold, but I must also admit I find it somewhat perplexing that some scholars, given the consensus that assumes a metaphor is dead and commonplace, can so suddenly decide that a metaphor is alive and important, especially when there is little systematic attempt to ascertain why it has significance or how it fits in with the rest of the text (and the context). Thus, one must ask, to what end does Euripides imagine a bold metaphor here? Why the drama explores this theme and how it is developed will become my concern.

The metaphor recurs through the *Heracles* as part of a larger network of associations of disease, purity and politics. It prepares the way for the madness of Heracles, his fall, and his restoration into society. In the play's first half, the metaphor appears three times, and then disappears once Heracles enters the house for a propitiatory sacrifice after he violently confronts and kills Lycus, at which point Heracles goes mad. Once he appears again all talk of illness centers on him, climaxing in Theseus' assertion that because Heracles is sick, he is no longer Heracles. Assuming that the poet does not casually repeat related language and imagery throughout a text, there must be some connection, so let us look at the drama's medical language beginning with the point just before Iris and Lyssa appear.

In order to establish a contextual framework for the systems of meaning in the *Heracles*, here I shall also first consider the disease metaphor in other Euripidean dramas, then possible allusions to the Asclepius myth and cult, as they are important factors in the drama's symbolic economy. Last I shall attempt to reintegrate the drama's medical, ritual and political dynamics.

NOSOLOGICAL IMAGERY IN EURIPIDEAN DRAMA

Several other tragic dramas, in particular the *Phoenissae*, deploy nosological imagery with respect to the city, and in order to establish a "grammar" for this imagery in the *Heracles* I need to examine them briefly. For example, the *Iphigenia at Tauris* several times speaks of the "sick house" (680, 693, 930); in the *Iphigenia at Aulis* all Hellas ails (411); and, in the *Andromache*, the house is again sick (548, 950) and all Hellas once more suffers a disease (1044). Since in tragedy the royal house can function metonymically for the city as a whole, the sick house can signify an ill *polis*. A quick comparative review with the other two tragedians demonstrates the singularity of Euripides' concerns. As I have shown already, Aeschylus presents glimpses of the sick city in his works, though the number of cases is small and located in an even relatively smaller body of work; Aeschylus leaves most of the metaphor's potential territory unexplored. Sophocles seems reluctant to engage in more open non-literal descriptions of illness. Thebes is ill in the *Antigone* and in the *Oedipus Tyrannus*, but only because plague really exists in the latter and is thought potential in the former; the *Antigone* does display a nascent sense of the metaphorical possibilities of the sick city, but they are underdeveloped here. The *Trachiniae* equates *eros* with illness (e.g. Deiainira's description of Heracles at learning of his passion for Iole, at 544), but, again, the field of reference remains with the individual. The sole instance of a metaphorically sick social body is in Sophocles' *Electra*, where the Chorus declares the heroine's house is sick (1070–71 τὰ μὲν ἐκ δόμων νοσεῖ), but with no further development of image. The fragments of Sophocles do not show much interest in disease.[4] While the fourteen (or thirteen, excluding *Prometheus*) surviving tragic dramas represent only a small fraction of the real output of Sophocles and Aeschylus, thus limiting the surety of any broader claims that can be made about it, the surviving group does seem to offer some indication of the tendencies of the poets working in the Theater of Dionysus during the fifth century. Barring the discovery of a miraculously huge cache of papyrus rolls or unexpected results from the opening of the *Oxyrhynchus Papyri*, this body of work will have to suffice.

It surely must be meaningful that neither of the extant Euripidean plays produced before the plague of 430–426 – that is, the *Medea* and the *Alcestis* – broadens the concept of disease beyond the individual or couple. Admittedly, this is also not a huge sample, but the earlier tendencies of Aeschylus and Sophocles, the fragments of the lost plays, and the dates of each drama's production, indicate that Euripides may have then become even more interested in the metaphor than we can show, so, before turning to the *Phoenissae*, let us quickly look at what the fragments indicate. All of the identifiable fragments that use illness as a metaphor for civic

---

[4] The fragments of lost dramas by Sophocles are readily available in Lloyd-Jones 1996. These fragments mention disease, but none with the kind of metaphorical associations discussed here: 149, 344, 589, 663, 698. Fragment 479 contains *limos* (famine) and a reference to *akos* (cure). Fragment 557 mentions healing (*iasthai*) troubles by weeping.

turmoil or moral decline come from dramas written around or after 415; that is, roughly about the time of *Heracles* and the *Phoenissae* or later and shortly after the construction of the Athenian Asklepieion.[5] These dramas are the *Antiope, Alcmaeon, Auge, Pleisthenes* and *Temenidae*.[6] Because the fragments are not as widely available or as well known as the complete dramas, especially in translation, I provide here the relevant passages:

> *Temenidae* (Fr. 728, Nauck)
> . . . φιλεῖ τοὶ πόλεμος οὐ πάντων τυχεῖν
> ἐσθλῶν δὲ χαίρει πτωνᾶσιν νεανίων,
> κακοὺς δὲ μισεῖ. τῇ πόλει μὲν νόσος
> τόδ᾽ ἐστί, τοῖς δὲ κατθανοῦσιν εὐκλεές.
>
> . . . War does not like to happen upon on all,
> but rejoices at the fall of good young men,
> and hates the bad. On the one hand, for the city
> this is a disease, but, on the other, for the dead it brings fame.

Here there is an almost Thucydidean portrayal of war as a disease. As it cuts down good and bad indifferently, war robs the *polis* of the nobility necessary for an ordered society. Imbalance results in the unmixed polity, and it grows ill. The language and sentiment here resemble lines 436–37 of the *Philoctetes*, produced a few years later.

> *Pleisthenes* (Fr. 626.6–7, Nauck)
> κώλυε δ᾽ ἄνδρα παρὰ δίκην τιμώμενον,
> πόλει γὰρ εὐτυχοῦντες οἱ κακοὶ νόσος.
>
> Hinder a man taking vengeance outside of justice;
> for when the bad are fortunate there is disease to the city.

> *Antiope* (Fr. 202, Nauck)
> ἐγὼ μὲν οὖν ἀ(ι)δοιμι καὶ λέγοιμί τι
> σοφόν, ταράσσων μηδὲν ὧν πόλις νοσεῖ.
>
> May I therefore sing and say something
> wise, disturbing nothing of the things which the city ails.

---

[5] On the date of the *Heracles* see Bond 1981: xxx–xxxiii. Bond favors a range of dates between 415 and 406 BCE, a range that entirely suits the concerns of my broader argument. Diggle's OCT (116) favors a date of around 415. As with most dates for Euripidean drama, the judgment of the *Heracles* relies on the analysis of the resolution of trimeters, which increase in frequency with time, and such analysis places the *Heracles* close to the *Trojan Women*, which was definitely produced in 415. Michelini 1987: 334–37 argues against the use of style to date Euripidean tragedy. Goebel and Nevin 1977: xxix–xxxi join the metric skeptics and doubt the presence of contemporary allusions, and thus they date the *Heracles* to a range of 424–414. Beta 1999: 156–57 contends that Aristophanes' *Wasps*, produced in 422, alludes to an older, now lost, version of Euripides' *Heracles*.

[6] I omit discussion of the content of the dramas. On the chronology and plots of these lost plays see Webster 1967.

Alcmaeon (Fr. 79, Nauck)

βροτοῖς τὰ μείζω τῶν μέσων τίκτει νόσους,
θεῶν δὲ θνητοὺς κόσμον οὐ πρέπει φέρειν.

For mortals things greater than the middle breed diseases;
and it is not fitting that men should bear the order of the gods.

Auge (Fr. 267, Nauck)

δεινὴ πόλις νοσοῦσ᾽ ἀνευρίσκειν κακά.
A sick city is very clever at discovering bad things.

These passages all seem to indicate that an imbalance of bad over good brings disease for the city, and most link the malfunctioning of the social and political orders to illness. Disease here is associated with disturbance in the city, and wise speech or song can bring a cure, presumably by restoring order. Clearly this was a group of connected ideas preoccupying Euripides during this period.[7] While it is difficult to draw conclusions about systems of imagery in particular texts from fragments, the *Heracles'* metaphorical economy does suggest that these passages might well have been part of a significant structure of meaning in each play and a substantial concern in late Euripidean drama as a whole.

NOSOS IN THE *PHOENISSAE*

Another relatively late drama (produced sometime between 411 and 409), the *Phoenissae*, displays a concern with *nosos* in the *polis* which strongly resembles that in the *Heracles*, which is appropriate because the *Phoenissae* represents a time of civic strife that its Athenian audience would have found very familiar, as the plot recasts the struggles of the family of Oedipus that Aeschylus and Sophocles had already dramatized.[8] Sophocles' first tragic drama about Oedipus presents the city of Thebes suffering from a real plague sent by the gods because of the unpunished murder of King Laius, while Euripides takes the concept of plague, elides the Theban plague

---

[7] If, as I maintain, the plague initially inspires the Euripidean interest in the disease metaphor which then increases in complexity as time passes, then it is entirely possible that Euripides' dramas influenced Plato's use of the metaphor at least as much as the Hippocratic texts did.

[8] On the differing views of the play's date see Mastronarde 1994: 11–14. On the *Phoenissae*'s evocation of current Athenian politics, particularly the problem of Alcibiades, see de Romilly 1965 and 1976. Kosak 2004: 174–89 discusses in detail the medical language in the drama.

I am avoiding the pitched battles that have been waged over the text of this play. In any case, the disputed passages do not affect or involve my argument to a significant extent. In general, I am in agreement with the more inclusive, conservative, view of the text held by Mastronarde 1994, as opposed to Diggle's more radical excisions.

staged by Sophocles, and disseminates it through the realm of the political, just as Thucydides depicts the diseased condition of Athenian, and later Hellenic, politics that resulted from the breakdown of the *polis* during the plague. Euripides' drama enacts the events of the day before the action of Sophocles' *Antigone*: the civil war between the sons of Oedipus. The intrafamilial struggle between the brothers Polynices and Eteocles over the control of Thebes, generated ultimately from the *nosos* afflicting Oedipus, evokes, if not symbolically represents, the growing factionalism of Athenian politics. Again, Euripides' drama is not "about" the problems generated by specific events – such as the return of Alcibiades – but it engages the energy generated by such contexts as part of its function and meaning. The particular form of the myth developed by Euripides, and the language used to embody it, textually both seem dependent on the specific historical and cultural context that I have been examining.[9]

Jocasta, who in Euripides' version of this myth did not commit suicide when she learned her first son and second husband were the same person, introduces the action at such a level of detail that it almost seems as if Euripides, in addition to constructing his standard explicatory prologue speech, is signaling to the audience as self-consciously as possible his differences from his predecessors. Polynices, having been deposed and expelled by his brother Eteocles, returns home to conquer Thebes with an army from Argos. Eteocles clings to the throne and ruthlessly asserts his power, sophistically equating any status other than that of ruler with slavery. The war begins and Tiresias warns a horrified Creon that only the sacrifice of the latter's virgin son Menoeceus, the last pure descendant of the Spartoi (the men sown by Cadmus from the dragon's teeth), can save Thebes from disaster. Menoeceus in turn kills himself to accomplish the civic salvation, an event which then launches a rapid-fire sequence of carnage that incurs the deaths of Polynices, Eteocles and Jocasta, who finally kills herself over her son's corpses. Antigone brings the blind aged Oedipus out from the house and Creon exiles him in order to save Thebes (again) from further harm. Antigone, rejecting Creon's threats that she must marry Haemon, threatens in turn to kill her betrothed, and so Creon sends her off with her father. Euripides thus crams as much of the myth's familial and political pathologies into his drama as possible, exploiting every opportunity for conflict.

---

[9] Mastronarde 1994: 5–6 and 28–30 observes how Euripides carefully rearranges the sequence of events in his plot, such as the separation of the fraternal duel from the main battle, in order to highlight certain aspects.

While no actual plague attacks Thebes in this drama, the *Phoenissae* offers a bounty of medical vocabulary. Before Menoeceus' self-sacrifice, words for illness are prominently associated in the text with imbalance and disorder.[10] As this drama seems to play itself off self-consciously against Sophocles' versions of the same events, it takes over the "sick city" metaphor that appears late in the *Antigone* and then reappears early in the *Oedipus Tyrannus*. Moreover, as I shall demonstrate, the sequence of the instances of *nosos* is not isolated from the rest of the text but is part of the larger structures of meaning in Euripides' drama. In the prologue, Jocasta describes how Oedipus, νοσῶν / ἀρὰς ἀρᾶται παισὶν ἀνοσιωτάτας, "being sick, hurled the most unholy curses at his sons" for their maltreatment of him (66–67). Indeed there seems to be a play in the sound of the last words of lines 66 and 67, with "sick," *nosôn*, playing off the description of the curses as "most unholy", *anosiôtatas*.[11] Jocasta's words attribute his willingness to harm his family members to the illness, or, perhaps, call this desire a disease in itself. Familial chaos, like civic anarchy, is a disease. Tiresias later repeats this type of description in a speech to Creon that ties the woes of Thebes to the persistent intrafamilial violence in the house of Laius (867–69):

> νοσεῖ γὰρ ἥδε γῆ πάλαι, Κρέον,
> ἐξ οὗ 'τεκνώθη Λάιος βίᾳ θεῶν
> πόσιν τ' ἔφυσε μητρὶ μέλεον Οἰδίπουν·

> For this land was sick long ago, Creon,
> from when with violence against the gods Laius made a child
> and sired wretched Oedipus to be a husband to his mother.

Thus begins a catalogue of the troubles in Laius' family, which climaxes with the description of the wrongs afflicted by Polynices and Eteocles on their father, which in turn reduce him to being "both ill and dishonored," νοσῶν τε καὶ ἠτιμασμένος (877). An imbalance of proper familial order, and hence civic order, is a *nosos*. The network of displacements moves the disease from Oedipus to the city to his children and back to the city. Polynices, upon his return, argues with his mother about the impending

---

[10] The translation by Craik 1988 generally avoids any inference of *nosos* as illness, with the notable exception of line 472, but there is no explanation why that instance is any different from the rest of the play. In her discussion of the play, Foley, on the other hand, occasionally implies a recognition of the metaphor's role – e.g., in her assessment of "the incurable state of Theban politics" (1985: 135) – but she does not develop the implications. Foley's discussion of the problematical nature of Menoeceus' sacrifice is very useful here.

[11] Euripides repeats this sound play twice in the *Orestes*, 282–85 and 480–81. In the *Heracles* the Chorus denounces the ἀνόσιον κάρα (255) of Lycus and, given the disease imagery in that drama, the sound play might be active there as well.

war, while she reports the arguments of Eteocles against him. Polynices says (471–72) that his brother's "unjust argument, being diseased (νοσῶν) needs wise drugs (φαρμάκων)." This is a fairly remarkable comment, for, as Mastronarde notes, this passage seems to be the only place in extant tragedy where even *logos* itself ails and requires a cure (Mastronarde 1994: 281); traditionally, poetry and song are conceived as healing the listener so this city's crisis warrants extraordinary medicine. This passage, if one combines it with the two instances of nosological language in the *Heracles* that I noted other scholars have recognized as unique and significant, must indicate the importance of this metaphor for Euripidean drama. In Thucydides, words fail to describe the calamity of the plague (2.50), while here language itself has caught the contagion. If political language ails, the *polis* then needs a different type of discourse that can still heal, and this points to the paeans later in the drama. Later in the same scene, Jocasta argues that Eteocles is mad (μαίνῃ, 535) and begs him to reject tyranny and instead honor Equality (Ἰσότητα τιμᾶν, 536). Thus, the drama clusters together illness, diseased language, *stasis* and tyranny.

Again, I observe the association of illness, imbalance and tyranny, a complex extended and enriched by a word used for civic and medical disturbances, *taragmos*, which occurs here as it does in the *Heracles* and participates and strengthens the similar network of disease metaphors; a fuller examination of this word occurs later in my discussion of the *Heracles*. The Pedagogue says that the Chorus of Phoenician women who are approaching arrived because (196) "upheaval (ταραγμὸς) came to the city", and the Messenger describes the din created by the brothers' fatal clash as a "huge commotion" (πολὺν ταραγμόν, 1406). The condition of the dramatic action and its resolution are a type of disturbance cast in language with both political and medical overtones. More nosological language occurs in the Pedogogue's final line before the parodos, as he observes of the approaching Chorus (200–01): "women take a certain pleasure in saying nothing healthy (ὑγιές) to each other."[12] The pejorative terms he uses to describe the Chorus – *ochlos*, "mob" – and his ascription of "unsanitary" language to them suggest that he is trying to scapegoat the foreigners for the internally bred civic illness of *stasis*. The accusatory aspersions cast on Polynices' "foreign marriage" further this scapegoating polarity. The unhealthy words of the Phoenician women are then recalled in the aforementioned complaint by Polynices how the language of his brother, the true fomenter of *stasis*,

---

[12] In his note on line 472, Mastronarde 1994: 281 points to this line for comparison, but without suggesting that there is any kind of noetic structure behind the recurrence.

is itself diseased. Thebes needs words that cure disease, not cause it, and later in the play, I shall observe shortly, it hears a paean, a song of healing. Thus, as the resolution of the play and the city's *stasis* approach, the disease imagery and its cure take on added force.

Only a literal *katharsis*, a purging cure, can save Thebes, and the drama hence enacts a healing of the diseased body politic. Tiresias, while hesitating before telling Creon that the cure is his son's death, first suggests that, unless the sons of Oedipus both renounce Thebes, there is (890) "one other device (μηχανή) of safety". This device is the sacrifice of Creon's son. Why should the dramatist choose this particular wording? Richard Martin has argued that healing, sacrifice and battle are closely tied together in Greek thought from archaic times, and that the root for *mêchanê, mêchos*, means a solution which consists of a healing, that in turn ends strife (Martin 1983: 32, 41).

Indeed, in one of the other extant tragedies depicting the war between Eteocles and Polynices, the Chorus celebrates man's newfound ability to escape from νόσων . . . ἀμηχάνων (*Antigone* 363); here, and elsewhere, *amêchanos* means "without remedy.[13] But this instance of *amêchanos* is not unique within the *Antigone*, since it is repeated early four times within the space of less than a hundred lines (79, 90, 92, 175) to denote the concept of the improper, unorderly actions that Antigone plans, Ismene resists and Creon denounces. Its instance at line 363 plays off those earlier cases and prepares the introduction of disease language that commences here and continues shortly later at line 421, when the Sentry describes the magical dust storm over the corpse of Polynices; once the disease imagery commences *amêchanos* disappears. Is this sequence in Sophocles coincidental? I do not think so.

While *mêchanê* and cognate words tend to mean primarily simple, often deceitful, contrivances, in at least two other passages in Euripidean drama it evokes its more archaic meaning, and in contexts similar to this one. The first comes in the *Alcestis* where the Chorus expresses its fear for their master and the hope that someone can save him: ὦναξ Παιάν, / ἔξευρε μηχανάν τιν' Ἀδμήτῳ κακῶν, "O lord Paian, find some *mêchanê* for the troubles of Admetus" (220–21). Several matters stand out here, not least of them the evocation of Apollo Paian. The *Alcestis* opens with Apollo connecting the play's action to his vengeance against the Cyclopes (and hence Zeus) for the death of his son Asclepius, whom Zeus punished for resurrecting

---

[13] *Amêchanos* is thought to mean "without remedy" also at *Il*.8.130; Hes. *Th*. 589; Archil. 66; A. *Eu*. 56; S. *El*. 140; Simon. 5.11; E. *Med*. 392, 447. At *Eu*. 645–46 Apollo further links *akos* and *mêchanê*. At the end of this chapter I argue that the verb *amêchanein* at *Her*. 1378 also could mean "I am without healing."

Hippolytus. Apollo's attempts to ward off death through substitution, and Admetus' own efforts to find a replacement, mirror the surrogacy of sacrifice and revenge. The designation of Apollo as Paian, "the Healer," thus also recalls the earlier activity of Asclepius, who by that time had also acquired that cult title. While the city of Admetus lacks war, the death of Alcestis is, ironically, a "healing" for the woes of Admetus, just as the sacrifice of Menoeceus, according to Tiresias, can save Thebes in the *Phoenissae*. I shall return to the *Alcestis* later, when the topic demands it.

A passage in another Euripidean drama, produced around 425 BCE and thus shortly after the plague, the *Andromache*, also combines war, healing and sacrifice in such a way as to suggest again the more archaic sense of *mêchanê*. This is not so clear or strong in comparison with the *Phoenissae*, but the clustering of the same ideas together again seems significant and meaningful. Peleus, having discovered the plot against the lives of his grandson's concubine, Andromache, and his great-grandson, expresses his outrage (547–49):

ὑμᾶς ἐρωτῶ τόν τ᾽ ἐφεστῶτα σφαγῇ,
τί ταῦτα; πῶς ταῦτ᾽; ἐκ τίνος λόγου νοσεῖ
δόμος; τί πράσσετ᾽ ἄκριτα μηχανώμενοι;

I ask you who oversees this sacrifice?
Why and how are these things happening? For what reason does
the house ail? What are you doing, contriving without trial?

Mêchanômenoi in the last phrase, obviously, translates awkwardly as "contriving" here, and refers to the plots of Menelaus and his daughter Hermione against her rival Andromache. The intended sacrifice of Andromache by Hermione produces *nosos* for the House of Peleus, while the language suggests it is intended as a cure. The language of disease is surprisingly persistent in the *Andromache* and points to the archaic meaning of *mêchanê*. Andromache calls infidelity a disease (220–22). Helen's daughter Hermione says that the "houses of men are ill" (949–50) from women who come from without to corrupt wives within. The domestic disturbances are magnified, however, when the Chorus, having learned of Orestes' murderous ambush against Neoptolemus, reflects on the Trojan War and the disasters of its aftermath and laments: "A plague, Hellas was enduring a plague" (νόσον Ἑλλὰς ἔτλα, νόσον, 1044). Reminded of the origins of the Trojan War when Hermione runs off with Orestes, the Chorus in this passage reactivates the Homeric association of war and plague, a connection strengthened by the presence of Apollo in *Iliad* Book 1 and at the death of Neoptolemus, who meets his end murdered by Orestes but also as a sacrificial victim at the altar of Apollo at Delphi. Orestes even uses the word *mêchanê* (995) to refer to his plot against Neoptolemus – μηχανὴ φόνου, "an instrument of murder" – a solution that "heals." Sick house and sick land meet an unlikely doctor wielding a cure for his own ailments which, however, also poisons the house of Peleus. Sacrifice, war and healing reconnect together through the death of Neoptolemus at the shrine of the healer Apollo and thus point toward the "instrument of safety," the death of Menoeceus in the *Phoenissae* a decade later.

PHARMAKON SÔTÊRIAS

Disease, war and sacrifice mark the terrain of Euripides' *Phoenissae*, and the sacrifice – or really, as we shall see shortly, the sequence of sacrifices – heals Thebes of the scars of its battles, external and internal. Thus, since healing, sacrifice and battle are all active parts in the play's discourse, Tiresias' language for the settlement already implies the sacrifice and participates in the drama's metaphorical structure, even leading it to its logical outcome. While initially refusing to spell out for Creon the nature of this solution, Tiresias adds another layer to the symbolic associations, by casting his prophecy as a "cure/drug of security," φάρμακον σωτηρίας (893).[14] The text, thus underscoring the connection between healing and sacrifice, moves in a mere three lines from μηχανὴ σωτηρίας to φάρμακον σωτηρίας. As Derrida has made more widely known, the Greek word *pharmakon* means both cure and poison. The wider scope of related words also shows that it implies a purging, a cleansing – in other words, some kind of *katharsis*.[15] So the sacrifice of Menoeceus is the *pharmakon* since it serves both as a cure for the city's *nosos* by initiating the war's final phase and as a poison for the royal house itself, thus preserving the ambivalence of *pharmakon*. And this is how Menoeceus himself sees his role, as he says in some of his final lines before his suicide: στείχω δέ, θανάτου δῶρον οὐκ αἰσχρὸν πόλει / δώσων, νόσου δὲ τήνδ᾽ ἀπαλλάξω χθόνα, "I am going, in order to give a not shameful gift of death to the city, and I shall release this land from

---

[14] On the ambivalence of the *pharmakon* see Derrida 1981: 61–172. Pucci 1980, following Derrida's lead (established in the 1972 French original), studies its role in Euripidean drama; in general now see Goldhill 1991: 255–61.

[15] Derrida 1981. The LSJ entry notes that *pharmakon* means "*healing remedy, medicine*, in Hom. mostly of those applied outwardly." Classical instances of the word imply an *internal* cure. Citing *Phoenissae* 893, the LSJ entry claims it can indicate "*a means of producing* something," a definition that has a potentially significant overlap with *mêchanê* as discussed above. Given the nosological language and imagery pervasive throughout the drama, I doubt its sense is restricted to a merely generic "means."

disease" (1013–14, if these lines are genuine[16]). Froma Zeitlin points out that Tiresias brings this idea of civic salvation to Thebes from Athens, where he has advised King Erechtheus to sacrifice his daughters to save the city, and thus it is only the democratic city that can inspire appropriate political behavior in Thebes: not that killing young girls is in itself commendable, a problem which Euripides further explores in the *Ion*, where the surviving daughter Creusa remembers these events with sorrow, but that placing the needs of the whole over the self-interest pursued by Eteocles can alone avert disaster (Zeitlin 1990b: 143–44). On an immediately political level, the disease of Thebes, exemplified by Eteocles' equation of not ruling with slavery, is the excessive attachment to one's private affairs that threatens the appropriate balance and mixture of the whole city's components.

If Menoeceus really is the "cure of safety" for the city, then his death should affect the previous discourse of disease, and, in fact, as Menoeceus kills himself for the city's cure, the nosological language begins to climax and change. The Messenger who appears after the final exit of Creon's son commences his report to Jocasta of the last battle by temporally, perhaps causally (given the possibility of both temporality and causation in ἐπεί, 1090), connecting the death of Menoeceus to Eteocles' decision to make his conclusive battle formations.[17] The final detail of this arrangement picks up the disease imagery once more, for Eteocles is concerned with a "weak/sick (νοσοῦντι) point in the walls" (1098). Again, normal Greek usage could simply deploy the participle to connote a debility in the armaments, but the reiterated insistence on disease and cures suggests a live, not dead, metaphor, perhaps a hypallage of the disease from the body politic to the walls that protect it; Euripides performs a similar maneuver later in the *Bacchae*, where the collapse of the house's walls during "the palace miracle" signifies Dionysus' initial penetration of Pentheus' "defenses." The walls of Thebes, like the city they protect, have become sick.

Following the self-sacrifice of Menoeceus, the cure begins to extend itself through the whole war, and songful language that can heal emerges to dispel the diseased political discourse of Eteocles. The armies of the two brothers line up in battle formations, and the war trumpets from Polynices' side intone a paean (1102), a type of song that can be used either for victory or

---

[16] See the doubts of Mastronarde 1994: 431–32. These lines are still suggestive and significant even if they are a later addition, for the interpolator was then responding to the larger metaphors of the play. Thus the interpolation would signify the force of the idea of the therapeutical sacrifice. Kosak 2004: 187 observes that Menoeceus' "cure" manages to be both homeopathic and allopathic.

[17] This sequence, which seems to occur finally only with Menoeceus' death, might suggest a solution to the vexed question of whether the death has any real effect.

for healing. As I shall demonstrate later in more detail with the *Heracles*, in tragedy the paean can be deployed ironically depending on the context of its use; its singers in this drama may mean a song of victory, but context demands that it become one of healing for the city as a whole. In the preceding ode, the Chorus, while narrating the destruction wrought by the Sphinx before Oedipus' arrival, describes the cries raised by the Thebans as ἰηΐήϊον βοάν / ἰηΐήϊον μέλος (1036–37), which can mean "a cry of mourning, a song of mourning." However, *iêiêion* also is used in paeanic healing prayers to Apollo and Asclepius, including elsewhere in tragedy, and since this occurs in the *Phoenissae* so close to the paean, it is entirely possible, even likely, that it also encompasses the cry of healing and certainly anticipates the later paean.[18] From *pharmakon* to the paean Thebes receives the full treatment for its diseased body politic by replacing the diseased language of Eteocles with a song of healing. The battle features one last instance of *nosos* (1171) and then this imagery ceases.

The disease imagery concludes, however, only once the carnage has commenced, thus suggesting the deaths of Menoeceus, Polynices, Eteocles and Jocasta function cathartically, literally so. In Greek culture blood sacrifices, *sphagia*, occur frequently before battle, as a preliminary to the bloodshed of the fighting itself (Burkert 1985: 60). The death of the male virgin Menoeceus is an obvious variation of the *sphagia* ritual of maiden sacrifice, but such language is not restricted to his suicide. Simultaneously with the move away from illness comes a sudden flurry of sacrificial language. Words derived from a Greek term for ritual killing, *sphazein*, (among which I include *phasganon*), move to the forefront,[19] as they virtually all occur around the point in the action where the nosological imagery climaxes and ends with Menoeceus' death. Now, it makes sense that Menoeceus is associated with sacrificial imagery (e.g. σφάξας, 1010), for he is, after all, a sacrificial victim, but such language attaches itself to Oedipus' sons as well. The descriptions of real animal sacrifices (174, 1110, 1255) serve to underscore the sacrificial overtones of human deaths. Oedipus' earlier thoughts of suicide, which prepare the ground for Jocasta's actual suicide, are cast as "sacrificial slaughter," σφαγάν (332). The Messenger reports that Jocasta, after the battle, sees her sons: "she saw them wounded and lamented their fatal slaughter (σφαγάς)" (1431–2).[20] Jocasta thus plays the role of the women at the sacrifice raising

---

[18] Healing: Pi., *Paian* 2.35; A. *Ag.* 146; Soph. *OT* 154, 1096. Since the *Oedipus Tyrannus* also includes another instance of this cry indicating mourning as well (174), it is apparent that tragic diction encompasses both.

[19] *Sphazein*: 173, 332, 913, 933, 945, 964, 1010, 1110, 1255, 1316, 1431; *phasganon*: 267, 521, 1404, 1577. On *phasganon* as a sacrificial knife see Mitchell-Boyask 1993.

[20] I take τετρωμένους . . . καιρίους as the object of ἰδοῦσα and σφαγάς as the object of ᾤμωξεν.

the cry of lamentation as the bull is struck, with the added twist that she will add her body to the altar. The sons' weapons become sacrificial knives, as they are called *phasganon* twice early and reciprocally (266, 521), and as the brothers seize their *phasgana* for their final rush toward one another (1404); during the duel itself, only as they approach each other for the final fatal lunges do their swords again become sacrificial knives. Note that these knives will soon end the clashing of their shields, whose noise is described as ταραγμόν in line 1406, and *taragmos*, as I shall argue shortly later, tends to denote medical and political disturbances. Jocasta takes one of these knives to bury into her own flesh as she commits suicide over their corpses, cutting her own throat like cattle at an altar (1457). The text casts each death in sacrificial language, which is in turn part of the nosological structure of meaning. The only sure *pharmakon* of safety for Thebes is not just the death of Menoeceus, but the destruction of its entire faction-ridden royal household.[21] Menoeceus' sacrifice merely initiates the final therapeutical bloodletting by enabling the purges of the others. And the audience, the citizens of Athens, behold this action and hear this language in a theater overlooked by the City Asklepieion, the home of the healing god. With the possible functions of disease imagery of Euripidean drama during this era established, I can return to the *Heracles*, another tragic drama with this dynamic relationship between text and context, the fuller implications of which will now become more apparent.

HERACLES II: TEXT AND CONTEXT

This detour through another chapter in the sordid mythical history of Thebes should help clarify similar Euripidean negotiations in other dramas from the years after the construction of the Asklepieion on the south slope of the Athenian Acropolis. The *Heracles* not only deploys the language of disease and cure on both the personal and civic levels, but it also keeps Asclepius hovering in the background. At no point does the text of the *Heracles* refer directly to Asclepius, but aspects of the Heracles myth include and are associated with Apollo's son, so a play where disease is an important metaphor, and performed in view of the healing god's shrine, may evoke Asclepius without naming him; further, the Athenians worshiped Heracles in cult as *Alexikakos*, "Averter of woe", a title he shared with Apollo in connection with anxieties produced by the great plague in Athens

---

[21] Seaford 1994: 317–18 comes close to the connection between the sacrificial and medical discourses but limits his consideration of the resonance of *nosos*.

(Woodford 1976; Kearns 1989: 14–15; Parker 1996: 175, 186). Of the three other extant tragic dramas that feature Heracles – the *Trachiniae*, *Philoctetes* and the *Alcestis* – the latter two name Asclepius, and indeed the language of illness marks all of the dramas where Heracles appears. In Sophocles the divinized Heracles appears *ex machina* to order Philoctetes to go to Troy where Heracles will send Asclepius to end "your illness" (*nosou*, 1437–38). Further, Asclepius' ambiguous status in Greek culture as sometimes hero, sometimes god, mirrors Heracles' duality as, in Pindar's words (*Nem.* 3.22), a *hêrôs theos*.

The only other tragedy to name Asclepius is the *Hippolytus*,[22] and there the character Theseus is often regarded as a mythological doublet for Heracles because he frequently accompanies Heracles on his exploits, as seen at the end of play I am currently examining, or engages in very similar activities, such as battling Amazons and Centaurs. Both heroes also inadvertently kill their own kin. But the boldest adventure they share is the journey to the world of the dead, the *katabasis*, which is traditionally held as the greatest of exploits possible for a mortal. This Heraclean tradition is so strong that Aristophanes, when he has his Dionysus seek a suitable disguise for his descent to the Underworld, casts him as Heracles seeking the hero's clothing to frighten off any potentially threatening denizens of Hades. In Euripides' *Heracles*, Theseus reminds us that is was Heracles who saved him when he himself was chained in Hades (1170). Moreover, in versions of the Hippolytus myth other than the one found in Euripides' extant play, Phaedra falls in love with Hippolytus while Theseus is in Hades; this is the case in Seneca's play.

Heracles' defiance of mortality links his mythical tradition to Asclepius, the hero who tried to save men from death, and Euripides' *Heracles* strengthens any possible associations by shifting the usual sequence of events to stress the connection between his descent to Hades to fetch Cerberus and his mad murder of his family. No other known literary source places the murders after the labors, and the juxtaposition of the return from Hades with this disaster suggests some deeper connection. By presenting Theseus as Heracles' savior in human terms at the end, in reciprocity for Heracles' release of him from Hades, Euripides further reminds us that Heracles enters the play having just violated that most precious of lines between men and gods, death. This is, after all, the second surviving Euripidean drama, after the *Alcestis*, that features Heracles returning a human from Hades.

---

[22] Asclepius is named by Heracles at the end of the *Philoctetes* (1437), and by Apollo at the beginning of the *Alcestis*. In the *Hippolytus*, the huge wave carrying the bull conceals the "rock of Asclepius."

Commenting on the gods' punishment of Heracles, Anne Burnett observes that Heracles "has robbed Death and played *sôter* to other mortals; he looks like another Asclepius, and having now in a sense conferred life, he cannot be left at large" (Burnett 1971: 179). Burnett's words are obviously convenient for my purposes, though they do not in themselves imply my larger point, and they raise an important question: what, exactly, does it mean to look like another Asclepius? Given the fatal consequences of being Asclepius in tragedy, which the *Alcestis* prologue indicates, imitating him is an activity fraught with danger, and the only one who can raise the dead safely is, as I (and Aristophanes) have already suggested, the dramatic poet. And when Euripides writes and stages his *Heracles*, Asclepius hovers thematically and literally in the background, looking over the shoulders of the spectators in the Theater of Dionysus. A later text, Statius' *Thebaid*, may indicate the deeper connection between Asclepius and Heracles, because in that epic one army sings a *Herculeum paeana* (4.157), a Herculean paean.[23]

Euripides clearly establishes the link between Heracles and Asclepius at the end of his earliest extant drama, the *Alcestis* of 438 BCE, when Heracles engages in an Asclepian resurrection. In the Prologue, Apollo explains his presence at the house of Admetus thus (3–7):

> Ζεὺς γὰρ κατακτὰς παῖδα τὸν ἐμὸν αἴτιος
> Ἀσκληπιόν, στέρνοισιν ἐμβαλὼν φλόγα·
> ὁ δὴ χολωθεὶς τέκτονας Δίου πυρὸς
> κτείνω Κύκλωπας· καί με θητεύειν πατὴρ
> θνητῷ παρ' ἀνδρὶ τῶνδ' ἄποιν' ἠνάγκασεν.

> For Zeus is responsible, having killed my son
> Asclepius, after hurling flame on his chest;
> enraged I killed the craftsmen of Zeus' fire
> the Cyclopes; and my father compelled me
> to serve a mortal man as recompense for this.

Concerned with establishing the justice of his two cases, against Zeus and for Admetus, who is himself trying to avoid death, Apollo significantly omits how Asclepius managed to anger Zeus so much, but the Chorus does allude to the myth which the audience could have known at least from *Pythian* 3.[24] The death of Asclepius makes the arrival of Heracles, the only mortal

---

[23] I am grateful to Ian Rutherford for suggesting this passage to me. I should also note that the subject of Statius' epic is the same as that of the *Phoenissae*, and Euripides' play must have been one of Statius' main sources. That Statius picks up the latent associations supports, I think, my arguments about the *Phoenissae*.

[24] Dale's 1954 commentary observes on these lines: "Apollo not unnaturally suppresses the information here."

capable of conquering Death (literally), all the more necessary and urgent. However, I do not think the full paradigmatic function of the Asclepius myth here has been sufficiently recognized. While, for example, Conacher observes rightly that Asclepius, in raising men from the dead, foreshadows Heracles' role in this play (Conacher 1967: 332),[25] fuller consideration of this prolepsis raises troubling questions about the play's ending beyond the nagging doubts some critics have had about whether the new woman is really Alcestis or whether Admetus in receiving her thus breaks his oath to Alcestis never to remarry. If the first thing in a drama the audience hears is that Zeus does not tolerate the resurrection of mortals and will punish the perpetrator, even if he is a god's son, then this surely has disquieting implications for the play's ending. Euripides leaves his audience, even with the most basic knowledge of Heracles' career, to wonder whether any of the disasters awaiting Heracles stem from his violation of the line between living and dead. The audience knows that Heracles' life has catastrophes that always equal his triumphs. He exits the stage quickly at the end, claiming to be in a hurry, but not saying to where, thus leaving his immediate and ultimate fates an open question. But Apollo has already suggested an answer to his ultimate destination. Thus, Sourvinou-Inwood notices the conflict between the punishment of Asclepius and what Heracles does during the play, though she resolves the conflict by positing that death is not overturned completely, merely "postponed." On the other hand, "this postponement is exceptional" (Sourvinou-Inwood 2003: 320–21).

While Aeschylean drama obliquely refers to Asclepian myth, Euripides' *Alcestis* is the earliest extant one to name Asclepius directly, and, by the time of the production of the *Heracles* around 415, all dramatic evocations of the god must have taken on added significance because the Asklepieion existed in some substantial state of completion at the upper western edge of the Theater of Dionysus. Even before the Chorus raises its paean song and Heracles falls ill, Euripides has already prepared its audience for the gestures to the Theater's Athenian location by evoking strongly, in the drama's earlier suppliancy scenes, before the arrival of Heracles, the Athenian cult of Zeus Soter, "the proprietor of the Stoa of Zeus in the Agora, the deity who had 'saved' their fathers from slavery in the Persian Wars" (Mikalson 1986: 90).

[25] Padilla 2000: 186 shows how this play "skews *charis* relations by incorporating the theme of death ... the figures of Apollo, Heracles and Alcestis possess the ability to be givers of life (*bios*), while Admetus is able to participate as a receiver of life ..." Padilla further points out (187) that "what Asclepius had effectively accomplished was the widening of a sphere of exchange to allow an inferior social group (mortals) to attain a possession (immortality) that had been restricted to, and controlled by, a superior social group (the gods)."

The god of healing, then, looked over the shoulders of the spectators and toward the chorus as it sang of the city's sickness in the *Heracles* and, later, the *Phoenissae*. If the circumstances of the performance of Greek tragedy have real significance for our understanding of the surviving texts, then I do not see how we can ignore this proximity of the healing cult to a site that witnessed so much talk of disease. The plague that began in 430 inspired the poets' use of illness, both literal and metaphorical, in drama, and the plague brought the cult of Asclepius to Athens, where it was installed next to the theater. Thus, a complex interrelationship between real plague, cult and Theater needs to be kept in mind when one approaches individual tragic dramas from this period. Remembering this context, let us return to how these matters unfold as Heracles enters the house.

In my discussion of the *Phoenissae*, I briefly observed the function of the potential ambiguities of paeans in tragedy, and now I develop this matter in detail, as the paean plays a fairly central role in the action of the *Heracles*. During the brief agitated scenes in the *Heracles* before the disaster occurs, there are several different evocations of the paean, the ritual song that, depending on context, means either a song of victory or one of healing, an ambivalence that Euripides' *Heracles* seems to exploit (Rutherford 1993: 73).[26] In his study of "paeanic ambiguity" in Greek literature, Ian Rutherford observes that Greek poets played on the ambiguity between the three classes of paean: apotropaic, celebratory, and hybrid songs that combine elements of the two. Paean is both the epithet for "the Healer", first applied to Apollo and then to his son Asclepius, and the name for a class of poetry, and in literature, Rutherford argues, there is a meaningful uncertainty, which is exploited by poets, between paean poem and Paean Healer; the latter is older and its function may be transferred to the former (Rutherford 1993: 87). Dramatic irony provides the tragedian with the means of using the audience's knowledge and expectations against the actions intended by the agents in the acting area, for the situation of a paean in a drama can allow the poet to exploit the different functions of the paeanic genre; for example, in Euripides' satyr play *Cyclops*, Seaford observes, the Chorus of satyrs mocks the Cyclops' apotropaic cries of pain as signaling instead their victory over him (Seaford 1984: 220). This ambivalence also allows the situation of paean cries in drama to take on added importance for the audience, and such is the case of the *Heracles*, which is one of the dramas where a "celebratory paian [precedes] a reversal in action" (Rutherford 1993: 89).

---

[26] On the paean in general see Käppel 1992 and Rutherford 2001.

Such a reversal can indicate more than dramatic irony or added poignancy in a drama where disease is an important metaphor. The city is sick with *stasis*, the play intones several times, and Heracles thus appears as a healer of this disease, so the Chorus' praise of Heracles in the second stasimon becomes, as Wilamowitz originally observed in his commentary, a paean, but with overtones that great scholar did not realize. The Chorus suggests (687–700) that Heracles is as worthy of paeans as Apollo, and a good deal of the thought of the last strophe applies as much to Heracles as Apollo, since both are "the son of Zeus" (Διὸς ὁ παῖς, 696) (Bond 1981: 246–47). Moreover, these evocations resonate in the aforementioned Athenian worship of Heracles as *Alexikakos*, "Averter of evil," due to the plague than began in 430. These associations continue in the immediately pursuant scene between Amphitryon and Lycus, where Heracles' mortal father lures the tyrant into a false sense of security with some rather black irony. Lycus states that Heracles can never return to save his wife Megara, to which Amphitryon responds (719): "No, unless one of the gods resurrects (ἀναστήσειε) him." Of course, in Greek tragedy the gods do not reverse death and explicitly frown on those, such as Asclepius, who try. But Heracles has, in fact, returned from Hades and immediately kills Lycus. Upon hearing the tyrant's cries of death, the Chorus thus first considers singing the celebratory paean, but perhaps, given the agitated atmosphere of the scene, also raises an apotropaic one, and then when Iris and Lyssa appear above the house (just after the Chorus has praised Heracles' escape from Hades), the terrified men cry out: ὦναξ Παιάν / ἀπότροπος γένοιό μοι πημάτων, "Oh Lord Paean, may you be an averter of woes for me" (820–21). This last prayer is thus, literally, apotropaic and shades, retrospectively, the paean that preceded it. Calling upon Apollo with a title that also designates Asclepius, they ask Apollo as the Healer to protect them from the two goddesses, one of whom is Madness, who, when besieging Heracles, is a type of illness; again, the position of the cult shrine just behind the shoulders of the audience would deepen and complicate the resonance of the address to Lord Paean, sung by the Chorus while facing the Asklepieion itself. The earlier triumphal paean has turned to its opposite: a desperate cry for help.

Heracles has not brought a cure to Thebes, but a worsening of the disease afflicting the city, and only his destruction can save it. He is both a threat to the city and its safety, cure and poison, the *pharmakon*. Yet the danger he poses to Thebes also means that he must be punished as the *pharmakos*. As I noted during the discussions of the *pharmakon* in the *Hippolytus* and the *Phoenissae*, there have been several important treatments of its ambivalent meanings (Derrida 1981: 61–172; Pucci 1980; Goldhill 1991: 255–61), but, to my knowledge, there has been no substantive examination of the possible verbal play in actual texts between *pharmakon* (φάρμακον) and *pharmakos* (φαρμακός).[27] Several of the oblique, inflected cases of the two words overlap, with only accentuation distinguishing them from each other, so that the audience could easily hear one suggested by the other.[28] There is also precedent for other verbal plays in tragedy between homologous or homophonous words differentiated only by accent; for example Sophocles' Heraclitean play on βιός (bow) and βίος (life) in the *Philoctetes*, wherein, because of Philoctetes' total reliance on his bow for survival, the loss of the former entails the end of the latter.[29] In the *Hippolytus* the Nurse cryptically refers to a drug that will cure Phaedra of her disease (τῆσδε φάρμακον νόσου 479); the ambiguity in the Nurse's language leaves vague the nature of this cure, allowing her to deceive Phaedra. However, given the duality of the *pharmakon*, this ambiguity, once opened, is difficult to shut down and the cure for Phaedra obviously becomes a poison. Yet the larger discourses that I have explored in that drama form wider resonances in the language; since the *pharmakon* is Hippolytus and Hippolytus becomes a *pharmakos* who is expelled from the city and destroyed violently outside of it, the Nurse's language names Hippolytus as a scapegoat for Phaedra's illness.[30] Words are not absolutes unto themselves, but mark ideas and networks of associations, and if similar words link related concepts, then we need to pay attention.

Given the homology between purging the body of unwanted elements through a drug and expelling an individual from the city to prevent famine or plague, and given the rhetoric of the sick city in the *Heracles*, I submit

[27] See Hughes 1991: 140, with bibliography. Burkert 1979: 65 notes that the connection is "mysterious." Lloyd 2003: 11 accepts that *pharmakos* is cognate with, and thus conceptually related to (especially in its ambivalence), *pharmakon*.

[28] In his note on line 893 of the *Phoenissae*, Mastronarde 1994: 409 observes that one scholar has mistaken "scapegoat" for "drug" in a translation and commentary. While a fifth-century Athenian obviously had a greater linguistic competence in his native tongue than a modern scholar, the almost identical, save for pitch accent, homonymicity probably tripped up, or at least momentarily aroused, those audience members listening to the actors.

[29] See Robinson 1969: 43–44; Vidal-Naquet, "Sophocles' *Philoctetes* and the Ephebia," in Vernant and Vidal-Naquet 1988: 168; and Rose 1992: 287.

[30] Mitchell 1991. As I noted earlier in the main discussion of disease language, in a fourth-century oration attributed to Demosthenes, *Against Aristogeiton*, the speaker's invective brings together a direct connection between plague (*loimos*) and scapegoat (*pharmakos*), asking the jury to convict (25.80) "the scapegoat, the plague" (ὁ φαρμακός, ὁ λοιμός). Given the tendency we have observed in fifth-century writers to avoid the word *loimos* the power of this language in the fourth century might have been remarkable. Since the scapegoat is both cause and cure, this passage further underscores the relationship between societal disorder and plague.

that there is such a connection between *pharmakon* and *pharmakos*. To the frightened cries of the Chorus, Iris answers in terms suggesting that Heracles is a surrogate victim for the city (824–26):[31]

πόλει γὰρ οὐδὲν ἥκομεν βλάβος,
ἑνὸς δ' ἐπ' ἀνδρὸς δώματα στρατεύομεν,
ὅν φασιν εἶναι Ζηνὸς Ἀλκμήνης τ' ἄπο.

For the city we have come as no harm,
but we attack the house of a single man
whom they say is born from Zeus and Alcmene.

The rhetorical composition of the lines of the Greek verse stresses and enacts the opposition between the safe city (*polei*) and the single man (*henos andros*) who will suffer; the contrast between the secure many and the endangered/dangerous one is paradigmatic of the scapegoat ritual. The further equation drawn between Heracles and Thebes strengthens this tie. The contrast between the salvation of the whole and the destruction of the individual recalls Amphitryon's earlier description of Heracles' military service for Thebes, where the solitary warrior defeated the whole armies of other cities (220–21):

Μιωνύαις ὃς εἷς πᾶσι διὰ μάχης μολὼν
Θήβαις ἔθηκεν ὄμμ' ἐλεύθερον βλέπειν.
He who having gone through battle alone against all the Minyans
made Thebes free.

The return, when the goddesses attack later, of the distinction between the one and the many stresses that Heracles, despite his successes, has relied excessively on the practices of the individual warrior and that his adherence to such values endangers not just himself but the city as a whole.[32] The goddesses thus clarify their mission to Thebes. Heracles is ultimately destroyed here in return for his singularity.

The vehicle of the divine assault on Heracles, his madness, returns us to the discussion of *taragmos*, roughly translated as "disturbance," that I postponed earlier.[33] The *mania* the gods will cast on him consists of

---

[31] Here I rely on the insightful study of this drama in Foley 1985: 147–204, but my stress on the surrogacy mechanism and cause, especially in the context of disease imagery, and my deemphasis of violence in sacrifice, depart from, or perhaps supplement, Foley's analysis.

[32] See George 1994: 153 on this passage, including Diggle's support for Elmsley's emendation of 220. Papadopoulou 2005: 137–50 stresses that Heracles is depicted in the play's language more frequently as a hoplite that many critics allow.

[33] Kosak 2004: 159–61 also discusses the word as a medical term in this drama, but without the linkages to political discourse.

παιδοκτόνους / φρενῶν ταραγμούς, "a pedicidal disturbance of his mind" (835–36). Amphitryon, when he sees Athena intervene in the potentially patricidal rampage of his foster son, cries from inside the palace: τάραγμα ταρτάρειον ὡς ἐπ' Ἐγκελάδῳ πέμπεις, "You are sending an upheaval from hell as you once did against Enceladus" (906–07). Amphitryon recognizes that only the gods could send such a disaster, yet, ignorant of the machinations of the other pair of goddesses, has only Athena to blame. This term *taragmos* and cognate words are used in fifth-century Greek to indicate mental, corporeal and political disturbance and anarchy, as seen in the Hippocratic texts, Aristophanes, Thucydides and Euripides (Smith 1967: 294–95; Döring 1876: 325–28; Croissant 1932: 71–74; Schamun 1997). *Taragmos* forms part of the same conceptual vocabulary as *stasis*, as it marks imbalance and instability. A brief glance at Thucydides' description of the *stasis* at Corcyra, which he saw as paradigmatic for the political upheavals then spreading throughout the Greek world, shows these relations. Introducing the main section of his diagnosis of this revolution, Thucydides wonders at the sheer profusion of disasters: καὶ ἐπέπεσε πολλὰ καὶ χαλεπὰ κατὰ στάσιν ταῖς πόλεσι, "Many harsh things fell upon the cities during the *stasis*" (3.82.2). This observation uses a verb, *epepese*, that also describes the onslaught of disease in Thucydides. Indeed, Thucydides' prose hints at the connection just a few chapters later when he very briefly catalogues the new attack of the plague: ἡ νόσος τὸ δεύτερον ἐπέπεσε τοῖς Ἀθηναίοις, "the plague for a second time fell upon the Athenians" (3.87.1). As I shall show later, this is not the last instance where Thucydides uses such language to describe a crisis. Returning to Corcyra, he extends his discourse of the ill civic body: ξυνταραχθέντος τε τοῦ βίου ἐς τὸν καιρὸν τοῦτον τῇ πόλει, "since life was completely confused in the city" (3.84.2). The force of the generalized language here is particularly striking, as "life" (*tou biou*) as some kind of abstract concept is disturbed, and not in one city or cities, but "the city" (*têi polei*). Thucydides diagnoses the cause of the city thrown out of balance as ἡ ἀνθρωπεία φύσις . . . ἀσμένη ἐδήλωσεν ἀκρατὴς μὲν ὀργῆς οὖσα, "human nature . . . gladly showed itself being not in control of its passion" (3.84.2). He does not baldly state that Corcyra, and then the rest of the Greek world, suffer from a *nosos*, since, given the dominance of language related to disease, he does not have to do so. As Kallet argues, Thucydides often "clusters" medical vocabulary to achieve a "specifically medical resonance" (Kallet 1999: 229). The Corcyra episode again shows the pervasiveness of the image of the diseased body politic in the late fifth century, and words such as *taragmos* point this discussion toward similar passages in tragedy.

Taragmos seems another one of those nosological terms that function contagiously in a text's language. Near the beginning of the *Phoenissae* (196) the Pedagogue tells how "tumult (*taragmos*) has entered the city" because of the encroaching war. Heracles, quickly assessing the dangers confronting Thebes once he arrives, asks his father (533): "Into what *taragmos* have I come?" Amphitryon in turn asks Heracles not to disturb (ταράξῃς 605) the city before Lycus is killed, which, given these associations, itself suggests that Heracles' presence is not necessarily entirely beneficial.[34] A fragment from a lost drama by Euripides (Fr. 202, Nauck) further shows the exact concinnity of these ideas (if the text is right): ἐγὼ μὲν οὖν ἅ(ι)δοιμι καὶ λέγοιμί τι σοφόν, ταράσσων μηδὲν ὧν πόλις νοσεῖ, "May I say something wise, disturbing nothing of which the city is sick." The *Heracles* shows the same essential metaphorical deployment; the city of Thebes is sick with *stasis*, and Heracles has the potential to disturb it further. And Heracles' reaction (565–73) to Megara's narrative of their own family's distress clearly shows the potential civic disaster: "I will fill the river Ismenus with corpses." Heracles would destroy the city for its breach of *philia* with him in not coming to aid his father, wife and children (George 1994: 152–54). Due to the intervention of the gods, such new disturbances do not fall on the city, however, but on Heracles, who recognizes this on his own when he awakes from his madness (1091–92): φρενῶν ταράγματι / πέπτωκα δεινῷ, "I have fallen in a terrible confusion (*taragmati*) of my mind." Now this greatest of heroes, one called upon with a paean, who entered to save the sick city, needs healing himself, as the illness has been displaced from the city to him. Heracles looks about him and cannot understand what has happened, and thus he asks in an extraordinary line (1107): "Who will heal (ἰάσεται) my ignorance?"[35] The only other time the idea of consciousness as disease occurs is in another drama where disease is an important metaphor, Euripides' *Orestes* (Smith 1967: 297). For Heracles not to feel diseased, he now needs a healer, who turns out to be Theseus, who can cleanse Heracles' hands of *miasma* (1324) but not his mind of disease. And as Theseus manages to convince Heracles to continue life, but as a common citizen (albeit with a good piece of land and a hero cult) in Athens, Theseus can declare (1414): "You are not the famous Heracles because you are sick (νοσῶν)."

Unless the drama's deployment of its language and imagery are casual and coincidental, the action has displaced the disease of *stasis* from the city

---

[34] Papadopoulou 2005: 34–48 discusses Heracles' internal instabilities, this drama's representation of his tendency to excessive violence, and the effect of his violent nature on those near him.

[35] On the more specific medical symptoms ascribed to Heracles see Bond 1981, especially his comments on line 1407.

to Heracles, and thus I must consider the significance of this transfer. Foley, whose insightful discussion of the sacrificial crisis in the *Heracles* focuses on violence and the killing of the hero's children while somewhat skirting the related question of whether Heracles himself is a surrogate victim, observes that the drama's crisis stems not so much from the hero's violent history, but that "in this play the sacrificial crisis seems more logically to derive from the community of Thebes and from the goddess who enacts the plans of its tyrant" (Foley 1985: 161). The disturbance in the city becomes the disturbance in the hero's mind, and the goddess Lyssa embodies this movement. Heracles, who before and after the attack on him seems quite sane, stable and rational, experiences his madness as a disease that has entered him from the outside. Thebes thus experiences a cure of its *stasis* through the internal *stasis* of Heracles, a cure that could be called allopathic – achieving health through the experience of a disease.[36] Alcmaeon's proto-Hippocratic teaching held that health depended on a proper balance of the body's different elements and it cast disease politically as a breakdown of *isonomia* where one element achieves a tyranny over the rest. To restore harmony the body must experience a *katharsis* of the element believed to be causing the instability. This last term, of course, is fraught with danger for the critic venturing anywhere near tragedy, due to the *stasis* surrounding Aristotle's *Poetics*. I shall postpone discussion of that issue until the end of my study. I do wish to stress here, however, that the frequency of disease as a metaphor, especially a political one, in the *Heracles* raises the question of the cure for the body politic.

TRAGIC DRAMA, SCAPEGOATING AND OSTRACISM

The presentation of the city as sick with *stasis* and the subsequent transfer of the disease to Heracles suggest a displacement of disorder on to a victim that typifies sacrifice and scapegoating, but here in a political matrix. Yet Athenian society engaged in two practices, one ritual, the other political, that attempted to maintain societal order through the expulsion of an individual; the two institutions had the same essential goal and structure, and both supported the ideology of the polis.[37] It is important to deploy a

---

[36] However, one could argue that here disease is used to cure a disease, which would be a homeopathic cure. On homeopathy, allopathy, Greek medicine, and tragic *katharsis* see Belfiore 1992.

[37] On the resemblance of the *ostrakismos* to the *pharmakos* see Burkert 1979: 70–71, who follows Gernet. On ostracism as a form of scapegoating see also Parker 1983: 269–71, although Parker seems to me excessively literally minded in questioning the structural resemblance of the two. Rejecting Gernet's theory, Mirhady 1997 ties ritual to ostracism through the figure of the hero-athlete, following

more open conception of the nature of ostracism, for, as David Rosenbloom observes, "[a]n *ostrakophoria* is not simply a political procedure; it is the manifestation of a political culture, a symbol-laden activity and decisive act of communal self-definition" (Rosenbloom 2004a: 57). The political expulsion, the *ostrakismos*, allowed Athenian citizens the opportunity to vote annually for another citizen, typically prominent, to be expelled for a year, and this practice aimed to prevent an elite individual from gaining excessive power. On the ritual side, the base *pharmakos* was chased from the city during the Thargelia, a festival dedicated to Apollo. The potential of expelling both high and low from the city corresponds to the tendency of scapegoating structures, in ritual and myth, to select marginal figures on either end of the spectrum of hierarchy. The language of the institutions, featuring terms like *pharmakon*, *katharma* and their derivatives, strongly evokes the tragic language of disease, cures and sacrifices.[38] Moreover, as I argued in a previous chapter, in Athens the *pharmakos* rite was given the etiology of the original purification of the city after the gods had punished it with plague and famine because of the death of Minos' son Androgeus, with the contemporary practice as a ritual repetition of this *katharsis* (Calame 1990: 309–13).

Solon (Fr. 9.3) once wrote that "[i]t is through big men that the city is destroyed," and tragedy could be seen as an expression of such Athenian ambivalence, if not fear. It might be significant ideologically that eventually the Athenians abused ostracism by turning it on someone whose contemptibility made him in some sense more suitable to be a *pharmakos* during the Thargelia, which then led them to abandon the practice in disgust.[39] That instance might have made them too aware of the ritual basis of ostracism and the ideological implications of split between the ritual language of the tragic scapegoats, who are always royal, and the "real" *pharmakoi*, who are poor or slaves; scapegoating, as Girard argues,

Fontenrose. Mirhady's thoughts on the modeling of ostracized figures on heroic myths (and vice versa) are valuable. Forsdyke 2000: 255 rejects the link between ostracism and scapegoating, maintaining, I believe, a too narrow view of ritual and neglecting how one societal discourse can affect another. Forsdyke 2005: 157–59, however, discusses parallels between ostracism and scapegoating and sees ostracism as collective ritual. Osborne's Introduction to Osborne and Hornblower 1994 provides a more inclusive conception of ritual in the life of the democratic *polis*. In general, most of the treatments of this topic underplay the homologies between the two acts of expulsion. Tragic drama seems to engage in both. Rosenbloom 2004a and 2004b traces out the homologies of ostracism and scapegoating, and their intersections on the comic stage and in the ostracism (and murder) of Hyperbolus.

[38] On marginality, the Thargelia and language see Bremmer 1983 and Parker 1983: 24–31. My thoughts on ostracism and tragedy are ultimately inspired by Burke 1959.

[39] On the abuse of ostracism in the case of Hyperbolus see Thucy. 8.73.3, Parker 1983: 270, Rhodes 1994, Rosenbloom 2004a and 2004b.

always depends on an element of *méconnaisance*. When famine or plague strikes a community in the Theater of Dionysus, a king suffers, but when such disasters fall upon a real *polis*, the scapegoat is definitely not one of the privileged.[40] If tragedy represents the way the Athenian *polis* thought about itself, then a certain amount of self-deception was at work.[41] One possible exception, but one which still shows the tendency of the many to blame the one, is how the Athenians, at least as Thucydides tells it, blamed Pericles for their misfortunes (2.69):

> After the second invasion of the Peloponnesians the Athenians underwent a change of feeling, now that their land had been ravaged a second time while the plague and the war combined lay heavily upon them. They blamed Pericles for having persuaded them to go to war and held him responsible for the misfortunes which had befallen them.

While the Athenians seem to have held Pericles responsible for the plague, the worst they could do to him was to fine him heavily; not exactly the severe punishment a *pharmakos* in the Thargelia would have experienced, or even an exile.[42] And, of course, Pericles was soon returned to power.

And for Oedipus, Hippolytus and Heracles – among other figures in the Theater of Dionysus whose role in their communities and in the eyes of the Athenian community watching them is persistently problematic – the price is much higher. The homology of scapegoating and ostracism, combined with the story pattern in tragic myth of the expulsion or destruction of the hero, suggests that Athenian tragic drama, as a creature of the democratic Athenian *polis*, formed part of the larger discourse of what Sara Forsdyke terms "symbolic ostracism." Forsdyke argues that the key to understanding the role of ostracism in the democratic *polis* lies not in the frequency of actual instances of ostracism but in "the annual proposal to hold an ostracism (often without actually holding an ostracism) to remind the aristocrats of the power of the demos to determine the political shape of the community" (Forsdyke 2000: 233). I would thus suggest here that tragic drama, because it depicts the destruction of royal households from myth, households to which elite families in Athens allied themselves or from which they claimed descent, forms part of the larger cultural discourse that

---

[40] It is striking that epic presents a lower-class scapegoat, the *Iliad*'s Thersites. On the implications of this see Thalmann 1988. Rosenbloom 2004a and 2004b, especially 2004b: 336–38, examines the slippages between ostracism and scapegoating, which were incurred by class-based factionalism, in the case of Hyperbolus.

[41] See Faraone 1992: 98–100 on how etiological legends that exhibit a scapegoat structure always focus on royal victims.

[42] On Pericles and the plague see Allison 1983.

enables the symbolic power of ostracism. Forsdyke further argues that the limiting of the number and the extremity of the terms of exiles helped legitimize and stabilize democratic rule in Athens; ostracism in democratic Athens was moderate (Forsdyke 2000: 253–58). The restriction of more severe forms of punishment to the tragic theater, while tragedy itself also engaged the audience emotionally with the sufferings of the heroes it would never countenance in the agora, could be seen as part of this more moderate tack, if tragic drama was in fact part of the discourse of ostracism in fifth-century Athens. The displacement of punitive power against aristocrats from the *demos* to the gods would thus be part of the mystification that enables a more ritualized theatrical scapegoating. Again, as Simon Goldhill observes, "[t]heatre is not so much a commentary on *ta politika* as part of it" (Goldhill 2000: 35). For example, Hippolytus' rejection of the norms of democracy and his refusal to adhere to the cooperative hoplite values held by the Athenian audience lead to disaster for him and his family, but safety for Troezen (and, by extension, Athens), by transferring his violent destruction outside of the city (Mitchell 1991; Mitchell-Boyask 1999). If I am right that the medical metaphor of *stasis* as disease is then displaced on to Heracles as he becomes mad, then he definitely serves as a *pharmakon/os* who falls from the heroic heights to life as a normal citizen with a defined and restrained place in the city in order to engender civic stability by acting as a cure for its ills. As Justina Gregory writes of Heracles' transformation, "Heracles' change of status incorporates a political message, for throughout the play immortality and heroic accomplishment are unobtrusively equated with aristocratic values, while mortality and ordinary human endeavor are linked to an egalitarian sensibility" (Gregory 1991: 163).[43] He must learn the virtues of interdependence and community.[44]

Given this discursive template of the one for the many, it is especially suggestive that Aristotle, in his famous discussion of ostracism in the *Politics*, cites Heracles as his main mythological example of the necessity of excluding the superior being in order to preserve equality (balanced by the story of Periander and Thrasybulus as a historical example):

It is said in mythology that the Argonauts left Heracles behind on account of the following cause: because the Argo did not want to take him with the other sailors on the grounds that he was surpassing so much (ὡς ὑπερβάλλοντα πολύ). *Pol.* 3.13, 1284a

[43] On democratic and aristocratic sensibilities in the *Heracles* see also Foley 1985: 177–200.
[44] George 1994 shows the iconographic import of the contrast between Heracles' bow and Theseus' hoplite spear, the former being a sign of the lone, independent warrior and the latter signifying the more corporately democratic ideal of group combat.

Mirhady cites this passage as part of his "mythological charter for ostracism" (Mirhady 1997: 14). And while this passage has received surprisingly little comment, it seems quite suggestive, with respect to the specific spin Aristotle gives the myth of Heracles' departure from the Argo, in the context of my discussion. Aristotle selects a political emphasis to this myth, eliminating the reason found in Apollodorus (1.9.19) that Heracles was too heavy for the Argo to carry, by selecting a verb (*huperballonta*) that stresses outdoing or exceeding others.[45] Further, this example likely alludes to the common trope of the ship of state that needs the cooperation of all for a successful "voyage." Heracles' presence endangers the equality, and thus the safety, of all. As Forsdyke observes, Heracles' abandonment is being compared by Aristotle to an ostracism in a manner that had become typical for how the Athenian imagination conceived of its heroes: "Indeed the tradition that the mythical Athenian hero Theseus was ostracized suggests that ostracism became a necessary attribute of heroes in the Athenian imagination" (Forsdyke 2005: 153).[46]

Thus, given the nosological metaphorical structure in Euripides' tragedy about this hero, it is appropriate that Theseus, the emblem of Athenian democracy in such dramas as the *Suppliants* and *Oedipus at Colonus*, provides the last words concerning illness, and does so in an immediately political context that evokes elites and the dynamics of expulsion and inclusion (1413–14):[47]

> Ἡρακλῆς
> ζῶ σοι ταπεινός; ἀλλὰ πρόσθεν οὐ δοκῶ.
> Θησεύς
> ἄγαν γ᾽· ὁ κλεινὸς Ἡρακλῆς οὐκ εἶ νοσῶν.

> **Heracles**
> In your view should I live so humbled? I don't think I did before.
> **Theseus**
> Very much so; you, being sick, are not the famous Heracles.

Theseus acknowledges, on the one hand, that Heracles' madness has humbled, if not humiliated, him to the point that Heracles' solitary life of heroic glory (*kleinos*) cannot continue, but, on the other, that moving Heracles toward a more democratic life means a cure for the *nosos*. But the *nosos* itself has been a cathartic first step in moving Heracles toward the cooperative

---

[45] The absoluteness of the participle, lacking any object or dependent clause, might suggest the action or state of being excessive, as opposed to exceeding others.

[46] See Ar. *Plut.* 627, Plut. *Thes.* 32–35. Rosenbloom 2004a: 57 adds: "Surviving an ostrakophoria was a rite of passage into the highest level of leadership in the fifth-century democracy."

[47] I should note here that text at the end of the *Heracles* is by no means certain. See Bond 1981: 412–13.

values of the Athenian *polis*. Before the final stichomythiac dialogue that climaxes with the final reference to Heracles' *nosos*, the hero beholds his murderous weapons and does not know whether to keep them with him or not. Even the word for his indecision is part of the nosological discourse of the drama, as *amêchanein* (ἀμηχανῶ, 1378) means in general "to be at a loss," yet, in this context, still evokes the medical associations of *mêchanê* that I discussed earlier. On the one hand, Heracles says, "I am at a loss as to whether I keep them or let them go," but he also could say, "I lack healing whether I keep them or let them go." He decides to retain them since, as Papadopoulou argues (Papadopoulou 2005: 179), "the weapons become symbolic of the gradual change in Heracles." The mighty Heracles has become vulnerable, and Theseus recognizes that his illness ends, for now at least, the life of heroic glory. Being humbled, *tapeinos*, means health, and thus "all the city of Athens," πᾶς Ἀθηναίων πόλις (1333), will honor Heracles once he goes there with Theseus; entry to and honor in democratic Athens is ultimately predicated on Heracles not being a bearer of the *nosos* of *stasis*. But when Heracles returns to the Theater of Dionysus a few years later, he becomes a source of healing for the hero of Sophocles' *Philoctetes* and, ultimately, the community of the Achaean army camped outside the walls of Troy. How that happens is my next subject.

CHAPTER 9

The Athenian Asklepieion and the end
of the Philoctetes

Fifteen to twenty years after the *Trachiniae* and roughly six after the *Heracles* of Euripides, Heracles returns to the Theater of Dionysus, though not as the lead role, in another tragic drama whose hero is a bearer of *nosos* and who stands in an ambivalent relationship with his community, and with no obvious connection to the city of Athens. However, one of the central paradoxes of Sophocles' *Philoctetes*, and of the efforts of modern interpreters to understand it, is the opposition between the drama's setting on the isolated, barren island of Lemnos, far from anything resembling a *polis*, and the pervasive consensus among a very diverse group of scholars that this work has something to do, however elusive it might ultimately be, with the nature of the Athenian *polis* at the end of the fifth century BCE (Jameson 1956; Calder 1971; Segal 1981; Greengard 1987; Vickers 1987; Rose 1992). My contribution to clarifying this relationship will be to reexamine the text's discourse of healing and cure in the light of the associations among disease, social strife, the language of democracy, and the cult of Asclepius, the figure who, according to Heracles at the end of the drama, will finally cure Philoctetes. Sophocles' vision of social healing reverses the Euripidean equation of the expulsion or destruction of the aristocratic hero, seen in such dramas as the *Hippolytus*, *Heracles* and *Phoenissae*, to stress the need to reintegrate the heroic, aristocratic mode into society, as part of a fundamentally democratic concern for the mixed or balanced polity.[1] The engagement of Sophoclean drama with the Athenian cults of Athena, Heracles and Asclepius and with the topography of the Acropolis provides the key to this interpretation.

Contrary to tradition, at the end of Sophocles' drama the god Heracles twice promises Philoctetes (1332–34, 1338–39) that he will send Asclepius to Troy in order to heal him, but what could Philoctetes' *nosos* and the promise of an Asclepian cure mean for an Athenian sitting in the Theater

---

[1] See Chapter 3, n. 37 above.

of Dionysus in 409 BCE? Because, in 409, the year of the production of the *Philoctetes*, it had been two years since Alcibiades' recall and Athens still continued in turmoil, the homology between the returns of the outcast hero of the Trojan War and of the controversial Athenian aristocrat has seemed an inviting target for many of the drama's investigators, even as the scholarly terrain moved away from searching for correspondence between dramatic and historical personage and toward a more general consideration of drama as an expression of *polis* ideology.[2] Hunting for Alcibiades has always been quite popular, though Jameson also suggested the younger Pericles for Neoptolemus, and Calder even linked Philoctetes with Sophocles himself. Rose's analysis of Sophistic influences on the drama correctly returned the discussion to considering the larger historical and cultural resonances of the drama's discourse (Jameson 1956; Vickers 1987; Calder 1971; Rose 1992). I argue for a different possible topicality for the play, through the invocation of Asclepius by Heracles at the end of the drama. More recently, Stephens reemphasized the importance of remembering "the stark realities of the audience's and Sophocles' recent and current experiences" (Stephens 1995: 156). The construction of the Athenian City Asklepieion adjacent to the Theater of Dionysus figured prominently in this reality.

LEMNOS AND ATHENS

Few Greek tragedies – save, perhaps, the *Hecuba* and *Prometheus Bound* – take such care as the *Philoctetes* does to divorce so completely their actions from the city and civilization, let alone from Athens itself, though the *Hecuba* at least manages to engage problems inherent in Athens' conduct during the Peloponnesian War. The young Neoptolemus and Odysseus arrive at the deserted island of Lemnos during the tenth year of the Trojan War because of a prophecy that Troy cannot be captured without the bow of Heracles and its owner, the hero Philoctetes, whom the Greeks had abandoned there a decade earlier because of the effects of a terrible snake bite he had suffered when he unwittingly stumbled into the shrine of the goddess Chryse. The action of the drama depicts the growing friendship between Philoctetes and Neoptolemus which results in the latter's refusal to keep the bow after he has stolen it. As the two ready their departure for Philoctetes' home instead of to the war at Troy, the god Heracles appears and convinces them to journey to Troy after all. Unlike the Euripidean tragedies

---

[2] The survey in Bowie 1997 of the problem of the relationship between Athenian history and *Philoctetes* is informative and very even-handed. For the relationship between ideology of the *polis* and Athenian drama see Connor 1989 and 1996, Goldhill 1990 and 2000, Seaford 1994 and 2000.

I have discussed thus far, though somewhat resembling the *Trachiniae*, the conflicts in the plot of the *Philoctetes* overtly concern neither the welfare of a city nor the healing of a faction-ridden community. While the schemes of Odysseus to return Philoctetes and his bow (or, after a while, just the bow) to the desperate Achaean army have been seen to represent the goals of the community, as opposed to the individualistic hero Philoctetes, even that community is distant (Beye 1970).

One of the major changes Sophocles made to the Philoctetes myth, as handed down to him by Aeschylus and Euripides, was to empty the island of Lemnos of its inhabitants, completely isolating from any aspect of society the hero Philoctetes, dumped there by the Greeks on the way to Troy because of the disturbances to their community from his wound; the extent of the depopulation of Lemnos becomes very evident when one considers that in the versions by the other two major tragedians the Chorus itself is composed of Lemnians, and not, as with Sophocles, sailors who serve under Neoptolemus.[3]

Sophocles drives this isolation home in the opening two lines of the play, which feature a tone-setting description of the island of Lemnos by Odysseus:

> ἀκτὴ μὲν ἥδε τῆς περιρρύτου χθονὸς
> Λήμνου, βροτοῖς ἄστιπτος οὐδ᾽ οἰκουμένη,
>
> This is the shore of the sea-girt land of
> Lemnos, untrodden by mortals and uninhabited.

Lemnos, readers of Thucydides would recall, figures early in Thucydides' plague narrative as the only named location of the outbreak of the plague before it reached Athens, and now here it becomes the remote, solitary home of a carrier of Philoctetes, who carries *nosos* with him. The dominant concern with the isolated nature of the island becomes even more apparent if one compares it to other Sophoclean openings such as the *Ajax*, which plunges us into Athena's rough urging of Odysseus to find Ajax, or the *Antigone*, which launches by immediately spelling out the cause of the heroine's distress. These dramas establish immediately their concerns with the relationship between heroes and their communities. In other words, in the *Philoctetes* Sophocles seems to have gone out of his way to move the drama's action out of the realm of the concerns of the *polis*, stressing instead the absence of any form of collective. This separation is especially apparent in the play's language, where words such as *erêmos*, "desolate," echo

---

[3] See Jebb's (1897) discussions in his introduction xxx–xxxi and the notes to verses 2 and 302.

thematically throughout the drama.[4] On the other hand, after Odysseus' evocation of Athena Polias, "Athena of the City," at 134 (an evocation to which I shall devote more attention later), words denoting civic collectives such as *astu* are completely absent and *polis* itself occurs only four other times: the first instance (386) features a gnomic utterance by Neoptolemus on the dependence of an army and a city on its leaders, which even Jebb has conceded might be a reference to the oligarchic revolution of the 400 in 411 BCE. In the second case, Philoctetes laments being *apolis*, "cityless" (1018), and later, when the now bowless Philoctetes contemplates suicide he cries ὦ πόλις, ὦ πατρία, "O city, O fatherland" (1213).[5] Finally, Heracles, appearing as a deity above the cave of Philoctetes, gives his orders to his former protégé that he should travel to the city of Troy (1423–24):

> ἐλθὼν δὲ σὺν τῷδ' ἀνδρὶ πρὸς τὸ Τρωικὸν
> πόλισμα, πρῶτον μὲν νόσου παύσει λυγρᾶς,

> By going with this man to the Trojan
> city, you will first cease from this terrible disease.

In the first straightforward reference to a city in the play, Heracles links Philoctetes' return to a *polis* to his healing, a linkage stressed by the quadruple alliteration of labial consonants in πρὸς τὸ Τρωικὸν πόλισμα, πρῶτον μὲν νόσου παύσει. The separation of Philoctetes from any city is both the effect of his wound and a symptom of the disease. His stubborn refusal to rejoin the army, according to Neoptolemus, reveals the conquest of his social nature by the island's savagery. Thus, paradoxically, the complete removal of the action from the city actually sharpens the focus on the *polis* and its discontents. Stripped of the complexities of *polis* life, its most elemental aspects become readily apparent. And, perhaps even more paradoxically, by removing the drama from any contact with a *polis*, Sophocles can gently refocus his audience on the one *polis* in view: Athens itself. In other words, while the *Philoctetes* abounds in topical references to Lemnos, it lies open, to paraphrase Taplin's 1987 study, to "remapping."

Thus, I shall contend that, while the scene is a rocky shore on Lemnos, the play is "set" in Athens and the drama accomplishes this maneuver because of the widespread connections between Lemnos and Athens during the fifth century. Such a double setting has precedent in Sophocles in his *Oedipus*

---

[4] *Erêmos* appears at 228, 265, 269, 471, 487, 1018. See Segal 1981: 296 and Jones 1962: 217.
[5] Forsdyke 2005: 11 observes that, in the fifth century, *apolis* is frequently a term for exile. In addition to *Phil.* 1018 Forsdyke cites Hdt. 7.104.4, 8.61.1 and Soph. *OC* 1357, as well as the similar *apopolis* and *aptolis* in A. *Ag.* 1410, Soph. *OT* 1000, *OC* 208 and *Tr.* 647.

Tyrannus, which is "full of expressions, emphases and references which suggests an Athenian rather than a Theban setting" (Knox 1956: 140).[6] Sophocles deploys a similar tactic in the *Philoctetes*. Lemnos itself appears to have been a particularly Athenian part of the Empire.[7] Athenians were the first Greeks to possess the island, an Athenian force led by Miltiades first occupied Lemnos around 500 BCE and the colonists who then inhabited Lemnos never ceased thinking of themselves as culturally Athenian (Parker 1994: 343; Hdt. 6.137–40). Pausanias records (1.28.2) that on the Athenian Acropolis there was a statue of Athena by Phidias: "the best worth seeing of the works of Phidias, the statue of Athena called Lemnian after those who dedicated it." Members of the audience of Sophocles' *Philoctetes* surely must have thought of this particular statue and the relationship between Athens and Lemnos while they watched the drama and heard Odysseus' evocation of a recognizable Athenian Athena. Lemnos is thus part of the equation that suggests Athens.

SOPHOCLES' *PHILOCTETES* AND ATHENIAN CULTS

The first key in recognizing the drama's concern with Athens lies in the evocation by Odysseus of Athena Polias. In the drama's opening scene, Odysseus rapidly and skillfully explains to his young comrade Neoptolemus the specific method, deceit, needed to capture Philoctetes and his bow. Departing from the scene with the explanation of a final fail-safe to back up the planned treachery, Odysseus closes the prologue with a prayer to the gods before the Chorus enters (133–40):

> Ἑρμῆς δ' ὁ πέμπων δόλιος ἡγήσαιτο νῷν
> Νίκη τ' Ἀθάνα Πολιάς, ἣ σῴζει μ' ἀεί.
>
> May Hermes the escorting deceiver lead us
> and Victory, Athena Polias, who saves me always.

Why does Odysseus turn to Hermes and Athena? While it makes perfect sense for Odysseus, at this hour of need, to pray to the two deities who help him the most, the trickster god of travelers and the warrior goddess

---

[6] One might also compare the pains Sophocles takes in the *Ajax* to link its hero to Athens, to the point where he is virtually called an Athenian; see Ormand 1999: 104–05.

[7] Sophocles would have become personally acquainted with the close bond between Lemnos and Athens when he served as a general during the Samian War; Thucydides 1.115.3–4 records how the Athenian leaders took aristocratic hostages from Samos and lodged them in Lemnos after establishing a democracy in Samos, but the Samian rebels stole the hostages back.

of wisdom, the presence of Athena Polias, "Athena of the City," is another matter.[8] In her appearance in the earlier drama *Ajax* Athena had played a role thematically appropriate from Homer's *Odyssey* as the protector of the hero and the enforcer of human limits; the last word of Odysseus' prologue speech in the *Philoctetes*, *aei*, might even nod at the same first word in the *Ajax*, which Athena herself utters.

It is very unclear, however, what Athena might have to do with the *Philoctetes* as Athena Polias. Athena of the City, one might ask, what city? How can Odysseus evoke a City Goddess when there is no city? The first part of the prayer to Athena, in her cult guise as Athena Nike, makes perfect sense, for Odysseus clearly and naturally desires victory in this expedition and in the Trojan War, but completing the reference to Athena as Polias warrants further study. While the evocation of Athena Polias in this cityless play is in itself remarkable, it becomes even more so when one considers that Athena never appears under this designation elsewhere in extant Greek tragedy – admittedly, a smaller corpus than ideal for forming such judgments securely. The only time in tragic drama that Athena receives her cult designation as protector of the city is when there is no city. A strange coincidence is that the sole instance where Aristophanic comedy mentions Athena Polias is in another drama from the same era (and where Alcibiades is also thought to lurk in the background), the *Birds*, where there is no city – or, perhaps more accurately, where the city is in the process of being founded, for this reference occurs when Pisthetaerus and Euelpides, having begun their founding of Cloudcuckooland, wonder which god should serve as protector of their city (*Birds* 828). That Euelpides first suggests Athena Polias shows the title's instantly recognizable function in the Theater of Dionysus in Athens.[9]

I shall now briefly explore the nature of the cult of Athena in Athens, for this foundation will help explain the prominence of Athena Polias at the end of the *Philoctetes'* prologue and, ultimately, its relation to the surprise ending of this drama. The *Philoctetes*, in fact, brings together various facets of the worship of Athena in Athens, especially those that were important late in the fifth century. Despite the modern perception of the greater centrality of Athena Parthenos in Athens, the ancient evidence, as Herington has shown, clearly indicates that "in the fifth century Athena Polias was

---

[8] Calder 1971: 169 insists this line is an interpolation, on the grounds that Athena would never consort with an Odysseus of this nature. Rose 1992: 309 argues against Calder compellingly.

[9] In *Birds* the mention of Athena Polias could also signal that the two comic heroes are beginning their unintended recreation of all they are trying to escape before it even starts!

the goddess of Athens par excellence" (Herington 1955: 26).[10] The adjective *polias*, Herington also observes, "originally meant 'she who dwells on the polis,' the old-fashioned name for the Acropolis." Athena Polias also was associated with two major structures on the Acropolis. First, the principal treasures of Athens, which were held in the Parthenon, belonged to Athena Polias. Second, Athena Polias was the name of the ancient wooden effigy in the Erechtheum, described by Pausanias (1.26.6). Given that the Erechtheum's construction was alluded to in a number of Athenian dramas (Calder 1969; Loraux 1993: 37–71, 172; Sourvinou-Inwood 2003: 25–31), the evocation of Athena Polias in the *Philoctetes* may well have been a further acknowledgment of this building's centrality in Athenian thought. Citing an inscription from 409/8, Herington proposed that the wooden statue of Athena Polias had been moved to the Erechtheum that year, roughly the time of the production of the *Philoctetes* (Herington 1955: 23). Moreover, Pausanias adds as one of his first visual details of this area a few sections later (1.27.1): "In the temple of Athena Polias is a wooden Hermes, said to have been dedicated by Cecrops." Images of Hermes and Athena, two gods naturally associated with Odysseus as wise trickster figures, are clustered close together on the Acropolis and in Odysseus' speech, thus suggesting that any reference here to Athena Polias in the Erechtheum could extend also to Hermes as well, and, as I shall observe below, Hermes, after Odysseus evokes him at the end of the prologue, creeps back in at the end of the *Philoctetes*, this time in association with Philoctetes himself. The combined reference to the two gods' effigies would of course strengthen the local flavor of the drama's setting.

Suggesting a topical, even a generally Athenian, reference to Athena Polias runs my argument afoul of the considerable wisdom of Jebb's commentary on the *Philoctetes*, so some consideration of his contrary opinion on these lines is required. Jebb rightly noted here that cults of Athena Nike and Athena Polias were spread elsewhere in the Greek world, so the references here to them are "not exclusively Athenian . . . Sophocles, though writing for the Athenians, is not making purely local allusions." But Jebb is often reluctant to see in Greek drama anything other than timeless, universal truths, and he strives here to minimize the possible Athenian relevance of these words. Jebb thus, while writing of the early attempts to link the play to the problem of Alcibiades, asserts: "Now, to suppose that Sophocles intended a political allegory of this kind, is surely to wrong him grievously

[10] On the development of the worship of Athena in the fifth century see Garland 1992, Chapter 5. Ridgway 1992 notes the challenges to parts of Herington's thesis that have been subsequently mounted, but these do not seem to affect his argument as it pertains to mine.

as a poet." While Jebb thus posits a vision of the poet rising above the messy fray of his time, he then concedes in the next sentence: "At the same time it must be recognized that the coincidence of date really is remarkable" (xli). And as I have already shown, Jebb seems perfectly comfortable with a Sophocles who can, as a poet, allude to the revolution of the 400 at lines 385ff., and, in his commentary on the *Oedipus Tyrannus*, he allows Sophocles to allude to the two temples of Athena on the Athenian Acropolis. So Jebb's own inconsistency suggests that there is more than one way to look at lines 133–4 of the *Philoctetes*, and the specifically Athenian nature of the references to Athena there are bolstered by the cult activities around the time of the production of this drama on the Acropolis. These are not "purely local allusions," but neither are they strictly universal. Athena Polias, as Herington stressed, simply was the dominant form of Athena in Athens and indelibly part of Athenian self-consciousness in the fifth century, so a creation and performance of a drama by an Athenian in Athens at a time of crisis merits attention, particularly when a prominent character prays to "Athena Polias, who always saves" him (134). Odysseus uses Athena Polias to stress that his actions benefit not himself but the greater good (though whether he is credible is another matter), and in turn he implies that salvation lies in the devotion to that common good.

Two further aspects of the worship of Athena on the Acropolis seem relevant to the concerns of the *Philoctetes*, the non-military nature of the cult of Athena Polias and the additional cult of Athena Hygieia. Odysseus first evokes Athena Nike, "Athena Victory," before turning to Athena Polias, but the underlying concepts of the two cults are not necessarily similar or compatible. Herington points out that the attributes of Athena as she was worshipped in the Parthenon and in the Erechtheum can be sharply distinguished, since, while in the latter sanctuary she was a peaceful goddess, depicted as unarmed and likely overseeing the fertility of the Attic land, in the former she was clearly more a warrior goddess, with Phidias' famous statue showing her in full battle array (Herington 1955: 44; Ridgway 1992). Here again events on the Acropolis seem to coincide with the language of this passage in the *Philoctetes*, for the famous carved parapet of the Temple of Athena Nike on the Acropolis was constructed around 410 BCE. Of course, the presence of the winged goddess Nike in the hand of the monumental statue of Athena Parthenos by Phidias adds to the martial nature of this Athena. Moreover, a number of architectural elements in the Temple of Athena Nike and the Erechtheum (the Temple of Athena Polias, as Ridgway 1992: 137 dubs it) correspond, suggesting further interconnections between the two figures as represented and worshipped on the

Acropolis. Odysseus thus briefly encompasses the two opposite yet complementary aspects of Athena as she was worshipped on the Acropolis in Athens, though the order of his words stresses Athena Polias, for it is she who "always saves" him. Devotion to Athena Polias, the peaceful Athena who guards the fundamental well-being of the *polis*, provides salvation for the hero, and, by extension, for the city as a whole.[11]

This concern with finding safety in Athena connects further with another aspect of the worship of Athena on the Athenian Acropolis that also pertains to the key theme of disease in Sophocles' *Philoctetes*. This is the cult of Athena Hygieia, "Athena Health," which was the most prominent healing sanctuary on the Acropolis before the arrival of Asclepius after the plague (Garland 1992: 132; Parker 1996: 175). In a sense, the ascription of healing powers to Athena seems a bit out of place, and peculiarly local to Athenian religion, but it may have simply arisen from her older fertility function in Attica. At no point in extant fifth-century poetry is she evoked thus and therefore she remains a somewhat murky figure. A later text, Plutarch's *Pericles*, records an anecdote about Athena Hygieia of typically Plutarchian charm and potential questionability (*Per.* 34.7–9). During the construction of the Propylaea one of the workmen fell from very high and was near death, and, as a result, "Pericles was much cast down at this, but the goddess appeared to him in a dream and prescribed a course of treatment for him to use, so that he speedily and easily healed the man. It was in commemoration of this that he set up the bronze statue of Athena Hygieia on the Acropolis near the altar of that goddess, which was there before, as they say." Pliny repeats an identical story (*HN* 22.44), which, combined with the chronology of construction and the location of the extant base, supports Plutarch's account. This dream is likely an etiological story to account for Pericles' construction of a statue to Athena Hygieia on the Acropolis (Ehrenberg 1954: 94), but there is not very much information beyond that story, and her cult appears to have been the main victim of Asclepius' popular arrival during the Peace of Nicias, since there are no extant dedications to Athena Hygieia dating later than 420. She does seem to have some kind of prominence in the 420s, after the great plague, since the monument to her was located next to the Propylaea and dates after 432, with an inscription that is thought to have been written in the early 420s (Ridgway 1992: 137). Thus, a surge in interest in Athena Hygieia could

---

[11] Rose 1992: 309 argues that the epithet Polias "implies broadly the supports of organized political life but also strongly suggests contemporary democratic Athens." Jameson 1956: 227 in turn asks: "Is it mere coincidence that these three gods, Hermes, Athena Polias, Athena Nike, whose moneys, controlled by the Treasurers of the Goddess, played an important part in Athens' war finances?"

have prepared the ground for the arrival of Asclepius. A further connection with Asclepius is that this cult title functions also as the name of Asclepius' daughter, who came to be worshipped prominently herself. Pausanias records that on the Acropolis there were two statues named Hygieia, one of Asclepius' daughter and another of Athena Hygieia (1.23.4). Elsewhere, Pausanias reports that at Tegea a statue of Athena is flanked by images of Hygieia and Asclepius (8.47.1). In Athens, the significance in the proximity of Athena Hygieia, Asclepius, and his daughter would have been further enriched by the snakes that were attributes of both deities, and we should not forget here that this was the very animal which wounded Philoctetes.[12] The text of the *Oedipus Tyrannus* offers a further connection, albeit more indirect, between Asclepius and Athena as healers. In the first stasimon, the Chorus, desperately praying to the gods to help save their city from plague, in the first strophe initially calls upon Apollo (the father of Asclepius) as "Delian Healer," Δάλιε Παιάν (154), before praying in the antistrophe to the trio Athena, Artemis and Apollo (158–62), grouped together as *aleximoroi*, "averters of death."[13]

Clearly, given the shared names and functions, there was some kind of deeper, significant relationship between Athena and Asclepius, and recognizing the full implications of this association requires a reconceptualization of the civic nature of the Asclepius cult on the Acropolis. We tend to think of health as an individual concern, yet for the densely populated *polis*, especially Athens during the plague years overcrowded because of the Peloponnesian War, it was a problem for the community as a whole on the literal level, and health quickly became a symbol for the general well-being of the body politic (Krug 1993: 120). Thus, Parker suggests, "Athena Hygieia's role was essentially prophylactic, and directed to the health of the community as a whole, not of individuals" (Parker 1996: 175). Sophocles' drama thus begins with the evocation of a deity in a specifically Athenian form and explicitly linked by Odysseus to his personal safety, a goddess who had until a mere decade before been prominently conceived as the primary deity overseeing the communal health of Athens, a function unlikely to have been completely forgotten because of the arrival of the figure of Asclepius, evoked at the end of the *Philoctetes*. The two healing deities thus provide a significant frame for the intervening action, and it is to the connection between frame and action that I turn after considering another significant element of the relationship between the *Philoctetes* and the Athenian Acropolis.

[12] Greengard 1987 links the snakes in the Asclepius cult and the *Philoctetes*. On snakes and healing see Kearns 1989: 16.
[13] This divine triad is repeated, without the epithet, at *OC* 1090–95.

ASCLEPIUS AND ASKLEPIEION: REMAPPING THE ACTION OF THE *PHILOCTETES*

As scholars have begun to work out the particularly Athenian nature of tragic drama and the importance of recognizing the "embeddedness" of this literature on the Acropolis, increased attention has come to the interplay between the topography of the drama's setting and the topography of the Acropolis. David Wiles (1997) has shown the need to include consideration of the performative space of the Theater of Dionysus when we try to determine the meaning and function of drama in fifth-century Athens.[14] The Asklepieion, constructed during the decade before the production of Sophocles' *Philoctetes*, was located at the north-west corner of the Theater of Dionysus (Aleshire 1989; Garland 1992: 116–35; Parker 1996: 177–81), and just as the temple ruins wrought by the Persians during their invasion in 480 and 479 would have produced a powerful political effect on the theater audience who looked over their shoulders during the performance of Aeschylus' *Persians* in 472 (Cartledge 1997: 19), so too would the new shrine to the healing deity, imported from Epidaurus during the Peace of Nicias (Mikalson 1984: 220), have meaningfully interacted with dramas where disease functioned as a metaphor. The introduction of Asclepius at the end of the *Philoctetes* is thus important as it reconfigured, at its first production, the performative space as Athenian, and improbably so, given that drama's stress on the physical realities of Lemnos.

A subtle network of references to Asclepius that has run throughout the text's center suddenly becomes prominent with the unexpected epiphany of Heracles at its end, but the epiphany, and the introduction of Asclepius, while unexpected, still come as a consequence of careful preparation by Sophocles in the drama's themes and language. Heracles himself was worshipped as *Alexikakos* ("Averter of evils"), a healing deity, and was strongly associated with Asclepius (Kearns 1989: 14–15; Parker 1996: 175, 186).[15] In building on the earlier themes of illness and cure, Heracles reminds the audience that the illness of Philoctetes extends beyond his physical body to his social relationship with the world. Heracles' speech twice links healing to Philoctetes' presence at the city of Troy (1423–24):

---

[14] See also Cartledge 1997. Wiles has an Athenocentric perspective, and one must allow that such dramas were quickly staged with success in other *poleis*, but my concern is the production of the *Philoctetes* in 409, in Athens.

[15] Greengard 1987: 7 and 91 elucidates the importance of the Heracles cult in Athens for the end of the *Philoctetes*, which he shows was (7) "similarly referential to and empowered by an external reality: in this case, the audience's predictable response to invocation of the religious cult of Heracles by the playwright."

ἐλθὼν δὲ σὺν τῷδ' ἀνδρὶ πρὸς τὸ Τρωικὸν
πόλισμα, πρῶτον μὲν νόσου παύσει λυγρᾶς,

By going with this man to the Trojan
city, you will first cease from this terrible disease.

Throughout the drama, Philoctetes' wound has been cast in language that
links it to his uncivilized existence, so Heracles seems almost to imply that
the main step in healing Philoctetes is the reentry itself into civilization.[16]
The shift in the adjective describing the illness, from "savage" (*agria*) to the
somewhat milder "terrible" (*lugras*) initiates this process; contact with the
divinized Heracles immediately ameliorates savagery. After further describing the future heroic exploits of Philoctetes and Neoptolemus, Heracles
returns to an explanation of how Philoctetes will be physically healed that
strongly echoes 1423–24 in its content, labial alliterations and the repetition of a form of *pauein*: ἐγὼ δ' Ἀσκληπιὸν / παυστῆρα πέμψω σῆς
νόσου πρὸς Ἴλιον, "and I shall send Asclepius to Troy to stop your disease"
(1437–38). The sudden appearance of Heracles at this point in the action
is matched in its unexpectedness by the announcement that Asclepius will
be the healer.

The naming of Asclepius here is yet another way in which Sophocles in
the *Philoctetes* either threatens to alter traditional myth, or actually does
so, and while the threat to send Philoctetes and Neoptolemus home is the
most obvious potential breach, the unprecedented inclusion of Asclepius
is neither insignificant nor unrelated to the rest of this drama, or even to
Athenian drama in general during the last quarter of the fifth century.[17]
The first fragment of Proclus' summary of the *Little Iliad* reports that
in that narrative Philoctetes is healed by Machaon, whom Homer's *Iliad*
identifies as the son of Asclepius (11.613–14). The Catalogue of the Ships
further has Machaon joined by his brother Podalirius as the two sons of
Asclepius at Troy (*Il.* 2.731). Neoptolemus, castigating Philoctetes for his
stubbornness and trying to persuade him to come to Troy of his own free
will, promises him healing by "the sons of Asclepius" (1333–34), who he
knows are at Troy, thus following the epic tradition. Since Neoptolemus
now has completely shown his hand to all the players, this promise cannot

---

[16] E.g. 173, 266. Neoptolemus' angry pleas to Philoctetes (1321–35) bring to fulfillment these associations
between Philoctetes' social isolation and his wound. See Segal 1981: 300–15.

[17] Scholars have paid surprisingly little attention to the presence of Asclepius in Heracles' speech.
Winnington-Ingram 1980: 302 merely notes the "inconsistency" of who will do the healing. The
two important articles by Deborah Roberts (1988 and 1989) on the ending of the *Philoctetes* say
nothing about the subject, while Greengard 1987: 91–93 at least recognizes than more is happening
in these lines than scholars have generally allowed.

be part of the set of mysteries and evasions that otherwise dog interpreters of this drama. Despite Sophocles' divergences from previous versions of the myth in other parts of the drama, such as the substitution of Neoptolemus for Diomedes and the presentation of Lemnos as a desert island, Neoptolemus and Sophocles are following and reaffirming the script handed to them from the epic tradition, and they lead the audience to expect that the drama's ending will stay true to form; thus, Heracles' words startle the son of Achilles as well.[18] What Heracles offers comes as a surprise, but not, upon closer reexamination of the previous parts of the drama, as a complete one.

First, given the divine cause of Philoctetes' wound and its specific origin with a snake, combined with precedent in dramatic versions of episodes from the Epic Cycle of a wound healed by the wounder, it seems appropriate that Asclepius, whose most prominent symbol was his serpent, be the healer of Philoctetes.[19] But another deity mentioned earlier in the *Philoctetes*, Athena, certainly had, as a result of her chthonic origins, strong associations with snakes, as seen frequently in Greek art, with the foremost example the huge snake coiled at her legs in Phidias' monumental statue in the Parthenon. Because of the First Argument and scholia on lines 194 and 1326 that identify Chryse with Athena, and the somewhat ill-defined nature of Chryse herself, one has cause to wonder whether Sophocles wants his audience to think about Athena here in some way.[20] The First Hypothesis

[18] Jebb 1897: xxxi conjectures that in Sophocles' lost *Philoctetes at Troy* "Asclepius was introduced as aiding the skill of his sons." He posits that *Philoctetes at Troy* was the earlier play and thus compares allusion to the *Antigone* at the end of the later *Oedipus at Colonus*. Jebb, however, does not account for the relationship between the traditional healing cited by Neoptolemus and the new version offered by Heracles. See Jebb on 1437 for the difference between the knowledge held by Neoptolemus and Heracles.

[19] A snake will be involved in both the attack on Philoctetes and his cure, so further suggesting that the logic of Asclepius' presence in the *Philoctetes* is the precedent of the Telephus legend on the Athenian stage, especially Euripides' *Telephus*, produced in 438 as part of the group that included the *Alcestis*. The *Telephus* likely told how Telephus, who had been earlier wounded by Achilles, now was needed by the Greek army to help them reach Troy. An oracle which indicated that he could be cured by his wounder led him to barter with the Greeks. While much is unknown about this drama, we do know that in it Odysseus persuades Achilles to heal Telephus. While the *Telephus* was produced almost thirty years before the *Philoctetes*, it seems to have stuck in the Athenian theatrical memory, as, in 425, Aristophanes plays it off in one of his most brilliant parodies of Euripides in the *Acharnians*, where Aristophanes takes Euripides to task, as he repeats in the *Frogs*, for dressing heroes in rags. The scenario of the rag-clad and wounded hero thus opens and closes the Trojan War. Note also that at *Acharnians* 423 Euripides offers Dikaiopolis the costume of Philoctetes, which Dikaiopolis rejects as insufficiently wretched before adopting Telephus for his persona. Presumably Aristophanes here is thinking of Euripides' own *Philoctetes* of 431. On Euripides' *Telephus* see Webster 1967: 43–48 and Heath 1987.

[20] On Chryse see Segal 1981: 308–12. Jebb 1897: xl and in the note on 1327 discusses briefly the scholia. Segal 1995: 110 observes how careful Philoctetes is to avoid speaking ill of, let alone cursing, the divinity that caused the wound.

begins with the assertion that Philoctetes received his wound at the altar
of Athena on the island which is also called Chryse.[21] While Jebb's notes
on line 1327 dismiss any full identification of Chryse with Athena, "yet,"
Jebb concedes, "the associations of the Erechtheum have suggested the
word οἰκουρῶν. The sacred serpent in that temple – representative of
Erichthonius and guardian of Athena Polias – was regularly called οἰκουρὸς
ὄφις."[22] It is possible that the later Alexandrian author of the Hypothesis
was influenced by such fifth-century language that so strongly points to
the worship of Athena in Athens. Chryse is not Athena, yet Sophocles can
exploit overlaps between the two as part of the redirection of the drama
to Asclepius and Athens; the goddess is Chryse, but she is also, in a sense
meaningful to the Athenian audience, Athena. As I discussed earlier, the full
meaning of Odysseus' prayer to Athena Polias depends on the audience's
awareness of the recent completion of the Erechtheum and the nature
of Athena Polias as a principal deity of Athens. As I shall argue below,
evocations of Athena and Asclepius as saviors in a specifically Athenian
context frame the action of the *Philoctetes*. Just as Asclepius supplanted
Athena Hygieia on the Acropolis, so too he succeeds her in the drama.
Thus, as a deity and a serpent wounded Philoctetes, so will a deity and a
serpent heal Philoctetes. With the broader context of Sophocles' *Philoctetes*
thus established, I shall now look again at how Sophocles prepares his
audience for Asclepius inside the drama.

POETRY AND PERFORMANCE

Language, poetic form and performative context set the stage for the arrival
of Asclepius. First, Sophocles carefully prepares his audience for the introduction of Asclepius at the end of the drama by beginning the first *kommos*
with a Hymn to Sleep (Hypnos), after Philoctetes has collapsed in pain and
handed the bow over to Neoptolemus (827–32):

> Ὕπν' ὀδύνας ἀδαής, Ὕπνε δ' ἀλγέων,
> εὐαὲς ἡμῖν ἔλθοις,
> εὐαίων εὐαίων, ὦναξ
> ὄμμασι δ' ἀντίσχοις
> τάνδ' αἴγλαν, ἃ τέταται τανῦν.
> ἴθι ἴθι μοι παιών.

---

[21] The Second Hypothesis omits mention of both Athena and Chryse.
[22] Jebb cites the entry in Hesychius for οἰκουρὸν ὄφιν, as well as Arist. *Lys.* 758 and Hdt. 8.41.

> Sleep, who knows no pain, Sleep, who knows no anguish,
> come in favor to us,
> come happy, and giving happiness, my lord!
> Keep before his eyes such light of healing
> as is spread before them now.
> Come, come to me, Healer!

Haldane has shown how the invocation ἴθι ἴθι μοι παιών ("Come, come to me, Healer") is intended to recall the paean song, and that the hymn as a whole should be read in light of Sophocles' association with the Asclepius cult (Haldane 1963: 54).[23] While Haldane's analysis of the generic aspects of this hymn remains pertinent and compelling, the references to Asclepius warrant redirection, as Haldane neither includes the immediate proximity of the Asklepieion to the Theater of Dionysus nor links the Hymn to the role of Asclepius at the drama's close. But, as I argued earlier, the tradition of the role of Sophocles in the introduction of Asclepius to Athens is at best questionable,[24] so to understand more fully this paean's role in the *Philoctetes* one needs to look again at the text as a whole and the topography of the Acropolis. Haldane offers the suggestion that "the short hymn must at every point have recalled to Sophocles' audience the liturgy of the new cult of Asclepius" (Haldane 1963: 56), but it is worth asking why Sophocles would care to remind his audience at this juncture of the drama. I thus submit that Sophocles is setting his audience up for the change in the traditional healer of Philoctetes and continuing to direct his public to think about the significance of the religious topography of the Acropolis. I shall set aside the role of the topography for a moment in order to discuss further how the poetic structure of the drama prepares the way for Asclepius.

Second, Sophocles uses meter in addition to genre to redirect his audience, as Heracles speaks in anapests that disrupt the marching trochaics of what had appeared to be the exit of Philoctetes and Neoptolemus from the stage. Neoptolemus has decided to honor his pledge to protect Philoctetes and take him home in a move that surely astonished the audience which took their roles in the sack of Troy as unchanging and unchangeable parts of the Troy saga; such radical revisions, or threats to make them, the audience typically expected from Euripides, not so much from Sophocles. But Sophocles has yet another surprise ready, Heracles, whom he had sent off to be divinized at the end of the *Trachiniae*. And, as with the *Trachiniae*, Sophocles signals these unusual and momentous events with adroit exploitations

---

[23] Rutherford 2001: 110 observes that the noun *aiglê* is especially associated with Asclepius.
[24] Lefkowitz 1981: 84. See also Chapter 7, n. 15 above.

of the possibilities of poetic meter. The abrupt shift from trochaics to the anapests in the apparent, though false, ending makes the entrance of Heracles as startling to the audience as it is to Philoctetes and his comrade. Meredith Hoppin has shown that the anapests in the final scene create a divine aura around Heracles, shift the discourse from the human to the divine plane in a religious ritual, and "break dramatic illusion and rupture the dramatic frame".[25] Hoppin builds on the work of Sylvia Brown, whose study of the functions of anapests in tragic drama was crucial to my earlier analysis of the exodus of the *Trachiniae*. The anapests remind the audience that it is watching a theatrical event and distance its members from the action they are watching. Hoppin shows how the power of the change to anapests then shifts the action to a higher mimetic reality so that the "second" ending has more authority and power than the first: "once the second ending is underway it is even more integral to the play than the first ending was" (Hoppin 1990: 161).[26]

The abruptness of Heracles' entrance and its consequent disruptive effect are strongly linked to Philoctetes' first attempt to leave at 538 and the subsequent attack of pain and sleep that prevents it, events that were marked by the first oblique introduction of Asclepius, as we have already seen, through the Hymn to Sleep. In the structure of the *Philoctetes* the divinity of Heracles' epiphany balances the god-sent assault of Philoctetes' *nosos*, since the paroxysm prefaces one mirror scene (893–96) and the epiphany succeeds the other (1402) (Hoppin 1990: 162).[27] Hoppin further shows the thematic links between paroxysm and epiphany, yet somehow misses the way Heracles' introduction of Asclepius as Philoctetes' healer completes the distant evocation of the son of Apollo in the Hymn to Sleep. Moreover, the Chorus closes its ode just before the attack of pain on Philoctetes with an evocation of the divinization of Heracles on Mt. Oeta (726–29), which, of course, points forward to the end of the drama when the god Heracles himself appears. What has been a prayer for temporary respite from pain in the Hymn to Sleep, a remote hope that some permanent cure might be found, finds final fruition in the promise of Asclepius in the last scene. The introduction of Asclepius thus is inextricably linked with the center

---

[25] Hoppin 1990: 160. Hoppin develops broader ideas on anapests from Brown 1977. For the sake of clarity, I shall be repeating some ideas about the anapest from my earlier chapter on the *Trachiniae*.

[26] Hoppin continues and buttresses the modern trend in criticism of seeing the ending as integral to the preceding action, as opposed to being merely ironic or gratuitous. For a survey of this controversy see Easterling 1978: 32–39. The controversy has continued beyond the publication of Easterling's article, though its basic terms have not changed.

[27] On the mirror scenes see Taplin 1971: 27–29.

of the drama, and Sophocles makes the change in the identity of the healer of Philoctetes, who had been announced by Neoptolemus at 1333–34, a necessary component of the plot.

The anapests momentarily disrupt, and then shift, the audience's attention, while the content of Heracles' speech binds the scene to what had preceded it, but the disruption could also redirect the audience to the real religious life of Athens around them. In tragedy the anapestic meter can indicate the accession to the realm of the gods and trigger the audience's renewed awareness of its presence at a production in the theater. Hoppin concludes (Hoppin 1990: 173):

> For those spectators who choose to participate fully in the second ending, its anapests have indeed fulfilled both functions. They have acknowledged that the play's action is a substitute operating at one remove, but they have decided to accept the action as the real event. They will believe in the god's intervention since, as at all religious rites, only the god's presence can make the rite effective.

But there is more than one god intervening here, indirectly, though significantly, and that additional god, in an important sense, is present. If indeed the new anapests do momentarily distance the audience, making it newly aware of watching a mimetic enactment while binding it anew to the moment's religiosity, then the audience, while hearing the content of those anapestic lines, would be more likely to be aware of the relationship between Heracles' promise to Philoctetes and the topography of the south slope of the Acropolis that surrounds the Theater of Dionysus.

When Heracles promises Philoctetes that Asclepius will come to Troy to heal the suffering hero's wound, Sophocles makes a special direct appeal to the surroundings of the Theater of Dionysus that, aside from references to the god Dionysus, is without parallel in Athenian tragic drama. Sophocles shifts the identity of the healer from tradition in order to take advantage of the adjacency of the Asklepieion. The topography of the south slope of the Acropolis plays a significant role in the end of the *Philoctetes* by engaging the dynamics of social and personal healing to extend that healing through the acting area, into the audience and beyond. I have already shown how disease imagery and paean songs in Euripides' *Heracles* and *Phoenissae*, produced within the five years before the *Philoctetes*, are meaningfully related to the construction of the Asklepieion at the north-west edge of the *theatron* of the Theater of Dionysus; in other words, *Philoctetes'* relationship to its environment is not unique, but its awareness of that relationship, as manifested in the instructions and gestures of Heracles, is. Perched above the *skênê*, Heracles commands the acting area, looking out over the other two

actors and Chorus, to the spectators and above them.[28] With the audience's
attention newly engaged by his unexpected appearance and directed by the
anapests that accompanied it, Heracles, I propose, points over the audience's
heads to the new home of the god Asclepius himself, a gesture that, in
keeping with the effect of the anapests, momentarily ruptures the dramatic
illusion, yet at the same time draws the city of Athens into the Theater of
Dionysus as part of the meaning of the drama. While actors certainly could
make plenty of unscripted gestures, the topography of the south slope of
the Acropolis and its relationship to the themes of this drama motivate a
gesture by Heracles toward the Asklepieion.

My proposal here finds support in the direction of the exit of Philoctetes
and Neoptolemus. Oliver Taplin has shown that Sophocles in the *Philoctetes*
does not use one of the two *eisodoi* flanking the orchestra, "while loading
the other with unprecedentedly complex and shifting meaning" (Taplin
1987: 72). Taplin does not specify which of the two *eisodoi* remains unused,
nor does he elaborate his claims for symbolic complexity, but I suspect that
full realization of this requires thinking about the *eisodoi* in relation to the
topography of the south slope of the Acropolis. David Wiles, following
Taplin's lead, has in fact sketched out the symbolism of the entrances, with
the left (audience's left and true east) unused entrance representing nature –
where Philoctetes hunts and gathers food – and the active (right and west)
entrance representing the path to the bay, and thus civilization and culture
(Wiles 1997: 153–54).[29] Wiles argues convincingly that the physical dynamic
of the *Philoctetes* is consistent with this normal left–right paradigm, and
he cites the reference by Neoptolemus to the rising of the sun in support.
Neoptolemus, trying to convince Philoctetes to leave the island with him,
reminds his suffering friend that he will never be healed (1330–31) "while
the sun which rises here sets there." "The 'here' of Lemnos," argues Wiles,
"seems to be defined by the actor's gesture as east, whilst Chryse, Troy and
elsewhere are defined as west." If we assume that Sophocles uses the real
orientation of the Theater, it is clear that Neoptolemus points first to the
east and then to the west, consecutively in two different directions, thus
anticipating the significant deictic gesture of Heracles. Both gestures rely
on the physical reality around the audience and both involve the healing of

---

[28] Mastronarde 1990: 283 places Heracles either on the roof of the *skênê* or "perhaps" on the crane.
Wiles 1997: 181 sees "no reason" why Heracles should not be on the roof. Given the attention paid
to the nature of Philoctetes' cave as represented by the *skênê*, placing Heracles above it while he ends
Philoctetes' domicile there would be both thematically and theatrically appropriate.

[29] Wiles shows how this polarity is paradigmatic in the staging of tragedy in the Athenian Theater of
Dionysus. Wiles' stress on polarities has not been universally accepted; see Revermann 2000.

Philoctetes. The exit then binds the gestures of Neoptolemus and Heracles further together, as Neoptolemus and Philoctetes exit together to the right, to the west, and toward the Athenian Asklepieion. The movement that comes as a consequence of Heracles' instructions in a sense reverses them as those instructions are enacted by the actors, for, essentially, Heracles does not just send Asclepius to Philoctetes in Troy, but he also dispatches Philoctetes to Asclepius in Athens. Moreover, the gestures of Neoptolemus are immediately preceded by his reference (1327–28) to Chryse, who, I noted earlier, should evoke (though not necessarily be equated with) Athena, and to Chryse's "roofless shrine," protected by a guardian snake, which was traditionally associated with the snake in the Erechtheum, the temple of Athena Polias.

This localization of the drama's reference balances, and perhaps thus helps explain, the curious evocation of Athena Polias by Odysseus that I discussed earlier. The Chorus itself might strengthen this connection because, as it exits the orchestra, chanting again in anapests, it prays to the Nymphs of the sea to be "saviors of homecoming (1471)." The noun σωτῆρας clearly echoes the verb σώζει, in the prayer of Odysseus to Athena Polias (134), "who always saves " him.[30] Already Philoctetes had unknowingly almost quoted and thus appropriated Odysseus' words in his own description of the fire in his cave, which "always saves" him (ὃ καὶ σώζει μ' ἀεί, 297), so, if one takes together all these instances, salvation develops as a key motif through the course of the drama. While Odysseus has achieved his goal, the larger concern of safety or salvation has shifted from the schemes of an amoral manipulator to Philoctetes, and, finally to the community as a whole, as represented by the Chorus of sailors, a collective of potentially great resonance for the Athenian audience, many of whom had served in the army, if not the navy itself.[31] Words thus echo from beginning to end, binding the parts of the drama together, as do the evocations of the Athenian Acropolis, and they do so in yet another way as well. In his farewell speech to the landscape of Lemnos, Philoctetes hails (1459–60) "the mountain of Hermes which echoed in response to my groaning while I was suffering." The name of Hermes, Athena's companion in the Erechtheum, thus appears for the second time in the drama, moving from Odysseus at the end of the prologue to Philoctetes at the close of the drama, and no longer simply a trickster god evoked by Odysseus as an escort

---

[30] The theme of salvation in the *Philoctetes* has been discussed from varying angles by Avery 1965, Jameson 1956 and Rose 1992.

[31] The specific identity of the Chorus as sailors has been disputed. Kosak 1999: 121 succinctly summarizes the arguments for and against, concluding that the chorus members are in fact sailors.

in his mission of deception; Hermes, in a sense, provided companionship to Philoctetes as much as to Odysseus, and the god is now drawn into the happier, more inclusive, vision of the world made possible by the promise of healing. The presence of the divinized Heracles here might also recall the invocation of Athena Nike at the end of the prologue (134), since it was Athena Nike who was represented on Athenian vases as escorting the transfigured Heracles to Olympus, an approach which the Chorus also commemorates earlier (727–28).[32]

SOPHOCLES' *PHILOCTETES* AND THE ATHENS OF 409 BCE

The dramatic space of the *Philoctetes*, thus remapped, raises new questions. What do these Athenian references mean for the audience members who sit in the Theater of Dionysus at Athens in 409 BCE? Given that Sophocles gives such an intense sense of the place of Lemnos, why would he then also point his audience toward their own city? As we have already seen, it certainly was not unprecedented for Sophocles, or for Euripides, to engage in a double setting for a drama's action, placing it in a city other than Athens, while constructing a clearly Athenian framework around the primary city through references to Athenian landmarks and institutions (Knox 1956; Mitchell-Boyask 1999: 49–59). This move allows the poet to universalize the action's significance while still keeping the audience aware that the drama is pertinent to their immediate concerns. Sophocles' emptying Lemnos of its inhabitants, working against the tradition of a normally populated island carried on by Aeschylus and Euripides, marks that depopulation as significant. The irony of the natural setting of this drama is that it makes much more visible, and thus highlighted, any reference to Athenian life and its problems.

Sophocles can also exploit the physical nature of the *theatron* to unite his audience with the characters and their concerns. David Wiles has shown how the open *theatron* and the immediacy of the acting area to the spectators incorporated the audience into the spatial field of the performance.[33] When actors address any group or the larger world, the audience becomes part of that community. Similarly, the *theatron* can be associated with a mountainous slope, such as Mt. Cithaeron, so important to Dionysus, or, as is the case at present, Mt. Oeta, or even the mountain of Hermes called

---

[32] See Jebb's note on line 1031 of his commentary on the *Trachiniae*.
[33] Wiles 1997, especially Chapter 10, "*Orchestra* and *Theatron*."

upon by Philoctetes at the end. Starting with the example of Mt. Cithaeron in the *Oedipus Tyrannus*, Wiles observes (Wiles 1997: 215):

The performance interpellates the slope of the Acropolis as much as the citizen body seated on it. On Philoctetes' lonely island of Lemnos, where there can be no public assembly, Mount Oeta across the sea seems in the same way to be associated with the *theatron*. Philoctetes gazes across the sea at the community from which he has been severed, and Heracles gazes at the site of his apotheosis.[34]

I have already demonstrated a certain permeability between dramatic setting and performance space operative in the semantics of the *Philoctetes*, so I can now consider a reversal of the identity of that distanced community and the hero's relationship to it. The audience can become inhabitants of Philoctetes' home city, but it can also associate itself with the Chorus of sailors who accompany Neoptolemus. An inanimate mountain cannot reciprocate the pangs of separation, but a collection of human beings can. Alienation from community has had its corollary in Philoctetes' wound that has made him savage, and on that slope where Philoctetes gazes is the temple of the god whom Heracles will send to Philoctetes as he becomes resocialized and thus healed at Troy. The *theatron* thus marks the separation of Philoctetes from home and community and the means of his healing and reintegration. Philoctetes can be saved by something, in a sense, visible to him, and visible to the audience. His troubles are over.

The troubles of the audience, on the other hand, are another matter. One of the primary crises afflicting Athens in the years immediately preceding the production of the *Philoctetes* was the role of Alcibiades in the government of Athens and in the conduct of the Peloponnesian War, with his recall in 411 so tantalizingly evocative of the Greek army's need for Philoctetes at Troy. Attempts by scholars since Lebeau in 1770 to match Alcibiades with one or several characters in Sophocles' drama have proved inconclusive or unsatisfactory (Jameson 1956; Calder 1971; Vickers 1987).[35] While we can never be certain how Sophocles wants his audience to think of Alcibiades when watching the *Philoctetes*, it does seem fairly safe to say that the question of Alcibiades and the strife within Athens energize the thematic concerns of the *Philoctetes*, and the drama itself feeds back into the civic discourse on the stability of the *polis*. As Bowie argues, "particular historical events are made homologous with mythical stories in such a

---

[34] Wiles does not mention Hermes' mountain.
[35] Bowie 1997: 56–61 judiciously surveys the question of whether the characters in Sophocles' drama are meant to represent any historical personages.

way that the action of the dramas provides various models for viewing the events" (Bowie 1997: 61).

One of the models operative here, I think, is the social drama of expulsion (and its opposite) to ensure communal health and stability. Sophocles reverses the Euripidean equation of the expulsion of the hero to heal the sick city, producing a drama wherein, instead, the community only finds salvation by reincorporating the previously expelled hero. Sophocles, at least in his earlier surviving dramas such as the *Ajax*, *Trachiniae* and *Oedipus Tyrannus*, had depicted the annihilation of the heroes whose very success as individuals had endangered the community. Perhaps Sophocles in particular presents a version of this idea already in the *Trachiniae*, where the problematic hero Heracles will not truly serve any community until after his apotheosis on Mt. Oeta; like Oedipus he must be destroyed as a human being first. The danger of earlier heroes was figured as a disease, a *nosos*, which must be purged from the body politic, but Sophocles, late in his career, felt impelled to enact dramas such as the *Philoctetes* and *Oedipus at Colonus*, in which heroes were reintegrated into their societies, thus enabling cures for both themselves and their communities. The Euripidean formula was characteristic of democratic Athenian ideology: the city cannot be stable in the presence of the aristocratic hero.[36]

Thus, one might ask with justification whether Sophocles in the *Philoctetes* is offering a rather "undemocratic" cure for the ills of Athens.[37] I do not think a simply reversible equation works here, for several reasons. Given the pervasiveness of the metaphor of the sick city and hero in Euripidean drama, Sophocles' almost total isolation of references to illness to the figure of Philoctetes alone becomes quite remarkable. Sophocles makes it quite clear that the Greek army is in dire need, that its leaders are at best driven by questionable motives and use less than admirable methods, but he refrains from any direct link between the *nosos* in Philoctetes and one in the body politic. In the face of the pervasive Euripidean exploitation of this metaphor, its absence here seems a deliberate, or at least motivated, choice by Sophocles, who appears interested here in another permutation of the relationship between the sick hero and the community.

---

[36] See Seaford 1993 and 1994 on the relationship between heroes and the Athenian *polis*. On the importance of exile and expulsion to the Athenian imagination see now Forsdyke 2005.

[37] Rose 1992 subtly explores the relationship between Sophistic beliefs and democratic ideology, concluding that the *Philoctetes* ultimately advocates a renewed aristocratic ethos, thus making the Sophoclean project "counter-revolutionary." It is impossible to think about this drama and contemporary politics without Rose's work, but it will quickly become clear that I think there are other ways to look at the relationship between the *Philoctetes* and the Athenian *polis*.

Expulsion as solution remains the effective pattern throughout the drama, until Heracles makes Philoctetes' reinclusion possible. We are never given a reason to doubt the claims of Odysseus that Philoctetes had disrupted the sacrifices, rituals and battle plans of the army; Philoctetes had introduced disorder to his community.[38] The harsh speech of Neoptolemus after persuasion to leave for Troy begins to fail stresses that Philoctetes violated – willingly or not – a sanctuary of the gods (1326–28) and that the wildness produced by his disease makes him incapable of engaging in productive verbal interaction even with those who seek to be his friends.[39] Exclusion extends even to the thinking of the excluded, for, in the central scene when the full violent attack of pain strikes Philoctetes, he begs Neoptolemus to cut off the wounded foot with his sword (an instrument Philoctetes himself lacks, 747–49). Later, when deprived of his bow, he again begs, this time the Chorus, for an amputation (1200–09). Had he the means, Philoctetes would do to his own body part what Agamemnon, Menelaus and Odysseus did to him. Philoctetes' language in these two moments does not resemble the way characters speak of his exile, which is dominated by forms of *ekballein*, "to throw out" (255, 1034, 1390–91), while at 747–49 and 1249 he uses verbs for cutting and striking. However, at 1201, Philoctetes speaks of "driving off" (ἀπῶσαι) his foot, a verb Sophocles deploys elsewhere for exile (*OT* 641, 670), as does Herodotus (1.173.2). In between these threatened amputations, Philoctetes speaks of himself as *apolis*, "without a city," a common word for exile in the fifth century (Forsdyke 2005: 11). Since Sophocles frequently personifies the wound on Philoctetes' foot (e.g. βρύχομαι, 745), he thus prepares an extension of the image of the wound as a separate being in the form of an exile. But the amputation does not occur; Philoctetes cannot drive away from his body his own limb. This could be Sophocles' way of signaling that the body of Philoctetes is a metaphor for the entire Greek army.

If the inseparable foot of Philoctetes stands for his relationship to army, then his reincorporation into it seems inevitable, and his exile, while long, only temporary; in other words, he was, essentially, ostracized, not banished. While the discourse of pollution and purgation suggests that Philoctetes served as a kind of ritual *pharmakos* figure,[40] his exile does evoke more effectively also the political, democratic, institution of ostracism. Evoking

---

[38] The reasoning behind the expulsion of Philoctetes is not in doubt, but the cowardly way in which it was carried out remains morally reprehensible by Greek standards as well as ours.

[39] Worman 2000 shows how Philoctetes' disease affects discourse in the drama.

[40] Worman 2000: 17 invokes this loaded term, but does not elaborate much on its implications for reading the *Philoctetes* as a whole.

ostracism in a discussion of a drama produced in 409 BCE runs against the fact that Athens had not used it since the ostracism of Hyperbolus in 415 and never would again, but six years is not enough time for such a significant institution to have disappeared from the active cultural memory and social narrative patterns of the Athenians;[41] I shall return to the end of ostracism at the end of this chapter, but for now I signal my larger awareness that one writes of ostracism in 409 with great caution, at the very least. It would also be foolish to imply that the army expelled Philoctetes because he became superior in virtue or power and thus a threat to their democracy, as typifies the victim of ostracism, but the temporary nature of his exclusion and his successful return to society suggest ostracism more than scapegoating. Moreover, the duration of Philoctetes' exile, approximately ten years, suggests several important models of exile in myth and history.[42] Athenians subject to ostracism were banished for ten years.[43] Plutarch reports that Solon, while in his prime, asked the Athenians for a ten-year leave of absence (*Sol.* 25.6), while the second exile of the tyrant Pisistratus lasted a decade. Homer, of course, shows how Odysseus spent ten years in a form of exile after the Trojan War before returning home to Ithaca, a better king for his experience than had he returned directly home. If Philoctetes was in fact intended to evoke Alcibiades or any other exiled aristocrat, it is important to remember that, as Forsdyke argues, exile through ostracism helped legitimize democratic rule through moderation (Forsdyke 2000 and 2005).[44] Again, one can hardly call the treatment of Philoctetes "moderate" (though he was expelled, not killed), yet drama, myth and history seem to engage here in a complex network whose parts shape and reshape one another. It is also important to remember that Philoctetes leaves Lemnos of his own free will, joyously journeying to Troy under the instructions of Heracles, to become a functioning member of heroic society again. Exile, which had threatened to ensavage Philoctetes permanently, has in its end brought him to a new understanding of his place in the world that had been impossible for his Sophoclean predecessors such as Ajax. A few years later, of course, Sophocles would return the ruined Oedipus from a different

---

[41] Ostwald 1955: 110 observes that there was no ostracism after Hyperbolus because of "the temporary and makeshift nature of the reforms by which the Athenian democracy was modified" after the disaster of the Sicilian Expedition. Rosenbloom 2004b: 351 argues that the rise of non-landed elites and the ascendancy of the agora and dikasterion contributed to end of ostracism.

[42] Mirhady 1997: 17 suggests the "etiological function of mythology" for ostracism, but does not mention Philoctetes.

[43] Rhodes 1994: 88 sees "no good reason" why we should think that the duration of absence from Athens required by ostracism was anything other than a decade.

[44] Rosenbloom 2004a and 2004b studies the relationship between comic drama and ostracism in a manner that complements my approach here.

kind of exile in the *Oedipus at Colonus*. An Athenian watching these dramas might see in them the resonance of his own city's institutions, wherein ostracism had previously been used moderately in support of the democratic regime.

The *Philoctetes* projects a reborn political body of the army that incorporates the harsh lessons Philoctetes and Neoptolemus have learned, while still inclusive of the able, if amoral, Odysseus. While, as Rose has demonstrated, Sophocles' drama seems to restore aristocratic prerogatives through a reaffirmation of the principle of inherited excellence (Rose 1992: 328),[45] the *Philoctetes* presents currents in its language, dissenting from aristocratic values, that are grounded in the principles of Athenian democracy. In other words, the Sophistic resonances in the language and tactics of Odysseus, and the renewed stress on inherited excellence, are not necessarily sufficient to turn Sophocles into some kind of fifth-century Neoconservative. On the other hand, the view that Sophocles turned committed democrat after his complicity, even if passive, in the oligarchic coup of the 400 in 411 BCE remains hard to prove conclusively, to say the least.[46] We have already seen how the *Philoctetes*, through its evocations of Athena Polias and inclusion of the Asklepieion in its semantic topography, combined with the identity of the Chorus as soldiers and sailors, participates symbolically in the discourse of Athenian political life, and examining the drama's language anew reveals terminology that is consonant with the democratic concerns of the *polis* that I examined in Euripidean drama earlier in this study.

Health, ultimately, seems linked to freedom in the *Philoctetes*. Before the paroxysm, in the ode that concludes with the allusion to Heracles' divinization, the Chorus laments the suffering of Philoctetes, which it feels is particularly undeserved because Philoctetes was ἴσος . . . ἴσοις ἀνήρ, "a man fair/equal to those who are fair/equal" (684).[47] As with the adjective *eleutheros* later in the drama, it is difficult to overlook completely the political connotations of *isos*, which has an especially strong connection with

---

[45] Segal 1981: 339 also concludes: "*Philoctetes* reflects a mood of declining trust in democracy."

[46] Calder 1971 presents the *Philoctetes* as a Sophoclean *apologia* for the coup. Such biographical readings do not offer much beyond mere speculation, but Rose 1992: 328 is too blankly dismissive of any and all democratic leanings in the text. Jameson 1971 reexamines the passages in Aristotle's *Rhetoric* that deal with arguments made by and against Sophocles after the oligarchic revolution and concludes that Sophocles must have prosecuted one of its main leaders, Peisander, after the restoration of the democracy. I find Jameson's argument and evidence convincing, and they show a Sophocles of a much more democratic mind while composing the *Philoctetes*. This article has not circulated as widely as it should have, and it is neither cited nor acknowledged by Rose. Scodel 2003: 37 agrees with Ostwald 1986: 340–41 that Sophocles is unlikely to have been oligarchic in his politics.

[47] See Kosak 1999: 120–21 on this language as typical of Athenian democracy.

the Athenian notion of citizenship. *Isos* and *isonomia* typically designate political relationships where all have an equal share in power (Vlastos 1947, 1953; Ostwald 1969). But Philoctetes' illness and isolation deprive him of equal status, and a way must be found for his reintegration with the army as an equal. He cannot return under compulsion, but must go freely. But, to be a "citizen," Philoctetes must be healthy; citizenship requires a cure. This is not the last time health and the language of fifth-century democracy are linked.

In the pivotal scene where Odysseus suddenly appears and violently tries to suppress the incipient hesitation in Neoptolemus over the seizure of the bow, Philoctetes laments his lost freedom (995–96):

> οἴμοι τάλας. ἡμᾶς μὲν ὡς δούλους σαφῶς
> πατὴρ ἄρ' ἐξέφυσεν οὐδ' ἐλευθέρους.

> Ah wretched me. Father clearly sired
> me to be a slave, not free.

Philoctetes responds here to Odysseus' insistence, so evocative of the Melian Dialogue in Thucydides, that "these things must be obeyed" (994). Crippled and deprived of his one means of independence, if not survival, Philoctetes has lost his freedom. His *nosos* has effectively stripped him of all status and rights and placed him in the condition of slavery. As Philoctetes begins to speak almost like a democrat, Odysseus responds immediately with the language of aristocracy, that Philoctetes' destiny is to be among "the best," τοῖς ἀρίστοισιν (997). Deprived of freedom, Philoctetes believes his only choice is suicide, throwing himself off the cliff where he lives, an act Odysseus prevents.

Philoctetes, then, early in his extended denunciation of Odysseus, reiterates the language of freedom but combines it with the discourse of disease (1006): ὦ μηδὲν ὑγιὲς μηδ' ἐλεύθερον φρονῶν, "O you thinking nothing healthy nor free." Jebb ad loc. notes that "the phrase οὐδὲν ὑγιές was a common one in Attic and is used often by [Euripides], though never by [Aeschylus], and only here by Sophocles." Nosological language does tend to be more predominant in Euripides than in the other two tragedians, but I should also note here that "nothing healthy" cannot be simply cast off here as a dead metaphor and translated as "nothing good," since, in tragedy, it is common only to Euripidean drama, and, moreover, its presence in the mouth of a diseased character in a drama where illness is used as a metaphor extensively cannot be thus minimized. An altered context can allow dead metaphors to be resurrected and inhabit human discourse with new force. And the combination of health and freedom extends the thinking of the previous reference to freedom only a few lines earlier.[48] As Philoctetes' accusations at 1006 suggest, Odysseus' designs and tactics are a symptom of illness in Odysseus; the *nosos* of Philoctetes is infecting in different ways all those who come in contact with him. At what is, arguably, the absolute emotional climax of the drama, the audience hears the protagonist insist on the importance of freedom after the Chorus has identified him in terms that suggest one of the cardinal principles of Athenian democracy.

If W. R. Connor is correct in his recent argument that the City Dionysia arose not under the Pisistratids but after the birth of democracy, his claim that "the festival itself was a celebration of freedom" (Connor 1989: 18) rings truer, I think, when we notice the centrality of references to freedom in the *Philoctetes* and other Athenian tragedies.[49] Sophocles does in this drama grapple with profound contemporary problems such as the influence of the Sophists and political instabilities after the oligarchic coup, but it is extremely unclear which "side" he takes here in the struggle between aristocrats and democrats. There is certainly abundant material to see, in Rose's words, an "ideological counteroffensive" that restores the old aristocratic tradition, but the drama stubbornly resists simple formulae about its politics, as even Rose has conceded is possible (Rose 1992: 326): "Sophocles' ideological counteroffensive is eminently indirect and cautiously circumscribed with what might almost be called escape-clause ambiguities." The audience in the Theater of Dionysus, especially its western half, sat roughly in between the sanctuaries of Dionysus Eleuthereus and Asclepius. The *Philoctetes* itself equates health with freedom, and the lack of compulsion in Heracles' command allows Philoctetes to leave the island with joy at the prospect of being, at last, healed by Asclepius. Odysseus may have been expelled from the stage, almost as a theatrical *pharmakos*,[50] yet it remains an inalterable part of myth, and thus part of the drama's parameters, that Troy's fall results from his ingenuity. The drama's characters look forward to a healthy mixed polity, projected from the deepest desires of the Athenian

---

[48] Words made from *eleuther-* are not common in Sophocles, with only twenty instances (exclusive of fragments), as compared to twenty-four in Aeschylus and fifty-nine in Euripides; the frequency per 10,000 words: 3.34 in Sophocles, 4.01 in Euripides and 5.98 in Aeschylus.

[49] Connor 1989: 23–24 argues further that the theme of freedom in tragedy has not been given due emphasis by scholars. Against Connor's arguments for a Cleisthenic reorganization of the Festival see Rhodes 2003: 106–07, with bibliography, and Sourvinou-Inwood 2003: 102–04, who is overconfident, I think, concerning the shape of the orchestra in the Theater of Dionysus. Rhodes' cautions against the overemphasis on democracy, as opposed to the *polis*, in studies of Athenian drama, are salutary. Even if Connor's arguments for a fundamental restructuring of the Dionysia late in the sixth century are wrong, it is not unreasonable to posit an incorporation of liberation as a primary interest of the Dionysia after the advent of democracy in 508.

[50] See Mitchell-Boyask 1996 on theatrical (as opposed to ritual) scapegoating.

audience. As in his final drama, the *Oedipus at Colonus*, Sophocles brings the beneficent powers of the lost, ruined hero to Athens during the darkest, most desperate years of the Peloponnesian War.

EPILOGUE: *PHILOCTETES*, FREEDOM AND THE THREAT OF TYRANNY IN 410

I have tried to show how the *Philoctetes* depicts the tensions of the Athenian *polis* after the oligarchic coup of 411 in the struggle over the terms of democracy such as freedom, equality and slavery. In the process, I suggested that the experience of Philoctetes seems modeled on a narrative of exile based in ostracism, a tool for preserving democracy that ceased to be used after 415. As Raubitschek explained, "the law of ostracism was one of the legal measures by which the Athenians sought to protect themselves against attacks from within" (Raubitschek 1951: 224). In this coda to my study of the *Philoctetes* I shall suggest that it could be read in the light of what seems to have replaced ostracism in 410, the law against the overthrow of democracy.[51]

From its inception in the late sixth century through its efflorescence in the fifth, the Athenian democracy continually feared the return of aristocratic rule and tyranny, and thus developed a series of laws to combat it. The first law against tyrants, which permitted the killing of anyone who attempted or abetted the institution of tyranny, was superseded by the advent of ostracism early in the fifth century, coinciding, according to Raubitschek, with the election of powerful, popularly elected generals. Ostracism was abandoned after the fiasco of Hyperbolus in 415 and the original law against tyrants was not invoked during the oligarchic revolution of 411, so clearly Athens, having quickly studied the lessons of that experience, decided it needed a new solution to the threat of tyranny. Thus Demophantus, a member of the board of *sungrapheis* (compilers) who were appointed to revise the laws, pushed through a resolution that reaffirmed and strengthened the Solonian law against sedition, which Andocides first quotes (1.95) before he asks for a reading of the *stêlê* on which was inscribed the law against the suppression of the democracy (97–98). The degree called for every Athenian to take an oath, accompanied by a sacrifice, in support of this law that he would do anything possible to avert the overthrow of the democracy, including killing

---

[51] On the decree of 410, and its role as the successor to the Solonian law against tyrants and ostracism, see Raubitschek 1951: 224–26, Ostwald 1955 and Rhodes 1981: 230–32. The main primary evidence for this decree is Andocides, *On the Mysteries* 97–99. In this section I am extremely grateful to Julia Shear, who pointed out to me the potential significance of this decree.

with impunity, and, moreover, he would succor the family of anyone who died in the defense of the democracy. And, in the penultimate sentence of the decree, we read: "All the Athenians shall take this oath over a sacrifice without blemish, as the law enjoins, before the Dionysia."

Since this decree was approved during the prytany of 410/9, Athenians had a long time, nine months, before the Dionysia to swear their oaths, but that this period ended at the Dionysia of 409, and that Sophocles was composing and rehearsing the *Philoctetes* as one of the nine tragic dramas produced at that Dionysia, both warrant further attention.

There are many oaths sworn in Greek tragedy, from Orestes' to avenge his father in Aeschylus to Hippolytus' vow of silence in Euripides, but the events of 411–410 create a more highly charged context for theatrical oaths sworn around then, and oath-swearing is a prominent feature in Sophocles' *Philoctetes*; indeed, the entire outcome, until Heracles intervenes, hinges on the decision of Neoptolemus to honor his oath to Philoctetes. The verb in Andocides' citation of the decree, ὀμόσαι (97, repeated in three different forms in 98), occurs three times in the *Philoctetes*, half of their instances in all of Sophocles.[52] The first occurs in Neoptolemus' (totally?) false account of his arrival at Troy, when all the Achaeans were swearing (ὄμνυντες 357) that Achilles was now alive again, so great was the resemblance of his son. Second, Philoctetes reacts to the Merchant's story of Helenus' prophecy that Odysseus is coming to fetch the bow by force or deceit with the question: "Has he sworn to fetch me back to the Achaeans after persuading me?" (625). The first two oaths are thus casual and wrapped in falsehood, and mark the moral shallowness of Neoptolemus early in the action and Odysseus' willingness to swear oaths about committing ignoble actions. But they do set the stage for the crisis of Philoctetes' raging denunciation of Neoptolemus after the truth begins to dawn on him. He laments "such things which the son of Achilles has done to me, who swore (ὀμόσας) he would take me home" (941). Neoptolemus was under oath (ἔνερκον 811) concerning the bow and Philoctetes' return home. But once Neoptolemus decides finally to help Philoctetes no matter what the consequences, he does so without the negative compulsion of oaths, but with the positive choice of friendship. I cannot establish conclusively here that Sophocles intends to evoke the oath-swearing of the previous nine months in Athens, but given the language of democracy that emerges in the second half of the *Philoctetes*, and its invocation of Athenian institutions throughout its action, I am more reluctant to deny any role to the decree of Demophantus

---

[52] *OC* 1145; *Tr.* 1185, 1188; *Phil.* 357, 623, 941.

in the resonance of the drama in the experience of the original Athenian audience than I am to assert a significant role for it. We should not forget that Sophocles was active in the reform and administration of the Athenian government after the disaster of the Sicilian Expedition in 413 as one of the ten Probouloi, just before the oligarchic coup.[53] He would have known the legislation of 410 well and many of his friends would have seen fit to swears their oaths before the Dionysia of 409, affirming their allegiance to the democracy of Athens. His *Philoctetes* is very much a child of its time.

[53] Thucy. 8.1.3; Arist. *Ath. Pol.* 29.2, *Rhet.* 1419a25.

CHAPTER 10

Conclusions and afterthoughts

Here I shall close with some general considerations about Athenian drama and society toward the end of the fifth century BCE. In this study, I have not sought even to imply that the readings presented here exclude all others or that Asclepius is the only key to understanding Greek drama, which is as complex an art form and, in Kenneth Burke's terms, a social action as any seen in the history of Western literature. I have, however, tried to ask a different set of related questions about tragedy in Athens than has normally been the practice among scholars in this field. What happens if we take nosological imagery and language seriously, and consistently so? Why does this imagery seem to increase in frequency after the plague at Athens and especially after the construction of the City Asklepieion on the south slope of the Athenian Acropolis, at the upper western edge of the Theater of Dionysus? What significance does the appearance of Asclepius and related themes have in tragedy? Why do Asclepius temples sit so often next to theaters? Do questions about disease imagery in Athenian drama give rise to new resonances and interpretive possibilities after the plague and the construction of the Asklepieion? These familial questions are part of a complex system of meaning generated from the conditions of performance. In Athens during and after the plague poets drew on traditional associations of healing and music to suggest a balm for the troubled audience. As civic strife during these years increasingly spread like a disease through Athens and the larger Greek world over the next decade, the dramatic poets drew on other established associations between the body and the body politic to develop an extended metaphor of disease in society, and these poets were conscious of the adjacency of the new healing shrine to their theater. By examining this disease, the city could have a chance of a cure. The theater could bring civic tensions to a new intensity; Laín Entralgo, summarizing Bernays, comments that "traditional medical doctrine in Greece taught that a purgative acts by first exacerbating and even bringing to a paroxysm the disease that it subsequently is to cure" (Laín Entralgo 1970: 189). Thus the *nosos* in the Theater of Dionysus could purify the *polis* of its *nosos*, or, to use a distinctly modern metaphor, "vaccinate" it against further strife and so produce a healthy body politic in the city of Athens.

Inside the Theater of Dionysus, the presence of paeans during the production of tragic dramas could also have participated in the transmission of *polis* values to the young of Athens through their performance, and this would have formed an important link to the relationship between drama and initiation discussed elsewhere (Winkler 1990; Padilla 1999). As observed throughout this study, Greek poetry from its inception concerns itself with healing, centering in the genre of the paean poem. The "song culture" of Athens, to borrow C. J. Herington's phrase (1985),[1] that produced Athenian drama drew deeply from both the traditions of choral lyric poetry and its own current society of song–dance performance, and one of these central traditions was the paean, a type of choral poem which, Ian Rutherford observes, groups of male adolescents or young men performed (Rutherford 1995: 114). In Athens, guilds under the aegis of cults of Apollo performed paeans around the temple of the Delian Apollo at the Athenian Thargelia (where the *pharmakos* ritual was observed) and held symposia at which the young Euripides is said to have served as a wine-pourer. Because Apollo's cult played such a central role for the *polis* in providing the focal center of activities demarcating masculinity, especially the passage from adolescence to life as an adult male citizen, the paean performances by these young males were an "expression of the social practices and values that the institutions stood for" (Rutherford 1995: 115). Peter Wilson further stresses that the choral groups were composed exclusively of citizens and thus embodied a "civic purity" (Wilson 2000: 80–81). The performance of the paean and initiatory practices in Athens were in this way deeply connected. A group of young males of military age enacted their identification with the god Paean/Apollo and thus their songs represented the health and safety of the *polis* itself. Tragedy's absorption and incorporation of the paean could have had tremendous resonance, especially if Winkler is correct that the chorus members in the Theater of Dionysus were ephebes and thus the same types of groups who participated in paean choruses (Winkler 1990; Nagy 1995; Wilson 2000: 77–79). With Apollo's son Asclepius, who shares the title Paean with his father, looking over the shoulders of the audience after 420 BCE, paean songs and the language of healing must be understood as part of the representation of *polis* life and values. We thus have a cluster of practices central to the discourses of the Athenian theater, healing,

---

[1] On the institution and function of choral groups and their competitions see Wilson 2000.

initiation and scapegoating, whose interconnections are strengthened because they all fall under the control of Apollo, the deity so involved also with civic stability and order. So intimately do these practices circulate together through the theater's discourse that a rupture in any one of the three brings disaster in the other two.

The performative context thus becomes crucial, and returns us unexpectedly to Aristotle's *Poetics*. I say "unexpectedly" because the *Poetics*, with its stress on plot, decidedly deemphasizes performance and context. Moreover, Aristotle in the *Poetics* says nothing about the tragedy and the *polis*, and nothing directly about drama's place in the City Dionysia (Hall 1996). Aristotle certainly omits Asclepius from his discussion of tragedy! However, the philosopher did provide a term with resonance in medical terminology as an important part of his definition of tragedy, and the word of course is *katharsis*. In the nineteenth century, Jacob Bernays, whose words opened this study, introduced an interpretation of *katharsis* as medical purification, in response to Lessing's theory that *katharsis* is moral purification. More recently, Leon Golden has argued that *katharsis* is intellectual clarification, and there has also been recent reemphasis on its ritual sense (Golden 1976).[2] Moreover, Elizabeth Belfiore has tried to shift the mechanism of tragic *katharsis* from homeopathy (like acts on like) to allopathy (unlike acts on unlike), with a focus on "psychic" *katharsis* in which tragedy induces in its audience a more balanced, "less shameful and thumetic" temperament (Belfiore 1992: 356).[3] The often heated controversy over what exactly Aristotle meant has essentially circled around these diverse readings, and while I approach this battlefield with the utmost caution, I would like to make a small suggestion that perhaps we need to take the language of tragedy itself in this matter more seriously when approaching Aristotle's terminology in the *Poetics*.[4] As Halliwell has observed, the medical and ritual senses of *katharsis* sometimes overlap, and since the Asclepius cult also combined the belief in the power of medicine with a recognition that ritual needs to supplement it, and because tragedy itself deploys medical language in a metaphorical, often ritual, sense, I think we need to look not just to other works by Aristotle, or to Plato, or to the Hippocratic works, but to the

---

[2] See also Chapter 7 in Parker 1983, and Burkert 1985: 75–84.

[3] Belfiore 1992: 257–90 discusses the cases against homeopathic and for allopathic *katharsis* and then builds toward a more general reading of tragic *katharsis* (337–60) which operates on the individual level in a manner I am arguing for the social and political.

[4] For recent surveys of the controversy, with fuller bibliography, see Belfiore 1992 and Halliwell 1986. In a readily accessible and handy volume Janko 1987 has collected the relevant passages on *katharsis* from the larger Aristotelian corpus. Belfiore 2000 could now serve as a model for using the language of tragedy to examine Aristotle.

texts of the dramas that Aristotle himself knew (Halliwell 1986: 186). More recently G. E. R. Lloyd restores the importance of the linkage between the discussions of *katharsis* in *Politics* 8 and the *Poetics*, pointing out how easily Aristotle's discourse moves from medical to religious to political contexts (Lloyd 2003: 187–91). As we have seen, the language of disease and cure in tragedy participates in several different cultural codes, ranging from the erotic to the religious to the political, and these resonate in Aristotle's language, whether Aristotle intended this or not. Thus, Aristotle, who excludes the political and social dimension of tragedy from the *Poetics* in order to focus on the individual, does not, perhaps would not, consciously bring in to his scheme a reading of the purification of the *polis* in the *Heracles* or the *Phoenissae* such as I gave above. A more modern Aristotelian such as Kenneth Burke, however, would. As Page DuBois observes, "While tragedy is a collective, poetic, ritual, and eminently democratic form, concerned with the social whole, with the dynamic interaction that is the city, the *polis*, Aristotle concerns himself with the management of individuals" (DuBois 2002: 23). An Athenian sitting in the Theater of Dionysus experienced dramas not just as an individual, but as part of a collective, and the pattern of seating in wedges according to tribe and social status reinforced the collective sense. Scholarly consideration of what Aristotle meant by *katharsis*, however, has continually focused on the emotional reactions of individuals as individuals, not as members of a political or social whole. I think we need to shift the semantic fields we use when we consider tragic *katharsis*.

What all this shows, if nothing else, I hope, is that a scholar-critic attempting to understand Greek tragedy must cast her or his net broadly and not assume that metaphors are dead, or that seemingly unconnected theories are in fact unconnected. Kenneth Burke's work is occasionally dug up and exhibited to a sometimes admiring but bewildered audience as an example of a critic whose ideas anticipated many of the ideas of structuralism and post-structuralism that have so changed the scholarly landscape over the past thirty years.[5] None of the essays in *Nothing to Do with Dionysos?* mention Burke, but most of them strive to prove Burke's contention that drama is a form of social action, that literature is equipment for living. To my knowledge, Kenneth Burke never discussed Asclepius and Greek drama as I have here, but I suspect he would have found it familiar territory. How *katharsis* functions in terms of the language of tragedy itself is

---

[5] This prolepsis is seen in the range of appreciations in the volume edited by White and Brose 1982. I have benefited especially from reading from that book the chapter by Donald Jennerman, "Kenneth Burke's Poetics of Catharsis."

outside the focus of my study, but I believe that it deserves further examination. Girard has shown how dramatic communities expel the scapegoat to save themselves from pollution, thus cleansing the tragic stage, but his somewhat ahistorical approach focuses on drama as an object, not as an action with effects on the society that engenders and then watches it. Burke in turn demonstrates how dramatic scapegoating heals the audience of certain social tensions.[6] The ritual and the medical, as well as the political, do in fact overlap in the language of Greek drama, as we have seen in this study, and thus drama acts as a form of social medicine which vaccinates the body politic, a *pharmakon* for the *polis*. In the pharmacy Euripides and Sophocles operate in the Theater of Dionysus, Asclepius is never far away. The poets of the Theater of Dionysus provided for their audience what the Assembly could not for itself, the doctor whom Nicias requested during the debate over the Sicilian Expedition. So much for the last of the three quoted passages that opened this study. Now for the first two.

"Who," Chremylus wonders in Aristophanes' *Wealth*, "is now the doctor in the city?" He wants to find one because, in his quest to discover whether virtue or vice leads to success, he has stumbled on Wealth, whom Zeus has blinded to prevent him from seeing and rewarding the good, thereby correcting the age-old social injustice of the success of the bad. In his last extant comedy, Aristophanes here plays on the tragic truisms of unjust suffering and unmerited fortune, and seems to be directly playing on Euripides' *Ion* because Chremylus has just been told by the Delphic oracle to take home with him the first man he meets while exiting the sanctuary, a clear allusion to the oracle's command in Euripides that the first person Xuthus will meet while leaving the temple will be his son. Chremylus thus asks about a doctor, and, lacking one, they proceed to the Asklepieion where the god himself heals Wealth's blindness, just as he probably did for Phineus in Sophocles' lost play about the Argonauts, and the healed Wealth then hails Athens in a parody of high tragic style. After the usual round of Aristophanic fantasy and fantasy-bred problems, Chremylus suggests installing Wealth to his former seat on the Acropolis, where he previously had kept Athena's treasure room filled. Aristophanes thus looks back to an era of greater civic prosperity, before Athens lost the empire that both produced its riches and eventually led to the destructive war with Sparta. Thus, it is significant that Asclepius is the key to the fulfillment of Aristophanes' comic vision both of a society where reward and punishment are doled

[6] Burke 1959 and "Coriolanus and the Delights of Faction" in Burke 1966.

out in just measure and of an Athens with its imperial wealth restored but without the headaches of empire.

The ultimate "author" of this healing is the comic poet Aristophanes who presents a "vision" of a newly wealthy Athens to his audience, and hence I suggest that the ultimate answer to Chremylus' question is that the dramatic poet is the doctor in the city, for this accords with earlier Aristophanic thought. Seventeen years previously, Aristophanes in the *Frogs* has Euripides and Aeschylus assert that the duty of poets is "to make men in the cities better" (1008–09). Dionysus will further finally resurrect one of the poets on the basis of which of them gives the best advice to the city (1419–21). Aristophanes might suggest that the poet can inject the right advice or display of virtue into the ailing body politic as a *pharmakon*, but his treatment of Euripides in the *Frogs* suggests that this particular tragic poet more likely infects Athens than cures it. This is not the place to engage the complicated matter of Aristophanes' attitude to Euripides, but I hope that it is very clear that Aristophanes focuses on a different aspect of Euripidean tragedy than I have, to say the very least. Through its tragic pharmacology, the drama of Euripides and Sophocles aims to heal the city, a cure, we know from Thucydides, that Athens needs.

During the controversy over the proposed expedition to Sicily, Thucydides' Nicias speaks more directly of the need for a doctor for the city of Athens, but, although he has in mind the president of the Assembly (6.14), the specific nature of the healing activity could almost just as well be ascribed to the dramatic poet. Sometime earlier in the century, the god Okeanos tells the bound, ailing and prideful Prometheus (*Prom.* 380): "words are the doctors of the ailing temperament," ὀργῆς νοσούσης εἰσὶν ἰατροὶ λόγοι. In Thucydides 6.14, Nicias then calls upon the president of the Assembly "to put this question to the vote and allow the Athenians to debate the matter once again", saying that in this way he "will be acting as a physician for [his] misguided city." Note here the confluence of political order, medicine and speech-making; the proper conduct of democracy through debate and vote effects health. The president of the Assembly thus allows the political debaters to "take the stage" and engage in an agon over the correct course of action. Cleon, in an earlier section of Thucydides' *History*, in fact calls the Athenians "spectators of speeches" (3.38.7). Because Assembly speeches and theatrical performances were both, as Ober and Strauss argue, "closely bound up in the mediation of competing values," and because of the similar spatial organizations of the Theater of Dionysus and the Pnyx (where the Assembly met), "the responses of Athenian citizens as jurors and Assemblymen were inevitably influenced by the fact of their having been members of theatrical audiences, and vice versa" (Ober and Strauss 1990: 238). Such congruities are operative here. Nicias seems to presume that the mere spectacle of the debate and the presentation of the facts of the expedition will be enough to inoculate Athens from the desire to harm itself further by attacking Sicily.

But when the *logoi* themselves are sick, as Polynices diagnoses his brother Eteocles' arguments in the *Phoenissae* (469–73), then a normal cure is impossible, and Thucydides himself seems to suggest as much in the language he uses to depict the aftermath of the debate over the Sicilian Expedition, when Nicias' pleas, combined by Alcibiades' persuasive power on the other side, work to the opposite effect from what Nicias intends (6.24.3): "A passion to sail fell upon everyone." "A passion fell upon", *erôs enepese*.[7] *Erôs*, the disease of Heracles in the *Trachiniae*, which I connected to Athenian *pleonexia*, becomes the disease of Athens in the debate over the Sicilian Expedition. Even without considering its prominence in the *Trachiniae*, *erôs* is a provocative word in the Theater of Dionysus during this era, as seen in two powerful dramas of the forbidden composed during the next decade. In Sophocles' *Oedipus at Colonus* the Chorus, after its initial horrified outrage against the blind stranger subsides, begins its questioning of Oedipus about his dark past with the confession "I long" (*eramai*) to hear. In the *Bacchae*, *erôs* is the word for Pentheus' lust to see his mother's alleged sexual activities on Mt. Cithaeron.[8] *Erôs* here is the fervent desire for what is forbidden by common sense, by respect, by, in a Greek term, *aidôs*, and it falls on its victims like a plague. In Sophocles' *Philoctetes*, another text involving war and illness, the verb *empiptein* (ἐμπέσοι, 699) designates attacks of the hero's *nosos*, as well as the paralyzing pity that Neoptolemus feels for the robbed Philoctetes (ἐμπέπτωκε, 965). Thucydides uses the exact same verb to describe the plague's first attack (1.48.2), as well as, we have already observed, its subsequent recurrence (3.87.1), and he may have been subtly driving the point home when he notes a few lines later in Book 6 that Athens was only just now recovered enough from the devastation of the plague to be able to mount such a large undertaking to Sicily. Thucydides here replicates the narrative sequence from Book 2 wherein something monstrously irrational falls upon Athens immediately subsequent to a speech, Pericles' Funeral Oration, that attempts to construct, through reason and language, a better Athens. The duplication thus seems

---

[7] See Kallet 1999: 232 and Wohl 2002: 192–95, who also sees the connections between the plague and the Sicilian expedition, through the motif of "diseased longing."

[8] Belfiore 1992: 344 cites these two passages as examples of the type of shamelessness that tragedy should purge.

through design, not coincidence. Nicias' plea is further extraordinary for Thucydidean discourse since it features a rare (for Thucydides) metaphorical use of medical language, as the word for doctor, *iatros*, here is the only occurrence in Thucydides which does not designate a real physician, while, as the passages from the *Prometheus Bound* (380) and the *Heracles* (1107) alone show, it was a common enough trope in the Theater of Dionysus. Clearly, Nicias' call for a doctor has gone unanswered. Where do healing *logoi* originate? The President and Assembly, being part of the real body politic, are not entirely immune from the civic illness. But the tragic poet, operating through the mediated forms of myth and theater, and standing utterly outside of the immediate patient, seems a better candidate for a physician for the misguided city. The audience which sits in both Pnyx and Theater of Dionysus needs to experience the paroxysm of disease in the latter before they deliberate in the former.

What follows the plague-like attack of *erôs* in Thucydides' narrative reads more like something out of the Theater of Dionysus, or even from René Girard's works, as the frenzied city discovers that someone has violated a number of Herms, religious statues, an event which plunges its citizens, egged on by the enemies of Alcibiades, into an almost paranoid search for the perpetrators, not least because this was an extraordinarily inauspicious event to have occurred on the eve of such a dangerous expedition. Fearing the gods, or, even worse, a threat to overthrow the democracy – a fear Thucydides returns to persistently – the Athenians enact, in Victor Turner's terms, another social drama, behaving like characters in Sophocles' *Oedipus Tyrannus* (Turner 1974, 1981). Thucydides hints that what can return Athens to civic stability is, literally, an arbitrarily chosen scapegoat, for the operative attitude among the Athenians is *hypopsia*, "suspicion," a word that runs throughout this episode. Once a number of citizens had been arrested and punished based upon these suspicions, Thucydides remarks (6.60.5): "And in this it was unclear whether those who suffered had been punished unjustly, but the rest of the city, however, was clearly benefited at that time." This would be fine grist for the mill of Girard's belief in the arbitrariness of the punishment of Oedipus, or for some of his successors such as Ahl who maintain that Oedipus is unjustly convicted on the basis of purely circumstantial evidence (Girard 1977: 68–88; Ahl 1991). Immediately after the initial mutilations of the Herms, Alcibiades' enemies believe they can pin the deed on him and "drive him out," expelling him from the city ostensibly for the good of the democracy. Barry Strauss thus contends, "Alcibiades was a figure of sinful pollution (*alitêrion*) or scapegoat (*pharmakos*) in the Greek tradition" (Strauss 1993: 151).[9] Thucydides does stress the arbitrariness of the scapegoating to an almost Girardean degree. As a solution, however, this expulsion was fairly short-lived, and Athens found itself again factionalized, unstable, and devastated by the disastrous Sicilian Expedition, and its dramas filled with allusions to the problem of Alcibiades. Perhaps the *Philoctetes* marks the exhaustion of this range of cultural performances seen in the dramas in both the Assembly and the Theater. Social dramas can only function so far as dramas, and society thus needs the healing powers of the theater itself.

[9] Wohl 2002: 191 also has recourse to the *pharmakos* to explain this episode.

Works Cited

Aélion, R. (1983) *Euripide: Héritier d'Eschyle* (2 vols.). Paris.

Ahl, F. (1991) *Sophocles' Oedipus: Evidence and Self-Conviction*. Ithaca.

Alcock, S. E. and R. Osborne (eds.) (1994) *Placing the Gods: Sanctuaries and Sacred Space in Ancient Greece*. Oxford.

Aleshire, S. B. (1989) *The Athenian Asklepieion: The People, Their Dedications, and the Inventories*. Amsterdam.

Allison, J. W. (1983) "Pericles' Policy and the Plague," *Historia* 32: 14–23.

Antonaccio, C. (1995) *An Archaeology of Ancestors: Tomb Cult and Hero Cult in Early Greece*. Lanham.

Avery, H. C. (1965) "Heracles, Philoctetes, Neoptolemus," *Hermes* 93: 279–97.

Balot, R. (2001) *Greed and Injustice in Classical Athens*. Princeton.

Barnes, J., M. Schofield and R. Sorabji (eds.) (1978) *Articles on Aristotle* IV. New York.

Barrett, W. S. (ed.) (1964) *Euripides: Hippolytos*. Oxford.

Baziotopoulou-Valavani, E. (2002) "A Mass Burial from the Cemetery of Kerameikos," in *Excavating Classical Culture: Recent Archaeological Discoveries in Greece. Studies in Classical Archaeology* I, ed. M. Stamatopoulou and M. Yeroulanou. Oxford: 187–201.

Belfiore, E. (1986) "Wine and Catharsis of the Emotions in Plato's *Laws*," *CQ* 36: 421–37.

  (1992) *Tragic Pleasures: Aristotle on Plot and the Emotions*. Princeton.

  (2000) *Murder among Friends: Violations of Philia in Greek Tragedy*. Oxford.

Bernays, J. (1880) *Zwei Handlungen über die aristotelische Theorie des Drama* (Berlin). Translated and excerpted as "Aristotle on the Effect of Tragedy," in Barnes, Schofield and Sorabji 1978: 154–65.

Beta, S. (1999) "Madness on the Comic Stage: Aristophanes' *Wasps* and Euripides' *Herakles*," *GRBS* 40: 135–57.

Beye, C. R. (1970) "Sophocles' *Philoctetes* and the Homeric Embassy," *TAPA* 101: 63–75.

Biggs, P. (1966) "The Disease Theme in Sophocles' *Ajax*, *Philoctetes* and *Trachiniae*," *CP* 61: 223–35.

Boedeker, D. (1992) "Hero Cult and Politics in Herodotus: The Bones of Orestes," in *Cultural Poetics in Archaic Greece*, ed. C. Dougherty and L. Kurke. Cambridge: 164–77.

Bond, G. W. (ed.) (1981) *Euripides: Heracles*. Oxford.

Bowie, A. M. (1993) *Aristophanes: Myth, Ritual and Comedy*. Cambridge.

(1997) "Tragic Filters for History: Euripides' *Supplices* and Sophocles' *Philoctetes*," in Pelling 1997: 39–62.

Bremmer, J. (1983) "Scapegoat Rituals in Ancient Greece," *HSCP* 87: 299–320.

Brock, R. (2000) "Sickness in the Body Politic: Medical Imagery in the Greek Polis," in Hope and Marshall 2000: 24–34.

Brown, S. G. (1977) "A Contextual Analysis of Tragic Meter: The Anapest," in *Ancient and Modern: Essays in Honor of Gerald Else*, ed. J. H. D'Arms and J. W. Eadie. Ann Arbor: 45–78.

Bruit Zaidman, L. and P. Schmitt Pantel (1992) *Religion in the Ancient Greek City*, trans. P. Cartledge. Cambridge.

Burford, A. (1969) *The Greek Temple Builders at Epidauros*. Liverpool.

Burgess, J. (2001) "Coronis Aflame: The Gender of Mortality," *CP* 96: 214–27.

Burian, P. (ed.) (1985) *Directions in Euripidean Criticism: A Collection of Essays*. Durham.

Burke, K. (1959) "On Catharsis or Resolution, with a Postscript," *Kenyon Review* 21: 337–75.

(1966) *Language as Symbolic Action*. Berkeley.

Burkert, W. (1972) *Lore and Science in Ancient Pythagoreanism*. Cambridge, Mass.

(1979) *Structure and History in Greek Mythology and Ritual*. Berkeley.

(1983a) *Homo Necans: The Anthropology of Ancient Greek Sacrificial Ritual and Myth*. Berkeley.

(1983b) *Anthropologie des religiösen Opfers: Die Sakralisierung des Gewalt*. Munich.

(1985) *Greek Religion*. Cambridge, Mass.

Burnett, A. P. (1971) *Catastrophe Survived: Euripides' Plays of Mixed Reversal*. Oxford.

Burton, R. W. (1980) *The Chorus in Sophocles' Tragedies*. Oxford.

Cairns, D. L. (1997) "The Meadow of Artemis and the Character of the Euripidean *Hippolytus*," *QUCC* 57: 51–75.

Calame, C. (1990) *Thésée et l'imaginaire athénien: Légende et culte en Grèce antique*. Lausanne.

(1997) *Choruses of Young Women in Ancient Greece*, trans. D. Collins and J. Orion. Lanham.

Calder, W. (1969) "The Date of Euripides' *Erechtheus*," *GRBS* 10: 147–56.

(1971) "Sophoclean Apologia: *Philoctetes*," *GRBS* 12: 153–74.

Camp, J. (2001) *The Archaeology of Athens*. New Haven.

Carpenter, T. H. and C. A. Faraone (eds.) (1993) *Masks of Dionysus*. Ithaca.

Cartledge, P. (1997) "Deep Plays: Theatre as Process in Greek Civic Life," in Easterling 1997: 3–35.

Caton, R. (1900) *The Temple and Ritual of Asklepios at Epidaurus and Athens*. London.

Cole, S. G. (1994) "Demeter in the Ancient Greek City and Its Countryside," in Alcock and Osborne 1994: 199–216.

Collinge, N. E. (1962) "Medical Terms and Clinical Attitudes in the Tragedians," *BICS* 9: 43–55.

Conacher, D. J. (1967) *Euripidean Drama: Myth, Theme and Structure*. Toronto.

Connolly, A. (1998) "Was Sophocles Heroised as Dexion?" *JHS* 118: 1–21.

Connor, W. R. (1977) "A Post Modern Thucydides?" *CJ* 72: 289–98.

   (1984) *Thucydides*. Princeton.

   (1989) "City Dionysia and Athenian Democracy," *C&M* 40: 7–32.

   (1996) "Civil Society, Dionysiac Festival, and the Athenian Democracy," in *Demokratia: A Conversation on Democracies, Ancient and Modern*, ed. J. Ober and C. Hedrick. Princeton: 217–26.

Cordes, P. (1994) *Iatros: Das Bild des Arztes in der griechischen Literatur von Homer bis Aristoteles*. Stuttgart.

Craik, E. M. (ed.) (1988) *Euripides: Phoenician Women*. Warminster.

   (2001) "Thucydides on the Plague: Physiology of Flux and Fixation," *CQ* 51: 102–08.

   (2002) "Medical Reference in Euripides," *BICS* 45: 81–97.

Croissant, J. (1932) *Aristote et les mystères*. Paris.

Currie, B. (2005) *Pindar and the Cult of Heroes*. Oxford.

Dale, A. M. (1948) *The Lyric Meters of Greek Drama*. Cambridge.

   (ed.) (1954) *Euripides: Alcestis*. Oxford.

Davies, M. (ed.) (1991) *Sophocles, Trachiniae: Introduction and Commentary*. Oxford.

Dawe, R. D. (ed.) (1982) *Sophocles: Oedipus Rex*. Cambridge.

Derrida, J. (1981) *Dissemination*, trans. B. Johnson. Chicago.

Des Bouvrie, S. (1993) "Creative Euphoria: Dionysos and the Theatre," *Kernos* 6: 79–112.

Dinsmoor, W. B. (1950) *The Architecture of Ancient Greece: An Account of Its Historic Development*. London.

Dodds, E. R. (1951) *The Greeks and the Irrational*. Berkeley.

Döring, A. (1876) *Die Kunstlehre Aristoteles*. Jena.

Dover, K. (ed.) (1968) *Aristophanes: Clouds*. Oxford.

DuBois, P. (2002) "Ancient Tragedy and the Metaphor of Katharsis," *Theatre Journal* 54: 19–24.

Dumortier, J. (1935) *Le vocabulaire médical d'Eschyle*. Paris.

Easterling, P. E. (1968) "Sophocles, *Trachiniae*," *BICS* 15: 58–60.

   (1978) "*Philoctetes* and Modern Criticism," *ICS* 3: 27–39.

   (ed.) (1982) *Sophocles: Trachiniae*. Cambridge.

   (ed.) (1997) *The Cambridge Companion to Greek Tragedy*. Cambridge.

Edelstein, E. and L. Edelstein (1945) *Asclepius: A Collection and Interpretation of the Testimonies*, 2 vols. Baltimore.

Ehrenberg, V. (1954) *Sophocles and Pericles*. Oxford.

Euben, J. P. (ed.) (1986) *Greek Tragedy and Political Theory*. Berkeley.

Falkner, T. M. (1998) "Containing Tragedy: Rhetoric and Self-Representation in Sophocles' *Philoctetes*," *ClAnt* 17: 25–58.

Faraone, C. A. (1992) *Talismans and Trojan Horses: Guardian Statues in Greek Myth and Ritual*. Oxford.

   (1994) "Deianira's Mistake and the Demise of Heracles: Erotic Magic in Sophocles' *Trachiniae*," *Helios* 21: 115–35.

Farnell, L. R. (1921) *Greek Hero Cults and Ideas of Immortality*. Oxford.

Finkelberg, M. (1996) "The Second Stasimon of the *Trachiniae* and Heracles' Festival on Mount Oeta," *Mnemosyne* 73: 129–43.

Finley, J. H. (1967) *Three Essays on Thucydides*. Cambridge, Mass.

Flashar, H. (1956) "Die medizinischen Grundlagen der Lehre von der Wirkung der Dichtung in der griechischen Poetik," *Hermes* 84: 12–48.

Fludernik, M., D. C. Freeman and M. H. Freeman (1999) "Metaphor and Beyond: An Introduction," *Poetics Today* 20: 383–96.

Foley, H. P. (1985) *Ritual Irony: Poetry and Sacrifice in Euripides*. Ithaca.

(1988) "Tragedy and Politics in Aristophanes' *Acharnians*," *JHS* 108: 33–47.

(1993) "Oedipus as *Pharmakos*," in *Nomodeiktes: Greek Studies in Honor of Martin Ostwald*, ed. R. Rosen and J. Farrell. Ann Arbor: 525–38.

Forsdyke, S. (2000) "Exile, Ostracism and the Athenian Democracy," *ClAnt* 19: 232–63.

(2005) *Exile, Ostracism and Democracy: The Politics of Expulsion in Ancient Greece*. Princeton.

Foucault, M. (1972) *The Archaeology of Knowledge*, trans. A. Sheridan. New York.

Fraenkel, E. (ed.) (1950) *Aeschylus: Agamemnon*. Oxford.

Frye, R. M. (1984) *The Renaissance Hamlet: Issues and Responses*. Princeton.

Gantz, T. (1993) *Early Greek Myth: A Guide to Literary and Artistic Sources*. Baltimore.

Garland, R. (1992) *Introducing New Gods: The Politics of Athenian Religion*. London.

George, D. B. (1994) "Euripides' *Heracles* 140–235: Staging and the Stage Iconography of Heracles' Bow," *GRBS* 35: 145–57.

Gibert, J. (1997) "Euripides' *Hippolytus* Plays: Which Came First?" *CQ* 47: 85–97.

Girard, R. (1977) *Violence and the Sacred*. Baltimore.

Gittings, C. (1984) *Death, Burial and the Individual in Early Modern England*. London.

Goebel, G. H. and T. R. Nevin (eds.) (1977) *Euripides: Heracles*. Madison.

Goff, B. (1990) *The Noose of Words: Readings of Desire, Violence and Language in Euripides' Hippolytus*. Cambridge.

Goheen, R. F. (1951) *The Imagery of Sophocles' Antigone: A Study of Poetic Language and Structure*. Princeton.

Golden, L. (1976) "The Clarification Theory of Katharsis," *Hermes* 104: 437–52.

Goldhill, S. (1986) *Reading Greek Tragedy*. Cambridge.

(1990) "The Great Dionysia and Civic Ideology," in Winkler and Zeitlin 1990: 97–129.

(1991) *The Poet's Voice: Essays on Poetics and Greek Literature*. Cambridge.

(1994) "Representing Democracy: Women at the City Dionysia," in Osborne and Hornblower 1994: 347–70.

(2000) "Civic Ideology and the Problem of Difference: The Politics of Aeschylean Tragedy, Once Again," *JHS* 120: 34–56.

Gomme, A. (ed.) (1956) *Thucydides History* II. Oxford.

Gould, J. (1985) "On Making Sense of Greek Religion," in *Greek Religion and Society*, ed. P. Easterling and J. Muir. Cambridge: 1–33.

Graf, F. (1992) "Heiligtum und Ritual: Das Beispiel der griechisch-römischen Asklepieia," in *Le sanctuaire grec*. Geneva: 159–99.

Greenblatt, S. (1980) *Renaissance Self-Fashioning*. Chicago.

(1988) *Shakespearean Negotiations*. Berkeley.

(2001) *Hamlet in Purgatory*. Princeton.

(2004) *Will in the World: How Shakespeare Became Shakespeare*. New York.

Greengard, C. (1987) *Theatre in Crisis: Sophocles' Reconstruction of Genre and Politics in Philoctetes*. Amsterdam.

Gregory, J. (1991) *Euripides and the Instruction of the Athenians*. Ann Arbor.

Griffin, J. (1977) "The Epic Cycle and the Uniqueness of Homer," *JHS* 97: 39–53.

(1980) *Homer on Life and Death*. Oxford.

(1998) "The Social Function of Greek Drama," *CQ* 48: 39–61.

Griffith, M. (1977) *The Authenticity of Prometheus Bound*. Cambridge.

(ed.) (1983) *Aeschylus: Prometheus Bound*. Cambridge.

Griffith, R. D. (1993) "Oedipus *pharmakos*? Alleged Scapegoating in Sophocles' *Oedipus the King*," *Phoenix* 47: 95–114.

(1996) *The Theatre of Apollo: Divine Justice and Sophocles' Oedipus the King*. Montreal.

(1998) "Corporality in the Ancient Greek Theatre," *Phoenix* 52: 230–56.

Haldane, J. A. (1963) "A Paean in *Philoctetes*," *CQ* 13: 53–56.

Hall, E. (1996) "Is there a Polis in Aristotle's *Poetics*?" in Silk 1996: 295–309.

Halliwell, S. (1986) *Aristotle's Poetics*. Chapel Hill.

Hammond, N. G. (1988) "More on the Conditions of Dramatic Production to the Death of Aeschylus," *GRBS* 29: 5–34.

Heath, M. (1987) "Euripides' *Telephus*," *CQ* 37: 272–80.

Heiden, B. (1989) *Tragic Rhetoric: An Interpretation of Sophocles' Trachiniae*. New York.

Henderson, J. (1991) *The Maculate Muse: Obscene Language in Attic Comedy*. Oxford.

Henrichs, A. (1995) "'Why Should I Dance?' Choral Self-Referentiality in Greek Tragedy," *Arion* 3: 56–111.

Herington, C. J. (1955) *Athena Parthenos and Athena Polias: A Study in the Religion of Periclean Athens*. Manchester.

(1979) *The Author of the Prometheus Bound*. Austin.

(1985) *Poetry into Drama: Early Tragedy and the Greek Poetic Tradition*. Berkeley.

Hoey, T. F. (1977) "Ambiguity in the Exodus of Sophocles' *Trachiniae*," *Arethusa* 10: 269–94.

(1979) "The Date of the *Trachiniae*," *Phoenix* 33: 210–32.

Holladay, A. J. and J. C. F. Poole (1979) "Thucydides and the Plague of Athens," *CQ* 29: 282–300.

(1988) "New Developments in the Problem of the Athenian Plague," *CQ* 38: 247–50.

Holt, P. (1989) "The End of the *Trachiniai* and the Fate of Herakles," *JHS* 109: 69–80.

Hope, V. M. and E. Marshall (eds.) (2000) *Death and Disease in the Ancient City*. New York.

Hoppin, M. C. (1990) "Metrical Effects, Dramatic Illusion, and the Two Endings of Sophocles' *Philoctetes*," *Arethusa* 23: 141–82.

Hornblower, S. (1987) *Thucydides*. London.

(1991) *A Commentary on Thucydides* I. *Books* I–III. Oxford.

Hughes, D. (1991) *Human Sacrifice in Ancient Greece*. London.

Jameson, M. H. (1956) "Politics and the *Philoctetes*," *CP* 51: 217–27.

(1971) "Sophocles and the Four Hundred," *Historia* 20: 541–68.

Janko, R. (ed.) (1987) *Aristotle: Poetics*. Indianapolis.

Jebb, R. C. (ed.) (1897) *Sophocles: The Plays and Fragments*, repr. 1932. Cambridge.

Jeny, H. (1989) "Troizen as the Setting of *Hippolytus Stephanephoros*," *AJP* 110: 400–04.

Johnston, S. I. (1999) *Restless Dead: Encounters between the Living and the Dead in Ancient Greece*. Berkeley.

Jones, J. (1962) *On Aristotle and Greek Tragedy*. London.

Jouan, F. (1970) "Le *Prométhée* d'Eschyle et l'*Héraclés* d'Euripide," *REA* 72: 317–31.

Jouanna, J. (1988) "La maladie sauvage et la tragédie grecque," *Métis* 3: 343–60.

Kallet, L. (1999) "The Diseased Body Politic, Athenian Public Finance, and the Massacre at Mykalessos (Thucydides 7: 27–29)," *AJP* 120: 223–44.

Kamerbeek, R. C. (ed.) (1970) *The Complete Plays of Sophocles*. Leiden.

Käppel, L. (1989) "Das Theater von Epidauros: Die mathematische Gurnidee des Gesamtentwurfs und ihr möglicher Sinn," *Jahrbuch des deutschen archäologischen Institutes* 104: 83–106.

(1992) *Paian: Studien zur Geschichte einer Gattung*. Berlin.

Kearns, E. (1989) *The Heroes of Attica*. London.

Kerényi, C. (1959) *Asklepios: Archetypal Image of the Physician's Existence*. New York.

Kirby, J. T. (1997) "Aristotle on Metaphor," *AJP* 118: 517–54.

Kirk, G. S., J. E. Raven and M. Schofield (eds.) (1983) *The Presocratic Philosophers*, 2nd edn. Cambridge.

Knox, B. M. W. (1956) "The Date of the *Oedipus Tyrannus* of Sophocles," *AJP* 77: 133–47.

(1957). *Oedipus at Thebes*. New Haven.

(1979). *Word and Action: Essays on the Ancient Theater*. Baltimore.

Kosak, J. C. (1999) "Therapeutic Touch and Sophokles' *Philoctetes*," *HSCP* 99: 93–135.

(2000) "*Polis Nosousa*: Greek ideas about the city and disease in the fifth century," in Hope and Marshall 2000: 35–54.

(2004) *Heroic Measures: Hippocratic Medicine in the Making of Euripidean Tragedy*. Leiden.

Kövecses, Z. (2005) *Metaphor in Culture: Universality and Variation*. Cambridge.

Krug, A. (1993) *Heilkunst und Heilkult: Medizin in der Antike*. Munich.

Laín Entralgo, P. (1970) *The Therapy of the Word in Classical Antiquity*, trans. L. J. Rather and J. M. Sharp. New Haven.

Lakoff, G. (1987) *Women, Fire, and Dangerous Things: What Categories Reveal about the Mind*. Chicago.

Lakoff, G. and M. Johnson (1980) *Metaphors We Live by*. Chicago.

Lateiner, D. (1986) "The Empirical Element in the Methods of Early Greek Medical Writers and Herodotus: A Shared Epistemological Response," *Antichthon* 20: 1–20.

Lefkowitz, M. R. (1981) *The Lives of the Greek Poets*. London
  (1989) "'Impiety' and 'Atheism' in Euripides' Dramas," *CQ* 39: 70–82.

Lesky, A. (1972) *Die tragische Dichtung der Hellenen*, 3rd edn. Göttingen.

Lewis, R. G. (1988) "An Alternative Dating for Sophocles' Antigone," *GRBS* 29: 35–50.

Lloyd, G. E. R. (1979) *Magic, Reason and Experience: Studies in the Origins and Development of Greek Science*. Cambridge.
  (1990) *Demystifying Mentalities*. Cambridge.
  (2003) *In the Grip of Disease: Studies in the Greek Imagination*. Oxford.

Lloyd-Jones, H. (ed.) (1996) *Sophocles: Fragments*. Cambridge, Mass.

Lloyd-Jones, H. and N. G. Wilson (1990) *Sophoclea: Studies in the Text of Sophocles*. Oxford.

Longrigg, J. (1963) "Philosophy and Medicine: Some Early Interactions," *HSCP* 67: 147–75.
  (1993) *Greek Rational Medicine: Philosophy and Medicine from Alcmaeon to the Alexandrians*. London.

Loraux, N. (1993) *The Children of Athena: Athenian Ideas about Citizenship and the Division between the Sexes*, trans. C. Levine. Princeton.
  (1995) *The Experience of Tiresias: The Feminine and the Greek Man*, trans. P. Wissing. Princeton.

Maass, M. (1972) *Die Prohedrie des Dionysostheaters in Athens*. Munich.

Machemer, G. A. (1993) "Medicine, Music, and Magic: The Healing Grace of Pindar's Fourth Nemean," *HSCP* 95: 113–41.

Mackie, C. J. (1997) "Achilles' Teachers: Chiron and Phoenix in the *Iliad*," *G&R* 44: 1–10.
  (1998) "Achilles in Fire," *CQ* 48: 329–33.

Macleod, C. W. (1983) *Collected Essays*. Oxford.

Martin, R. P. (1983) *Healing, Sacrifice and Battle: Amechania and Related Concepts in Early Greek Poetry*. Innsbruck.

Mastronarde, D. J. (1979) *Contact and Discontinuity: Some Conventions of Speech and Action on the Greek Tragic Stage*. Berkeley.
  (1990) "Actors on High: The Skene Roof, the Crane and the Gods in Attic Drama," *CA* 9: 247–94.
  (ed.) (1994) *Euripides: Phoenissae*. Cambridge.

McCall, M. (1972) "The *Trachiniae*: Structure, Focus and Heracles," *AJP* 93: 142–63.

Meiggs, R. (1972) *The Athenian Empire*. Oxford.

Michelini, A. N. (1987) *Euripides and the Tragic Tradition*. Madison.

Mikalson, J. (1984) "Religion and the Plague in Athens, 431–423 B. C.," in *Studies Presented to Sterling Dow* (GRBS Monographs 1): 217–25.

(1986) "Zeus the Father and Heracles the Son," *TAPA* 116: 89–98.

Miller, H. W. (1944) "Medical Terminology in Tragedy," *TAPA* 75: 156–67.

Mirhady, D. C. (1997) "The Ritual Background to Athenian Ostracism," *AHB* 11: 13–19.

Mitchell, R. N. (1991) "Miasma, Mimesis and Scapegoating in Euripides' *Hippolytus*," *ClAnt* 10: 94–118.

Mitchell-Boyask, R. (1993) "Sacrifice and Revenge in Euripides' *Hecuba*," *Ramus* 22: 116–34.

(1996) "Dramatic Scapegoating: On the Uses and Abuses of Girard and Shakespearean Criticism," in Silk 1996: 426–37.

(1999) "Euripides' *Hippolytus* and the Trials of Manhood. (The Ephebia?)," *Bucknell Review* 43: 42–66.

Morgan, T. E. (1994) "Plague or Poetry? Thucydides on the Epidemic at Athens," *TAPA* 124: 197–210.

Morris, I. (1987) *Burial and Greek Society*. Cambridge.

(ed.) (1994) *Classical Greece: Ancient Histories and Modern Archaeologies*. Cambridge.

Mossman, J. (1995) *Wild Justice: A Study of Euripides' Hecuba*. Oxford.

Mueller-Goldingen, C. (1985) *Untersuchungen zu den Phönissen des Euripides*. Stuttgart.

Mullens, H. G. (1939) "*Hercules Furens* and *Prometheus Vinctus*," *CR* 53: 165–66.

(1941) "The Aeschylean Interpretation of *Hercules Furens*," *CJ* 36: 229–32.

Müller, C. W. (1984) *Zur Datierung des sophokleischen Oedipus*. Wiesbaden.

Murnaghan, S. B. (1987–88) "Body and Voice in Greek Tragedy," *YJC* 1: 23–43.

(1992) "Maternity and Mortality in Homeric Poetry," *ClAnt* 11: 242–64.

Nagy, G. (1979) *The Best of the Achaeans: Concepts of the Hero in Archaic Greek Poetry*. Baltimore.

(1995) "Transformations of Choral Lyric Traditions in the Context of Athenian State Theater," *Arion* 3: 41–55.

Neils, J. (ed.) (1992) *Goddess and the Polis: The Panathenaic Festival in Ancient Athens*. Princeton.

Nussbaum, M. (1986) *The Fragility of Goodness: Luck and Ethics in Greek Tragedy and Philosophy*. Cambridge.

Ober, J. and B. Strauss (1990) "Drama, Political Rhetoric and the Discourse of Athenian Democracy," in Winkler and Zeitlin 1990: 237–70.

Olson, S. D. (1996) "Politics and Poetry in Aristophanes' *Wasps*", *TAPA* 126: 129–50.

Ormand, K. (1999) *Exchange and the Maiden: Marriage in Sophoclean Tragedy*. Austin.

Osborne, R. and S. Hornblower (eds.) (1994) *Ritual, Finance, Politics: Athenian Democratic Accounts Presented to David Lewis*. Oxford.

Ostwald, M. (1955) "The Athenian Legislation against Tyranny and Subversion," *TAPA* 86: 103–29.

(1969) *Nomos and the Beginnings of the Athenian Democracy.* Oxford.

(1986) *From Popular Sovereignty to the Sovereignty of Law: Law, Society, and Politics in Fifth-Century Athens.* Berkeley.

Otto, W. (1933) *Dionysos: Mythos und Kultus.* Frankfurt.

Padel, R. (1992) *In and Out of Mind: Greek Images of the Tragic Self.* Princeton.

Padilla, M. (ed.) (1999) *Rites of Passage in Ancient Greece: Literature, Religion and Society* (Bucknell Review 43).

(2000) "Gifts of Humiliation: Charis and Tragic Experience in *Alcestis*," *AJP* 121: 179–211.

(2002) "Myth and Allusion in Sophocles's *Women of Trachis* and Euripides's *Herakles*," in *Approaches to Teaching the Dramas of Euripides*, ed. R. Mitchell-Boyask. New York: 138–48.

Page, D. L. (1953) "Thucydides' Description of the Plague of Athens," *CQ* 3: 97–119.

Papadopoulou, T. (2005) *Heracles and Euripidean Tragedy.* Cambridge.

Papagrigorakis, M., C. Yapijakis, P Synodinos and E. Baziotapoulou (2006) "DNA Examination of Ancient Dental Pulp Incriminates Typhoid Fever as Probable Cause of the Plague of Athens," *IJID* 10: 206–14.

Parke, H. W. (1977) *Festivals of the Athenians.* London.

Parker, R. (1983) *Miasma: Pollution and Purification in Early Greek Religion.* Oxford.

(1994) "Athenian Religion Abroad," in Osborne and Hornblower 1994: 339–46.

(1996) *Athenian Religion: A History.* Oxford.

Parry, A. (1969) "The Language of Thucydides' Description of the Plague," *BICS* 16: 106–18.

Parry, H. (1986) "Aphrodite and the Furies in Sophocles' *Trachiniae*," in *Greek Tragedy and Its Legacy: Essays Presented to D. J. Conacher*, ed. M. Cropp, E. Fantham and S. E. Scully. Alberta: 103–12.

Pelling, C. (ed.) (1997) *Greek Tragedy and the Historian.* Oxford.

Peradotto, J. (1992) "Disauthorizing Prophecy: The Ideological Mapping of *Oedipus Tyrannus*," *TAPA* 122: 1–15.

Pickard-Cambridge, A. W. (1946) *The Theatre of Dionysos in Athens.* Oxford.

(1968) *The Dramatic Festivals of Athens*, 2nd edn., revised by J. Gould and D. M. Lewis. Oxford.

Podlecki, A. J. (1966) *The Political Background of Aeschylean Tragedy.* Ann Arbor.

(1998) *Perikles and His Circle.* London.

Pohlenz, M. (1954) *Die Griechische Tragödie.* Göttingen.

Pohslander, H. P. (1963) "Lyrical Meters and Chronology in Sophocles," *AJP* 84: 280–86.

Polignac, F. de (1995) *Cults, Territory and the Origins of the Greek City-State*, trans. J. Lloyd. Chicago.

Price, J. (2001) *Thucydides and Internal War.* Cambridge.

Pucci, P. (1977) "Euripides: The Monument and the Sacrifice," *Arethusa* 10: 165–95

(1980) *The Violence of Pity in Euripides' Medea.* Ithaca.

Raaflaub, K. (1989) "Perceptions of Democracy in Fifth-Century Athens," *C&M* 40: 33–69.

Raubitschek, A. E. (1951) "The Origin of Ostracism," *AJA* 55: 221–29.

Raven, D. S. (1965) "Metrical Development in Sophocles' Lyrics," *AJP* 86: 225–38.

Reckford, K. (1972) "Phaethon, Hippolytus and Aphrodite," *TAPA* 103: 414–16.

(1974) "Phaedra and Pasiphae: The Pull Backward," *TAPA* 104: 307–28.

(1977) "Catharsis and Dream-Interpretation in Aristophanes' *Wasps*," *TAPA* 107: 283–312.

Redfield, J. M. (1975) *Nature and Culture in the Iliad: The Tragedy of Hector.* Chicago.

(1990) "Drama and Community: Aristophanes and Some of His Rivals," in Winkler and Zeitlin 1990: 314–35.

(2003) *The Locrian Maidens: Love and Death in Greek Italy.* Princeton.

Rehm, R. (1992) *Greek Tragic Theatre.* London.

Reinhardt, K. (1933) *Sophokles.* Frankfurt.

Renehan, R. (1992) "The Staunching of Odysseus' Blood: The Healing Power of Magic," *AJP* 113: 1–4.

Revermann, M. (2000) "Structured Space," *CR* 50: 410–12.

Rhodes, P. J. (1981) *A Commentary on the Aristotelean Athenaion Politeia.* Oxford.

(ed.) (1988) *Thucydides History* II. Warminster.

(1994) "The Ostracism of Hyperbolus," in Osborne and Hornblower 1994: 85–98.

(2003) "Nothing to Do with Democracy: Athenian Drama and the Polis," *JHS* 123: 104–19.

Ridgway, B. S. (1992) "Images of Athena on the Acropolis," in Neils 1992: 119–42.

Roberts, D. H. (1988) "Sophoclean Endings: Another Story," *Arethusa* 21: 177–96.

(1989) "Different Stories: Sophoclean Narrative(s) in the *Philoctetes*," *TAPA* 119: 161–76.

Robinson, D. (1969) "Topics in Sophocles' *Philoctetes*," *CQ* 19: 34–56.

Roebuck, C. (1951) *Corinth* XIV. *The Asklepieion and Lerna.* Princeton.

Romilly, J. de (1965) "Le Phéniciennes d'Euripide ou l'actualité dans la tragédie grecque," *RP* 39: 28–47.

(1976) "Alcibiade et le mélange entre jeunes et vieux: Politique et medicine," *WS* 10: 93–105.

Rose, P. W. (1992) *Sons of the Gods, Children of the Earth: Ideology and Literary Form in Ancient Greece.* Ithaca.

Rosenbloom, D. (2002) "From *Poneros* to *Pharmakos*: Theatre, Social Drama, and Revolution in Athens, 428–404 BCE," *ClAnt* 21: 283–346.

(2004a) "'Poneroi' vs. 'Chrestoi': The Ostracism of Hyperbolos and the Struggle for Hegemony in Athens after the Death of Perikles, Part I," *TAPA* 134: 55–105.

(2004b) "'Poneroi' vs. 'Chrestoi': The ostracism of Hyperbolos and the struggle for hegemony in Athens after the death of Perikles, Part II," *TAPA* 134: 323–58.

Rusten, J. (ed.) (1989) *Thucydides: The Peloponnesian War. Book II.* Cambridge.

Rutherford, I. (1993) "Paeanic Ambiguity: A Study of the Representation of the Paean in Greek Literature," *QUCC* 44: 77–92.

(1995) "Apollo in Ivy: The Tragic Paean," *Arion* 3: 112–35.

(2001) *Pindar's Paeans: A Reading of the Fragments with a Survey of the Genre.* Oxford.

Rutherford, R. (1982) "Tragic form and Feeling in the *Iliad*," *JHS* 102: 145–60.

Ryzman, M. (1992) "Oedipus, *nosos* and *phusis* in Sophocles' *Oedipus Tyrannus*," *AC* 61: 98–110.

Schamun, M. C. (1997) "Significaciones de τάραγμα (perturbacíon) en *Heracles* de Euripides," *Synthesis* 4: 99–112.

Schwinge, E.-R. (1962) *Die Stellung der Trachiniae im Werk des Sophokles.* Göttingen.

Scodel, R. (2003) "The Politics of Sophocles' *Ajax*," *SCI* 22: 1–42.

Scott, W. (1996) *Musical Design in Sophoclean Theater.* Hanover.

Scullion, S. (1998) "Dionysos and Katharsis in *Antigone*," *ClAnt* 17: 96–122.

(2002) "Tragic Dates," *CQ* 52: 87–111.

(2003) "Euripides and Macedon, or the Silence of the *Frogs*," *CQ* 53: 389–400.

Seaford, R. (1981) "Dionysiac Drama and the Dionysiac Mysteries," *CQ* 31: 252–75.

(ed.) (1984) *Euripides: Cyclops.* Oxford.

(1986) "Wedding Ritual and Textual Criticism in Sophocles' *Women of Trachis*," *Hermes* 114: 50–59.

(1993) "Dionysus as Destroyer of the Household: Homer, Tragedy and the Polis," in Carpenter and Faraone 1993: 115–46.

(1994) *Ritual and Reciprocity: Homer and Tragedy in the Developing City-State.* Oxford.

edy: A Response to Jasper Griffin,"

An Interpretation of Sophocles. Cam-

hae. Princeton.

nd the Limits of Human Knowledge.

ture, Society. Cambridge, Mass.

Sidwell, ... he ΝΟΣΟΣ Theme in Aristophanes' *Wasps*," CQ... 41. 9–31.

Silk, M. S. (1985) "Heracles and Greek Tragedy," *GR* 33: 1–22.

(ed.) (1996) *Tragedy and the Tragic: Greek Theatre and Beyond.* Oxford.

Smith, W. D. (1967) "Disease in Euripides' *Orestes*," *Hermes* 95: 291–307.

Sorum, C. E. (1978) "Monsters and the Family: The Exodus of Sophocles' *Trachiniae*," *GRBS* 19: 59–73.

Sourvinou-Inwood, C. (1997) "Tragedy and Religion: Constructs and Reading," in Pelling: 161–86.

(2003) *Tragedy and Athenian Religion.* Lanham.

Stephens, J. Ceri (1995) "The Wound of Philoctetes," *Mnemosyne* 48: 153–65.

Stillwell, R. (1952) *Corinth* II. *The Theatre.* Princeton.

Stinton, T. C. W. (1977) "Interlinear Hiatus in Trimeters," *CQ* 27: 67–72.

Strauss, B. (1993) *Fathers and Sons: Ideology and Society in the Era of the Peloponnesian War.* Princeton.

Sutton, D. (1984) *The Lost Sophocles.* Lanham.

Swain, S. (1994) "Man and Medicine in Thucydides," *Arethusa* 27: 303–28.

Taplin, O. (1971) "Significant Actions in Sophocles' *Philoctetes*," *GRBS* 12: 25–44.

(1977) *The Stagecraft of Aeschylus*. Oxford.

(1987) "The Mapping of Sophocles' *Philoctetes*," *BICS* 38: 69–77.

Thalmann, W. G. (1988) "Thersites: Comedy, Scapegoats, and Heroic Ideology in the *Iliad*," *TAPA* 118: 1–28.

Thomas, R. (2000) *Herodotus in Context: Ethnography, Science and the Art of Persuasion*. Cambridge.

Thomson, G. (1941) *Aeschylus and Athens*. London.

Turner, V. (1974) *Dramas, Fields, and Metaphors*. Ithaca.

(1981) "Social Dramas and Stories about Them," in *On Narrative*, ed. W. J. T. Mitchell. Chicago: 137–64.

Tyrell, W. and L. Bennett (1998) *Recapturing Sophocles' Antigone*. Lanham.

Valk, M. van der (1985) *Studies in Euripides: Phoenissae and Andromache*. Amsterdam.

Vernant, J.-P. (1983) *Myth and Thought among the Greeks*, trans. J. Lloyd and J. Fort. London.

(1988) "Ambiguity and Reversal: On the Enigmatic Structure of *Oedipus Rex*," in Vernant and Vidal-Naquet 1988: 113–40.

(1990) *Myth and Society in Ancient Greece*, trans. J. Lloyd. New York.

Vernant, J.-P. and P. Vidal Naquet (1988) *Myth and Tragedy in Ancient Greece*, trans. J. Lloyd. New York.

Vickers, M. J. (1987) "Alcibiades on Stage: *Philoctetes* and *Cyclops*," *Historia* 36: 171–97.

(1991) "A Contemporary Account of the Athenian Plague (Aristophanes *Clouds* 694–734)," *LCM* 16.4: 64.

Vidal-Naquet, P. (1986) *The Black Hunter: Forms of Thought and Forms of Society in the Greek World*, trans. A. Szegedy-Maszak. Baltimore.

Vlastos, G. (1947) "Equality and Justice in Early Greek Cosmologies," *CP* 42: 156–78.

(1953) "*Isonomia*," *AJP* 74: 337–66.

Vojatzi, M. (1982) *Frühe Argonautenbilder*. Würzburg.

Walsh, G. (1984) *The Varieties of Enchantment: Early Greek Views of the Nature and Function of Poetry*. Chapel Hill.

Webster, T. B. L. (1967) *The Tragedies of Euripides*. London.

(1969) *An Introduction to Sophocles*. Oxford.

West, M. L. (1979) "The Prometheus Trilogy," *JHS* 99: 130–48.

(ed.) (1985) *The Hesiodic Catalogue of Women: Its Nature, Structure, and Origins*. Oxford.

White, H. and M. Brose (eds.) (1982) *Representing Kenneth Burke*. Baltimore.

Whitman, C. H. (1951) *Sophocles: A Study in Heroic Humanism*. Cambridge.

Wilamowitz-Moellendorf, U. von (ed.) (1889) *Euripides: Herakles*. Berlin.

Wiles, D. (1997) *Tragedy in Athens: Performance Space and Theatrical Meaning*. Cambridge.

(2000) *Greek Theatre Performance: An Introduction*. Cambridge.

Wilkins, J. (ed.) (1993) *Euripides: Heraclidae*. Oxford.

Wilson, P. (2000) *The Athenian Institution of the Khoregia: The Chorus, the City, and the Stage.* Cambridge.

Wilson, P. and O. Taplin (1993) "The Aetiology of Tragedy in the *Oresteia*," *PCPS* 39: 169–80.

Winkler, J. (1990) "*The Ephebe's Song: Tragoidia and Polis,*" in Winkler and Zeitlin 1990: 20–62.

Winkler, J. and F. I. Zeitlin (eds.) (1990) *Nothing to Do with Dionysos? Athenian Drama in Its Social Context.* Princeton.

Winnington-Ingram, R. P. (1969) "Tragica," *BICS* 16: 44–54.

(1980) *Sophocles: An Interpretation.* Cambridge.

Wohl, V. (2002) *Love Among the Ruins: The Erotics of Democracy in Classical Athens.* Princeton.

Woodford, S. (1971) "Cults of Heracles in Attica," *Studies Presented to George M. A. Hanfmann* (Fogg Art Museum, Harvard University Monographs in Art and Archaeology 2): 211–25.

(1976) "Heracles Alexikakos Reviewed," *AJA* 80: 291–4.

Worman, N. (2000) "Infection in the Sentence: The Discourse of Disease in Sophocles' *Philoctetes*," *Arethusa* 33: 1–36.

Young, D. (1968) *Three Odes of Pindar.* Leiden.

Zeitlin, F. I. (1985) "The Power of Aphrodite: Eros and the Boundaries of the Self in the *Hippolytus*," in Burian 1985: 52–111.

(1990a) "Playing the Other: Theater, Theatricality and the Feminine in Greek Drama," in Winkler and Zeitlin 1990: 63–96.

(1990b) "Thebes: Theater of Self and Society in Athenian Drama," in Winkler and Zeitlin 1990: 130–167.

Index